A LOCOMOTIVE ENGINEER'S ALBUM

A LOCOMOTIVE

The Saga of STEAM ENGINES in America.

ENGINEER'S ALBUM

Fifth in the OLD RAILROAD Series

by Locomotive Engineer

George B. Abdill.

ALLEGHENY ASSEMBLAGE. The dapper trio shown here at Allegheny, Pennsylvania, represents the exhibit of the Pittsburgh Locomotive Works at the Exposition of Railway Appliances held in Chicago in 1883. At left is No. 108 of the Pittsburgh & Western, a 4-4-0 with 17 × 24 inch cylinders and 66 inch drivers; head-on to the camera is No. 990 of the Pennsylvania R.R., a Consolidation with 20 × 24 inch cylinders and 50 inch drivers; the husky 4-6-0 at right is No. 152 of the Pittsburgh, McKeesport & Youghiogheny.

Aside from minor structural differences the engines all reflect the clean lines of the Pittsburgh Works; the P. & W. engine has a wagon-top boiler and extended front end and both she and the "P-Mickey" tenwheeler have wooden stave pilots, while the Pennsy's 2-8-0 has the horizontal metal slat pilot and sports a set of classification lamps on her smokebox.

The reader is not the only one to enjoy this view of spanking new steam locomotives posed against a background of Allegheny City's shady, tree-lined streets and homes—note the barefoot urchin perched in rapt admiration on the lumber pile at far left. (Courtesy of Smithsonian Institution)

BONANZA BOOKS • NEW YORK

Dedication.

This one is for my littlest helper,

Karen Anne Abdill

The pictures on the next page

PANORAMA OF THE PAST. Photographer John A. Mather exposed a glass plate negative to record this scene on the Oil Creek Railroad near Pioneer, Pennsylvania, shortly after the close of the Civil War. His picture captures the spirit of railroading in that era of iron men and woodburning locomotives, the Schenectady-built 4-4-0 being typical of motive power then in use and the old combination wood and iron truss bridge in the background a fine example of the style then common throughout the United Sates.

Some doubt exists as to the actual identity of the locomotive pictured here; she is a Schenectady product, with brass dome casing, brass hand rail brackets, boiler check covers, and brass-bound polished boiler jacket, and the number on her sand box appears to be "11"; the tender, however, apparently carries the number "13", but tenders were occasionally exchanged when they or the engines they belonged with were temporarily shopped for repairs. (Photo courtesy of Pennsylvania Historical & Museum Commission, Harrisburg, Pennsylvania)

S.P. MONEY SAVER. The 4-4-0 shown here was built by Schenectady in 1880, Shop No. 1210, as Engine No. 37 of the Southern Pacific Railroad of Arizona. She later became S.P. 117, as pictured, then later renumbered S.P. 1331 and in 1920 was sold to the San Joaquin & Eastern.

The photograph shows the locomotive after she had been equipped with the primitive feedwater heater designed by General Master Mechanic A. J. Stevens and applied in the road's shops. This device, intended to cut fuel costs and improve the efficiency of the locomotive, was called a "boiler economizer" by Stevens; in the large dome added just behind the stack, and behind the tube sheet, there was a series of baffles and perforated plates. Water from the injector or crosshead pumps entered the dome near the top and filtered down through the baffle plates, being heated by the dry steam in the dome before being discharged into the main body of the boiler. The device worked but did not prove as economical as desired, and while a number of S.P. engines were equipped with it, the boiler economizer was soon removed from the motive power of the system.

Polished to a high gloss when this view was taken, old No. 117 sported elaborate scroll designs on her domes and sand box, and was well supplied with brass eagles, candle sticks, and a shiny star suspended beneath her big oil headlight. (Courtesy of Southern Pacific)

MASS TRANSIT. October 9th, 1893, marked the 22nd anniversary of the great Chicago fire and the occasion was marked by a "Chicago Day" celebration at the World's Columbian Exposition in Jackson Park. Transportation routes to the Exposition grounds were jammed with throngs of people and the capacities of the various companies were taxed to the breaking point.

The famous old Alley Elevated line, the Chicago & South Side Rapid Transit Company, had all 180 of its cars in service and the Forney type engines of the road departed with trains at intervals of 3 minutes throughout the entire day. The crowds from the western part of the city were mainly handled by the Chicago & Northern Pacific company's trains, while large numbers from the south-southwest area of Chicago arrived on the cars of the Calumet Electric Street Railway. Cable and horse cars of the Chicago City Railway Co. groaned with their burden of humanity and additional crowds rode to the Exposition grounds on the boats of the World's Fair Steamship Company.

The Illinois Central established a record on the day by carrying more than 541,000 people. Over double tracks linking the Van Buren Street Station with the fairgrounds the I.C. ran trains of specially-designed cars with side doors for speedy loading and unloading; the accompanying photo shows 8 of these 300 cars disgorging passengers at Van Buren Street Station. In addition, the Illinois Central had 166 suburban coaches in service and during the peak of the rush pressed 60 through passenger coaches and 40 excursion coaches into Exposition grounds service.

When the dust settled at midnight, over 761,000 people had attended the World's Columbian Exposition on "Chicago Day." (Courtesy of Illinois Central Railroad)

Foreword.

Within the pages of this book lie the pictorial story of the Iron Horse in North America, a stirring saga of railroading that goes hand in hand with the history and development of our nation.

Through the wonderful medium of the camera it has been possible to record the growth of the steam locomotive, from birth pangs to the peak of its existence, from the cradle to the grave. Come with a locomotive engineer and stroll through the scenes of yesteryear, through the shadowy roundhouses of history and out along the gleaming ribbons of silver that reached from the Atlantic to the Pacific, Canada to Mexico.

The illustrations in this album come from a wide variety of sources; from private collections generously shared, from the files of locomotive builders, the archives of national institutions, and from the historical records of various railroads. In selecting the photographs the author has endeavored to choose those that best tell the story of mechanical growth, including the primitive Iron Colts of the 1830's, the rapid advances to better and more efficient designs, and the crowning achievements of engine builders. Chapters have been devoted to exhibition power, displayed at a number of expositions, and to odd and unusual locomotives, to speed queens, freight hogs, and the humble switchers.

Brief histories of many early railroads have been included in the caption material, along with thumbnail sketches of some of the country's obscure pikes. The bulk of the material covers the era from the beginnings of steam railroading to the turn of the century, and special effort has been made to avoid duplicating any of the material in the author's four previous pictorial books on historic railroading.

A major portion of this volume is aimed at what has been termed the "nuts and bolts" segment of railroad enthusiasts, those whose interests lie primarily in the locomotive engine. While a number of the pictures reveal early cars, stations, bridges, and other adjuncts of American railroading, the majority of the illustrations depict the mechanical steed that has fascinated generations of American males. Many of the photographs portray locomotives fresh from the factory in those classic poses known as builder's photos, while others capture the Iron Horse in his habitat, spewing cinders, steam, and smoke over a colorful variety of scenery that embraces nearly every portion of the North American continent.

To the many who contributed pictures and information for this work, the author is truly grateful. Special thanks are due Mr. H. M. Ghormley, long-time railroad machinist and a retired employee of the Cincinnati, New Orleans & Texas Pacific, for his generous use of photos from the collection of the late W. A. Anderson; equal thanks are owing Mr. Herb Broadbelt for prints from the builder's negatives of the Baldwin Locomotive Works collection, and to Mr. John H. White, Jr., of the Smithsonian Institution.

The author is also grateful for the use of photographs or information from the following: Mr. Fred Jukes, Mr. Raymond B. Carneal, Dr. S. R. Wood, Phil Blackmarr, Bernard Corbin, Jack Slattery, Benjamin F. G. Kline, Jr., William Batman, A. F. Zimmerman of the Brotherhood of Locomotive Engineers, Lester L. Leavitt, Arthur Petersen, Franklin A. King, Roy D. Graves, Harold S. Walker, Beaumont Newhall of George Eastman House, and Chas. Fisher of the Railway & Locomotive Historical Society.

A special tribute is due to the late Henry C. Ritchie, Archivist for the Schenectady History Center, whose unstinting cooperation made possible the reproduction of the many photographs from the American Locomotive Works collection of glass plate negatives.

Others who have lent encouragement and aided in various ways include T. W. Bernard, George Kirby, I. M. Dunn, L. E. Whetstine, D. L. Chase, David Clune, L. E. Davis, Don Roberts, Guy Dunscomb, David L. Stearns, E. U. Gogl, Don Bryans, and many others.

The author is indebted to President John Barriger of the Pittsburgh & Lake Erie, and to the public relations staffs of the many railroads who aided in this project, along with the Oregon Historical Society, the Douglas County Historical Society, and the Oregon Game Commission, and to Jay Golden and Edward Kenny for photographic work.

To those who have helped and have been overlooked in the foregoing list, my sincere apologies; I deeply appreciate all the many kindnesses extended to me.

Lastly, a loving thank you to my wife, Annette Abdill, whose tender care and inspiring confidence has made my journey over the rails of yesteryear a most pleasant one.

The pictures on the next page

WOLVERINE STATE FLYER. This view, taken in Chicago in the 1870's, shows the graceful 4-4-0 passenger locomotive QUICKSTEP, No. 74 of the Michigan Central Railroad, heading a string of varnished cars. The bare trees, bundled crew, and the trampled snow bear mute witness to the chill of the Windy City in winter, while grey clouds scud above the Pullman Palace Car Company building in the background.

The Michigan Central was organized by the State of Michigan under an act of the Legislature in 1837 and acquired an 1832 incorporation known as the Detroit & St. Joseph R.R. Company. A standard gauge line was opened from Detroit (Campus Martius) to Dearborn early in 1838, to Ypsilanti in the same year, and to Ann Arbor in 1839. In 1846 further State expenditures were prohibited and a private company was chartered to purchase the State road; this new organization retained the Michigan Central name and completed the road in 1852. The road had reached Battle Creek in 1845 and entered Kalamazoo in 1846 under State control; the new Michigan Central company of 1846 completed the line to Niles in 1848, to Michigan City in 1850, and in May of 1852 reached Kensington, Illinois, where a connection was made with the Illinois Central R.R. and entrance to Chicago gained by use of 14 miles of Illinois Central track.

The baggage car coupled behind the QUICKSTEP is lettered "American Merchants Express Co." and bears the legend "Great Central Route." (Courtesy of the Smithsonian Institution)

SPRINGTIME IN THE '90'S. The fleecy clouds drifting across the Minnesota sky and the shrinking remnants of winter's snow in the rutted road beside the depot platform are harbingers of springtime in the Jim Hill country.

The passenger train halted at the Great Northern's station at Cokato is headed by Engine 127, a Schenectady eight-wheeler of 1882 manufacture with a flanger bolted to her stave pilot. Her fireboy watches the bustle of train-time activity and awaits the conductor's high-ball that will send the trim 4-4-0 and her consist of wooden varnish scurrying on her way.

The combination of warm sun and rich earth will soon cloak the naked trees in greenery and the wheat will grow tall and deliver its seed to the reapers; farmers' wagons will toil into town under the hot sun of harvest time and the wooden elevators across from the frame station will bulge with the golden yield. The town band will mount the circular bandstand at far right to serenade the good citizens of the Wright county village under the mellow glow of the autumn moon, perhaps disturbed occasionally by the Great Northern freight switching the elevator tracks.

With the wheat on its way to Pillsbury's mills, the winter's supply of coal in the shed, and a tidy stack of gold double eagles hidden away in the base of the mantel clock, the sturdy farmer can pause in his evening chores to harken to the cry of wild geese heading south and the distant wail of a Big G engine, secure in the knowledge that God is in Heaven and Jim Hill is running a close second in the affairs of Minnesota. (Barnes Studio, Cokato, courtesy of Great Northern Ry.)

IN THE GOLDEN AGE. Few institutions have ever captured the fancy of Americans so widely as the strings of varnished passenger cars burnishing the bright ribbons of rail the length and breadth of the nation, headed by a steam locomotive.

The fame of many named trains was often restricted to the area they served but that of the OVERLAND LIMITED was widespread and the story of that classic flyer has recently provided Lucius Beebe, the dean of rail literature, with enough material for a complete book on the subject.

In this magnificent photograph taken about 1911, the westbound OVERLAND LIMITED sweeps around a gentle curve on the Union Pacific at Granite Canyon, Wyoming. Thirteen cars are included in the consist of the speeding varnish as she heads toward the Golden Gate; behind lie the endless reaches of the Great Plains with the horizon fading to infinity.

The haze of coal smoke drifts acridly on the breeze where once the bison and the Indian dwelt in solitude before the Iron Horse invaded their vast domain, and a clear block signal beckons the OVERLAND westward in the golden age of steam railroading. (Courtesy of Union Pacific Railroad)

Table of Contents.

The picture on the next page

ALL ABOARD! This photo presents the typical American railroad scene in the years just prior to the turn of the century, indeed the epitome of transport via the steam cars.

   The little American type spews a pillar of black smoke as her fireboy raises a head of steam preparatory to departure. She retains the oil headlight of an earlier era, along with a wooden pilot, but sports a slotted-knuckle automatic coupler in the Janney fashion.

   Her string of wooden coaches are innocent of air conditioning and recall the era of Pintsch gas lamps, hard seats, and cinders in the eye.

   Soon the skipper will lift his hand in the familiar highball, the slack will ease out, and the varnish will be on its way, to the accompaniment of clanging bell, wailing whistle, and the clack of rail joints. Forgotten the minor discomforts, lulled by the motion of the rushing cars and perfumed by occasional whiffs of coal smoke from the barking stack.

   Settle back, relax, and enjoy the constantly changing views as the pounding drivers speed us along the highroad of nostalgic adventure.

JOHN BULL. This venerable iron colt was built in 1831 by Robert Stephenson & Co. of Newcastle-upon-Tyne, England, for the Camden & Amboy Rail Road & Transportation Co. and arrived in Philadelphia in August of 1831 aboard the ship, *Allegheny*. It was taken by sloop to Bordentown and assembled by Issac Dripps, a youthful mechanic who later rose to fame in the ranks of the Pennsylvania Railroad, successors to the Camden & Amboy. Aboard the locomotive with Dripps on the trial run was Robert L. Stevens, president of the road who had gone to England in 1830 to purchase the JOHN BULL.

The inside-connected 0-4-0 had 11 × 20 inch cylinders and 54 inch drivers, the latter having cast iron hubs, wrought iron tires, and locust wood spokes. Although fitted with connecting rods, these were reportedly never used, due to the sharp curves on the road; other sources state the side rods were removed when the 2-wheeled pilot was added. The cab and the tender shown in this early view are later additions; no tender came with the JOHN BULL and Isaac Dripps improvised one from a 4-wheeled car, an empty whiskey cask serving as the tank and the water delivered to the pump by means of a tin pipe and several sections of leather hose fabricated by a Bordentown cobbler.

The JOHN BULL was on display at the Philadelphia Centennial Exhibition in 1876, at the Exposition of Railway Appliances in Chicago in 1883, and ran to Chicago and back under her own power for the World's Columbian Exposition in 1893, drawing two ancient coaches. Restored to resemble its original appearance, the JOHN BULL reposes in the National Museum, along with a model of the 1831 design. (Courtesy of Smithsonian Institution)

AN ALBUM OF OLD-TIMERS

Railroading and the art of photography were both born in the same era but the advent of the steam locomotive antedated the processes of Isidore Niepce and Louis J. M. Daguerre slightly, with the result that actual photographs of the earliest locomotives do not exist. It was not until Scott Archer introduced the collodion process using wet plates in 1851 that photographs of locomotives appeared in any quantity, but from that time on the Iron Horse was a favored subject of pioneer cameramen who posed the metal steeds before their cumbersome equipment to record their appearance. To those sturdy spirits who spent tedious time in the preparation of their plates and developed them on the spot in portable dark-rooms the succeeding generations of lovers of steam locomotives owe an everlasting debt of gratitude.

By the time the photographic art had reached the practical stage many of the earlier locomotives had faded and vanished, but a few of the breed lingered on and their likenesses were captured by the magic of the camera.

The following chapter of the book is devoted to pictures of these primitive survivors and the improved models that followed in their wake. Here are the imported British engines and the early products of American builders, the improved types of the 1840-50 period, and fancier versions of the Civil War period. Some of the earlier engines, especially those from England, had been rather extensively rebuilt before their images were recorded and in most cases the stacks, cabs, and various other appurtenances are of American origin and were added after the engines had been used for some time, thus changing the original appearance of the locomotive to some degree.

As the steam locomotive and its iron paths spread up and down the eastern seaboard and began to penetrate the frontiers to the west an increasing number of locomotive builders began constructing engines and the products of a number of these early manufacturers are represented in the pictures in this album.

The first locomotives were rather crude affairs, built for service and lacking in the refinements that were added as the art of railroading progressed. The pioneer British engines were built without cabs and the engine crew braved the elements from an exposed position on the footplate. American designers followed this practice in the beginning but soon devised a sheltering roof to ward off sun, rain, and snow. Early cabs were frequently a roof supported by upright posts; to these were added storm curtains that could be unfurled when conditions required. The rigors of New England winters made a more substantial shelter necessary and crude wooden cabs were applied; the style and construction of these cabs are illustrated in early photographs and the pictures reveal that these early additions were of artless design and often of rough finish.

As the skill of locomotive builders flourished the cab became an integral part of the engine and talented craftsmen designed and assembled them. By the time the Civil War divided the nation the locomotive cab had become a thing of beauty, created by artisans and fashioned from selected hardwoods, carefully joined to withstand the strains of hard service.

In presenting this selection of early locomotives the author has subscribed to the theory that a picture tells a story better than a thousand words, hence the caption material has been kept to a minimum and contains pertinent information without literary frills.

This style follows throughout the entire book, with an occasional anecdote directly related to the photograph or the road under discussion.

It has been left for the reader to place himself at the throttle and visualize for himself the thrill of exhilarating speed, smoke, and noise that these progenitorial locomotives embodied. While the general opinion is that early engines operated at slow speeds, this notion seems to be refuted by Emory Edwards in his book, "Modern American Locomotive Engines," published in 1888. Mr. Edwards, a mechanical engineer, states that Engineer William Pettit ran the Baldwin engine, IRONSIDES, built in 1832, at the rate of 62 miles per hour and that Dr. Patterson of the University of Virginia and Mr. Franklin Peale were aboard the engine on that occasion and timed the run. On her first trip the IRONSIDES made 28 miles per hour, using but a portion of her power and easing off at road crossings. An Edward Norris engine of Crampton style named the LIGHTNING ran a reported 60 miles per hour on the Utica & Schenectady R.R. in 1850, a feat equalled by the CARROLL OF CARROLLTON, a single-drivered Ross Winans engine built in 1849 for the Boston & Worcester Railroad.

Mr. Edwards reproduces the following interesting account from J. H. Jackman, the man who ran this 7-foot drivered engine over a century ago:

"Since I run her in 1849, I have traveled many thousand miles on locomotives, and have seen some high speeds made, still I have never seen the locomotive that could lay right down to it and out-run the CARROLL OF CARROLLTON. When I run her we made many stops, and therefore could not make better time than locomotives having small driving wheels. But give me fifty or sixty miles on a clear run and I could out-run a thunder-storm if it was going our way. In those days we had no air-brakes, and to run at such high rates of speed sometimes became dangerous. I remember one instance, in the night time, of rounding a curve at about sixty miles per hour when a danger signal met my view. I shut off steam and whistled down brakes, but they did not seem to check me. I whistled again; still the speed kept up. I gave the third signal for brakes, and then reversed my engine, saying to her, 'Do your duty, my beauty, or in twenty seconds it is good-by to railroading.' We came to a stand-still eighty rods from a train on the main track, having run one mile and a quarter from the place where I first discovered the red light. A locomotive engineer, to avoid trouble, must take time by the forelock. . . ."

Engineer Jackman's final observation is as true today as it was then, as any engineman can testify. But let us have done with talk and swing aboard the engines waiting on the following pages, steam up and ready to ramble across the pages of history.

The picture on the next page

PINE TREE STATE PIONEER. The ancient little 2-2-0 shown here is the PIONEER and was the first locomotive on the first railroad in the State of Maine. She reportedly was built by the Stephenson Works in England in 1832, shop number 26, and was delivered to America where she was in service on the Boston & Worcester R.R. as their METEOR, and in 1835 was sold to the Bangor & Piscataquis Canal & Railroad Company for their 12-mile line then being constructed up the western shore of the Penobscot River from Bangor to Old Town, Maine. This line was a descendant of the Old Town Railway, chartered in 1832 but never completed; the Old Town Ry. property passed to the Bangor & Piscataquis County R.R., later absorbed into the Bangor & Piscataquis Canal & Railroad Company. The latter road was reorganized as the Bangor, Old Town & Milford R.R., was extended across the Penobscot to Milford, and was sold to the European & North American R.R. about 1870 and abandoned to kill the threat of competition.

The Bangor & Piscataquis was completed in November, 1836, and the PIONEER was operated over its wooden rails faced with strap iron, replaced in 1849 with 36-pound double-chair rails purchased second-hand. The PIONEER, which some sources believe was built for the road by Stephenson, lasted until 1865; a second engine soon joined her on the road, hauling cargoes of boards, lath and shingles from the chain of mills along the line. This second engine, the BANGOR, was built in England by the Rothwell Locomotive Works and was a cab-less 2-2-0 carrying shop number 6, built in 1836. The PIONEER is typical of early British engines, having a boiler lagged with wood and an outside frame with inside-connected cylinders. Her wheels were of wood, with iron tires and hubs. (Courtesy of Smithsonian Institution)

ENGLISH IMPORT. The Little Schuylkill Navigation, Railroad & Coal Company was incorporated in 1826 and by 1832 had completed 28 miles of standard gauge track laid with strap iron rails between Port Clinton and Tamaqua, Pennsylvania. The first motive power was a pair of 0-4-0 engines named the COMET and the CATAWISSA, the latter shown here; the cab, stack, pilot, and sand box were probably added in later years of operation in America.

Both locomotives were built by Edward Bury of Liverpool, England, the COMET being Bury's 6th engine and the CATAWISSA his 10th; both had inside-connected 11 × 16 inch cylinders and 54 inch drivers. The COMET was reportedly destroyed at an early date but the CATAWISSA was still on the Little Schuylkill property when it was leased to the Philadelphia & Reading R.R. in 1863; in 1871 the P&R sold the CATAWISSA to the American Dredging Company.

The Little Schuylkill acquired a pair of 4-2-0 engines built by Baldwin in 1836, construction numbers 46 and 47; these engines were named TAMAQUA and TUSCARORA. Railroad historians believe the little 0-4-0 engine ANTHRACITE, built by Garrett & Eastwick of Philadelphia in 1837, may have also come to the Little Schuylkill; in 1840 it was reportedly hauled up the Quakake Valley by teams from Tamaqua to Rockport on the Lehigh River, where it operated on 5 miles of track of the Buck Mountain Railroad running from Rockport to the Buck Mountain mines. (Courtesy of Reading Railway Company)

PREHISTORIC POWER. The ancient 0-4-0 shown here illustrates the primitive motive power in use on the Baltimore & Ohio R.R. in the late 1830's, when railroading in the United States was still in its infancy. This engine was an improved "grasshopper" type, similar in design to the earlier models built by Davis & Gartner of York, Pennsylvania. The Baltimore & Ohio used a number of these "grasshopper" types, constructed by builders such as Charles Reeder, Gartner, and Phineas Davis in the Mount Clare shops of the road in Baltimore. Davis served as Master of Machinery on the B&O and is generally credited with the designing of the "grasshopper" type vertical boiler locomotive.

The engine shown here was named the ANDREW JACKSON when built in February, 1836, and was originally No. 2, but was renumbered 7 in 1850, shortly before this photo was probably taken; in 1884 she was renumbered 2 and in 1892 she was altered by Major Pangborn to represent the original ATLANTIC, the first "grasshopper" on the B&O which had been built in 1832, for display at the Columbian Exposition at Chicago in 1893. George Gillingham and Ross Winans, the latter a former New Jersey horse dealer, built several similar engines for the B&O, starting in April, 1836. Other B&O "grasshoppers" bore such names as TRAVELER, ARABIAN, MERCURY, JOHN QUINCY ADAMS, JOHN HANCOCK, and MARTIN VAN BUREN. The last three of these, together with the ANDREW JACKSON, were in active service around Mount Clare until 1892, then being turned over to Major Pangborn for remodelling to resemble various other pioneer B&O engines for the Chicago Exposition. (Courtesy of Baltimore & Ohio R.R.)

BOSTON & WORCESTER RAILROAD, chartered on June 23rd, 1831, was the first railroad in Massachusetts to offer regular service. It commenced operation of 8 miles of standard gauge track, Boston to Newton, in April of 1834 and by July of 1835 it had reached Worcester, 43½ miles from Boston. The age-dimmed photo shown here depicts the JUPITER, an inside-connected 4-4-0 built for the B&W by Hinkley & Drury in April, 1845, Shop No. 39; she had 14 × 18 inch cylinders and 66 inch drivers. The original JUPITER of the B&W was an 0-4-0 built by Stephenson in England in 1834 and was scrapped in 1845. The ancient sign admonishes "Railroad Crossing— Look Out For The Engine While The Bell Rings." (Courtesy of George Eastman House)

RUTLAND & BURLINGTON R.R. was originally chartered in 1843 as the Champlain & Connecticut River R.R., being renamed Rutland & Burlington in 1847. The 120 miles of standard gauge road from Bellows Falls to Burlington, Vermont, was opened in December, 1849. Engine No. 8, the PITTSFORD, was built by the Taunton Works in 1850, bearing Taunton's construction number 49. (Courtesy of Dr. S. R. Wood)

NOVA SCOTIA ANCIENT. The 0-6-0 pictured here is the SAMSON, built in the summer of 1838 at New Shildon, Durham, England, by the noted Timothy Hackworth. The SAMSON was one of three identical locomotives built by Hackworth for the General Mining Association of Nova Scotia, the other two being named HERCULES and JOHN BUDDLE. The 0-6-0 operated on the line known unofficially as the South Pictou Railroad or Albion Mines Railway, hauling coal over the six miles of track between the Albion mines at Stellarton and the docks at Pictou harbor.

The 56½ inch gauge SAMSON was unique in many ways, having no frame and the driving boxes being bolted to brackets riveted to the belly of the boiler. Her two cylinders of 15¼ × 18 inch bore and stroke were mounted vertically, and her 48 inch drivers were of the cast iron plate style. Her boiler, lagged with wood, was of the return flue type and her fire door was located below her stack, while her engineer reigned from the open deck at the opposite end of the boiler; note the two iron chairs on the deck of the 17-ton monster in this pre-1890 photograph. An 1883 photo elsewhere in this work shows the SAMSON with a coach coupled behind her 4-wheeled tender; when operated thus, she could have laid claim to being the ancestor of latter-day cab-in-front locomotives, save for the fact that she had no cab!

Although often credited with being the first locomotive in Canada, the SAMSON was preceded by the DORCHESTER of 1836 and the JASON C. PIERCE of 1837, the former built by Stephenson in England and the latter by William Norris in the United States; both of these pioneers operated on the Champlain & St. Lawrence Railroad. (Courtesy of Smithsonian Institution)

The ROGER WILLIAMS was built in Lowell, Mass., and reportedly pulled the first train over the road from Providence to Stonington; the engine was named in honor of the great religious liberal, Roger Williams, who founded the Rhode Island Colony and the city of Providence. When first built, the engine was a 2-2-0 type with 11×16 inch cylinders and weighed 9 tons; the boiler was 7½ feet long with 76 tubes each 2 inches in diameter. The ROGER WILLIAMS was rebuilt by Master Mechanic Wm. E. Rutter in 1846, who extended the boiler 3 feet, replaced the single pony truck with a 4-wheel truck, and added the set of 36 inch trailing wheels as shown in this photo, making the engine a 4-2-2 type. He also replaced the original cylinders with a set measuring 13×16 inches; when rebuilt the locomotive weighed 12 tons. (Courtesy of Smithsonian Institution)

RHODE ISLAND PIONEER. The locomotive shown here is the ROGER WILLIAMS of the New York, Providence & Boston R.R., a line chartered in 1832 and completed from Providence, Rhode Island, to Stonington, Connecticut, in 1837; the line later acquired the New London & Stonington R.R., completed in 1858 between Stonington and Groton, opposite New London. The road later became the Stonington Division of the New York, New Haven & Hartford; branches, built under separate charters, included the Westerly Granite Quarry R.R., Newport & Wickford R.R., Warwick R.R., Narragansett Pier R.R., and the Wood River Branch R.R.

READING RELIC. The 0-6-0 type locomotive UNITED STATES, built for the Philadelphia & Reading Railroad, was one of 22 engines built by Baldwin & Whitney in 1844. Matthias W. Baldwin constructed his first locomotive in 1831 and in 1839 joined with George Vail and Geo. W. Hufty, forming the firm of Baldwin, Vail & Hufty; Hufty withdrew in 1841 and Vail in 1842. Baldwin then joined with Asa Whitney, formerly Superintendent of the Mohawk & Hudson R.R.; in 1846 Whitney withdrew and formed the Philadelphia firm of A. Whitney & Sons, engaging in the manufacture of railroad wheels.

In 1842 Baldwin devised an 0-6-0 type, the first two pair of drivers combined in a flexible truck; the first engine of this design went to J. Edgar Thomson's Georgia Railroad, where it proved very satisfactory. In 1844 Baldwin & Whitney built six 18-ton engines for the Philadelphia & Reading, three of which were fitted with iron boiler tubes, the first used by the firm; in August of 1844 the Reading conducted experiments between Richmond and Mount Carbon, using the ONTARIO with copper tubes and the NEW ENGLAND, equipped with the new iron boiler tubes. Although not entirely conclusive, the tests indicated very little difference in the evaporative qualities of the two metals under operating conditions.

The first Baldwin engines with cabs and sand boxes were built for the Philadelphia & Reading R.R. in 1846; the cabs consisted of four iron posts supporting a wooden roof. Reading crews added curtains, similar to those shown on the UNITED STATES.

The flexible truck design permitted heavier engines and in 1844 Baldwin & Whitney built three locomotives for the Western R.R. of Massachusetts weighing 20 tons each. (Courtesy of Reading Railway Co.)

OH, PIONEER! The grim walls of the State Prison at Auburn, New York, form the backdrop for this photo of an early locomotive that probably belonged to the Auburn & Rochester Railroad. Details are lacking, save for a notation on the back of the original photograph stating it was taken in 1872 and that the little 4-2-0 formerly pulled a two-car passenger train between Auburn and Rochester before being relegated to yard service at Auburn.

The Auburn & Rochester, later consolidated with the Auburn & Syracuse to form the Rochester & Syracuse R.R., eventually was absorbed into the New York Central & Hudson River Railroad; the Auburn & Rochester was chartered in 1836, opened between Rochester and Canandaigua in 1840, and completed into Auburn in 1841. The first engine on the road was reportedly a Rogers, Ketchum & Grosvenor 4-4-0, built in 1840 and followed by four 4-2-0's built in the same year by Norris. The quaint oldster shown here may well be one of these early Norris engines, with the addition of such refinements as the cab and the odd type of pilot; the Bury boiler, with the firebox placed behind the main axle, was a Norris feature that gave their locomotives increased weight on the driving wheels. (Courtesy of Mr. Hugh Ghormley)

VENERABLE HINKLEYS. The two 0-4-0 locomotives pictured here are the LION, at left, and the TIGER, both built by Holmes Hinkley of the old Boston firm of Hinkley & Drury. The LION was built in 1846 and the TIGER is reportedly of earlier vintage; both were used on the Machiasport Railroad, a standard gauge line chartered in 1842 and opened in 1843. The line was 7.75 miles in length, running between Machiasport and Whitneyville, Maine, and was later known as the Whitneyville & Machiasport Railroad; it was constructed of wooden sleepers faced with strap iron ⅝ths of an inch in thickness, and was used by a Maine mill company to carry lumber from mills on the Machias River to the port at tidewater.

The LION weighed about 9 tons, had 9¼ × 17 inch cylinders, about 42½ inch wheels, and cost a reported $2,700. The road was closed in the 1890's when timber grew scarce, and the engines were sold to Thomas Towle of Portland, Maine, for junk. The TIGER was evidently scrapped, but Alderman E. E. Rounds of Portland raised enough cash to save the old LION and she was exhibited during a 4th of July celebration at Portland in 1898, then stored on city property until 1905 when it was given to the University of Maine. In 1929 it was installed in the then-new Crosby Mechanical Laboratory and some missing parts replaced, making the oldster able to operate on compressed air with its wheels jacked up clear of the rail. Safely preserved for posterity to marvel over in the University of Maine's Crosby Mechanical Laboratory at Orono, Maine, it is the only known Hinkley engine still in existence. (Courtesy of the Smithsonian Institution)

EAST NORTH EAST. One of the most northeasterly lines in the United States was the little St. Croix & Penobscot Railroad, a standard gauge pike extending 22 miles from Calais to Princeton, Maine. Calais, located at tidewater on the St. Croix River, was a shipping point for lumber sawed from the logs of the pine forests along that stream; shortly after 1800 a "sluice" was constructed there to aid in moving lumber from the mills to the docks.

The St. Croix & Penobscot R.R. was formed in 1870 by the consolidation of the Calais & Baring R.R. and the Lewey's Island R.R.; the former was chartered in 1837 and opened in the spring of 1851, the latter chartered in 1855 and opened in 1858.

The 0-4-0 shown here is the G. M. PORTER, named in honor of President George M. Porter of the St. Croix & Penobscot; he was a resident of St. Stephens, New Brunswick, on the eastern shore of the St. Croix River. The engine was built in 1858 and is devoid of headlight, indicating that her operations were conducted mostly during the hours of daylight. She was a wood-burner and her 4-wheel tender appears to carry lengths of pine logs left "in the round," or unsplit. (Courtesy of Smithsonian Institution)

NEW HAMPSHIRE CENTRAL R.R. was the proud owner of the REINDEER, a 4-4-0 built by John Souther of Boston, Mass., about 1850. Note the heavy outside frame, circular steam chest, and the typical ribbed Souther dome casing, looking for all the world like a modern trash can; the primitive cab does not appear in style with the finish of the rest of the engine, being of crude design and extremely plain. The name of the REINDEER is lettered on the skirt above the drivers, along with a painting depicting a reindeer dashing across a snowy landscape, hauling a Laplander on his sled. The locomotive is posed on a covered turntable, a device rendered essential in New England where winter snows could quickly fill a turntable pit. (Courtesy of George Eastman House)

BAY STATE OLDSTER. The quaint 4-2-2 pictured here is the UNCLE TOM of the Boston, Clinton & Fitchburg Railroad, a road formed in 1869 by the consolidation of the Agricultural Branch R.R. and the Fitchburg & Worcester R.R.; the Agricultural Branch R.R. was completed between Framingham and Northborough, 15 miles, in 1855 and was leased to the Boston & Worcester Railroad. The Fitchburg & Worcester R.R., chartered in 1846, opened 14 miles of track from Fitchburg to Sterling Junction in February, 1850.

The Boston, Clinton & Fitchburg later acquired the Mansfield & Framingham R.R., and in 1876 was consolidated with the New Bedford R.R. to form the Boston, Clinton, Fitchburg & New Bedford Railroad. The New Bedford road included 11 miles of the old Taunton Branch R.R., chartered in 1835 and opened between Taunton and Mansfield in 1836.

The UNCLE TOM was an inside-connected engine with a number of colorful touches, including the cast figures of a colored post-boy on her running board and a cock perched on her sand box; an oil painting decorates her cab panel and a waterbucket is hung on the rear of her tank, the latter reminiscent of the days when water was "jerked" with buckets from trackside springs and streams. The brake shoes on her driving and trailing wheels appear to be simply large blocks of wood fitted to the brake hangers. Her name may indicate the popularity of Harriet Beecher Stowe's novel in the hot-bed of the Abolitionist movement in the era preceding the Civil War. (Courtesy of Smithsonian Institution)

READING'S ROCKET. The 0-4-0 shown here was built in England by the British firm of Braithwaite, Milner & Company in 1838 for use on the Philadelphia & Reading Railroad, reportedly being the third locomotive placed on that road.

The little inside-connected engine was equipped to burn wood, but was later converted to use anthracite coal for fuel. Her cylinders were 10½ × 16 inches, her original weight was slightly over 8 tons, and she went into service early in 1838; the ROCKET pulled passenger trains until 1845, then was assigned to the Construction & Roadway Department for maintenance work until 1865, after which she was used as a switcher at Reading and at Port Richmond (Philadelphia) until retired in March of 1879.

This photo shows the ROCKET in retirement at Reading, bearing Philadelphia & Reading No. 1 on her boiler-top tank; the tank, wooden cab, stack, and drivers are not original, as the cab, tank, and bell were added in 1862 and it is believed her original driving wheels were replaced at that time. In 1893 she was restored to resemble her original appearance and was exhibited at the Columbian Exposition in Chicago, later being exhibited in St. Louis at the Louisiana Purchase Exposition in 1904 and then placed in the Columbia Avenue Station of the Reading in Philadelphia. Since 1933 the restored ROCKET has been on display at the Franklin Institute in Philadelphia.

Note the string of old 4-wheeled coal "jimmies" on the high line dump in the background of this photograph. (Courtesy of Smithsonian Institution)

The Days of 1865

By F. G. Rosenberry.

Penn. Yard Clerk

BUCKEYE PIONEER. The Little Miami Railroad was chartered in 1836 and construction began the following year on the 4 foot 10 inch gauge track running northeast from Cincinnati, the rails reaching Springfield in August of 1846. The Little Miami R.R. joined with the Columbia & Xenia R.R. in 1853 in a contract that united the two roads to provide a continuous through line from Cincinnati to Columbus, Ohio, the Columbus & Xenia having been opened in February of 1850. This partnership was dissolved in 1868 and the Little Miami leased the Columbus & Xenia, along with the Dayton & Western R.R., a 41-mile line opened on October 11, 1853, between Dayton, Ohio, and Richmond, Indiana; to connect up with the Dayton & Western, the 16-mile long Dayton, Xenia & Belpre R.R. linking Xenia with Dayton was purchased. The Little Miami R.R. connected with the Mad River & Lake Erie R.R. at Springfield when the latter line reached there in 1848, forming the first through rail connection between Lake Erie and the Ohio River. The Little Miami and leased roads were leased to the Pittsburgh, Cincinnati & St. Louis Railway in 1869 and the properties were transferred to the Pennsylvania Company, which was formed in 1870 to manage the network of roads west of Pittsburgh in the interest of the Pennsylvania Railroad; early lines included in this control were the Pittsburgh, Ft. Wayne & Chicago Ry., the Erie & Pittsburgh R.R., the Cincinnati & Muskingum Valley Ry., and others.

The engine pictured here is the DR. GOODALE of the consolidated Little Miami & Columbus & Xenia R.R., a 4-4-0 built by Moore & Richardson, the Cincinnati Locomotive Works, in 1853. Note the odd design of her metal pilot and the early application of extended valve stems, the latter visible on the front of both steam chests. (Courtesy of Smithsonian Institution)

RUTLAND & BURLINGTON R.R. was reorganized in 1853 and emerged as the Rutland Railroad. In 1870-71 it was leased to the Central Vermont R.R., along with its leased affiliates, the Vermont Valley R.R., the Vermont & Massachusetts R.R., and the Addison R.R.; the first two of these leased lines formed a route from Bellows Falls to Grant's Corners, via Brattleboro. Shown here is the Rutland & Burlington's No. 15, the CHESTER, a pretty inside-connected 4-4-0 woodburner built by Taunton in 1850. Note the plug-hatted official posed in studied nonchalance for this scene in the pastoral Vermont countryside. (Courtesy of Dr. S. R. Wood)

PENNSYLVANIA PASTORAL. The ancient 0-6-0 shown here is the ECONOMY of the Darlington Cannel Coal Railroad, a short line constructed in the western reaches of Pennsylvania in the 1860's by a sect called the "Economites." The road ran from New Galilee to Cannelton, Pa., and was later extended to Lisbon, Ohio, as the Pittsburgh, Marion & Chicago; this road was later reorganized as the Pittsburgh, Lisbon & Western R.R., owned by the Wheeling & Lake Erie.

The old ECONOMY was built in March, 1852, for the Ohio & Pennsylvania R.R. by Baldwin, shop number 466; when new she had 13½ × 18 inch cylinders, 42 inch drivers, and weighed 15 tons. She was equipped with the flexible beam truck patented by Baldwin in 1842, an innovation which was hailed as a vast improvement over previous locomotive designs. In 1859 the Baldwin Works rebuilt this engine, under shop number 844, for the Pittsburgh, Fort Wayne & Chicago, successors to the Ohio & Pennsylvania R.R. line; her new specifications included 14½ × 18 inch cylinders and 44 inch drivers, while her weight was increased to 17 tons. Note the early type of six-wheeled tender in this old photo of the ECONOMY, each set of wheels being carried in the jaws of boxes fixed rigidly to the tender frame. (Courtesy of Dr. S. R. Wood)

CENTRAL POWER OF THE 1850's. New York Central locomotive No. 57, named the W. R. GIFFORD, was constructed by the Schenectady Loco. Works in September, 1854, and bore Schenectady shop number 96; she is shown here on a decked turntable, with Engineer Hank Milligan posed in her gangway. The GIFFORD is typical of the woodburning motive power in use on the Central in the 1850's.

An interesting document issued in that era is the running expense and repair statement for the month of November, 1858, covering the Western Division of the N.Y.C. under the supervision of Master Mechanic David Upton and Assistant Supt. J. Collamer. This sheet lists all the locomotives on the division by name and number; in addition it lists the builder of each machine, including such firms as Rogers, Ketchum & Co., Blanchard & Kimball, Norris Brothers, the Detroit Locomotive Works, John Brandt of Paterson, N.J., Schenectady, Boston Loco. Works, and two engines built by the Auburn State Prison. The engineer of each engine is named, and the class of service and terminals of runs given for each; the 63 locomotives on the division racked up a total of 119,152 miles during the month, burning 2,854 cords of wood and using 6,991 pints of tallow and machine oil. A shop force of 109 men were employed

to repair the power, manning shops at Rochester, Buffalo and Niagara Falls, and 16 wipers were employed to keep the engines clean.

The report goes into great detail regarding miles run and cars handled by each locomotive, amounts of wood, oil and waste used, and the cost of wages, material and repairs to each engine. Engine 144, the WINNEBAGO, with Engr. Levi Lewis, ran 3,124 miles in November, 1,633 on passenger and 1,491 on freight, between Buffalo and Rochester; she burned 40¼ cords of wood and used 134 pints of oil. (Anderson collection, courtesy of H. M. Ghormley)

READING WORKHORSE. The Philadelphia & Reading Railroad built the TENNESSEE, shown here, in their Reading Shops in 1852. The 2-6-0 weighed about 60,525 pounds and had her single pair of truck wheels located behind the cylinders; she was fitted with two steam domes, the throttle being located in the forward dome, and carried her supply of sand in the box hung pannier-fashion astride her boiler.

The Reading's first engine was the NEVERSINK, a Baldwin of 1836 whose boiler exploded in 1846; she was followed by the DELAWARE, built by Ross Winans. Next came the ROCKET, FIREFLY, SPITFIRE, PLANET, DRAGON, and COMET, all built by Braithwaite between 1836 and 1838. These were followed by the GOWAN & MARX, an early 4-4-0 built by Eastwick & Harrison in 1839; this engine reportedly hauled forty times its own weight on the Reading-Philadelphia run in 1840. On January 1st, 1842, the first Reading train ran between Pottsville and Philadelphia, hauled by the HICHENS & HARRISON, Baldwin's 139th locomotive, built in 1839.

President John Tucker took charge of the Reading in 1844 and bolstered the line's economy by leasing mines, sending long trains of coal rumbling down to Port Richmond on the Delaware. The route of the Reading down from the Pennsylvania coal fields was largely selected by Moncure Robinson, a brilliant civil engineer from Virginia; backers in constructing the original line were Isaac Hiester and Geo. DeBenneville Keim of Reading, and Edward Biddle of Philadelphia.

The pioneer 5-ton wooden coal cars gave way to iron hoppers and locomotives increased in size to handle the heavier traffic, many of the engines being built in the Reading's shops; by 1883 the road was moving approximately 8 million tons of coal per year. (Courtesy of Reading Railway)

OHIO EIGHT-WHEELER. This 4-4-0 belonged to the Cincinnati, Hamilton & Dayton Railroad and was named the D. McLAREN, in honor of a CH&D Superintendent. Although reputedly built by the road in their Cincinnati shops in October, 1856, she bears a strong resemblance to motive power constructed by the Cincinnati firm of Moore & Richardson, proprietors of the Cincinnati Locomotive Works. Her pilot is of unusual design, being formed of metal straps and closely resembling Moore & Richardson pilots; she weighed about 19½ tons and had 66 inch driving wheels.

The Cincinnati, Hamilton & Dayton R.R. was chartered as the Cincinnati & Hamilton in 1846 and underwent a name change in 1847. The road between Cincinnati and Dayton, Ohio, was opened in 1848, and consisted of nearly 60 miles of track laid to a gauge of 4 feet, 10 inches. A "straddle" was later made over this route by laying a set of rails outside the CH&D tracks, and the trains of the Atlantic & Great Western R.R. operated on this 6-foot gauge "straddle." The CH&D operated, by ownership or lease, the Dayton & Michigan R.R., the Cincinnati, Richmond & Chicago R.R., and the Cincinnati, Hamilton & Indianapolis R.R., these systems comprising an additional 283 miles of track. Also operated over CH&D trackage in the 1870's were 50 flat cars and 50 box cars of the Saginaw & Cincinnati Lumber Transportation Co., used in lumber service between Saginaw, Michigan, and Cincinnati, Ohio.

The D. McLAREN was a woodburner and this rare old photo shows her posed in front of a pile of wood for the evident purpose of replenishing her fuel supply. (Courtesy of Smithsonian Institution)

B. & O. ANTIQUITY. The photograph reproduced here is of Civil War vintage and shows Baltimore & Ohio Railroad No. 16, a 4-4-0 named the P. E. THOMAS. This ancient tea-kettle was originally built by William Norris for the B. & O. in 1838 as a 4-2-0 type, later being rebuilt as a 4-4-0 at the Mount Clare shops in 1848.

The Washington Branch of the Baltimore & Ohio R.R. was authorized in 1831 and the line from Relay, Maryland, to Washington, D.C., was completed in August of 1835.

In the beginning, the power of the Washington Branch was separately numbered, the No. 1 being named the LAFAYETTE. This 4-2-0 was built by Wm. Norris in 1837 and was the first engine on the B&O lines to have a horizontal boiler; she was followed by the sister engines PHILIP E. THOMAS and J. W. PATTERSON in 1838, bearing Washington Branch numbers 2 and 3, respectively. These engines were called the "One Arm Billy" locomotives and carried 10 × 20 inch cylinders and 48 inch driving wheels. They proved so satisfactory that the B&O received four more from Norris, the WILLIAM COOKE, built in December of 1838, and the PATAPSCO, MONOCACY, and POTOMAC, all built in 1839. Two other Norris engines were added to the B&O roster in 1839, being the 4-4-0's

PEGASUS and VESTA. The first B&O 4-4-0 was the ATLAS, built for the road in 1839 by Eastwick & Harrison of Philadelphia, Pennsylvania. (Courtesy of Smithsonian Institution)

BRITISH EXPORT. The locomotive shown here is the ADAM BROWN, No. 55 of the Great Western Railway of Canada. She was built in Birkenhead, England, by the Canada Works, a firm formed by Messrs. Peto, Brassey, Betts and Jackson, contractors for Canada's Grand Trunk Railway. This firm built about 56 engines for the Grand Trunk Ry. and four for the Great Western Ry. of Canada between 1854 and 1858; these were of two classes, a 2-2-2 type for passenger service and a 2-4-0 for freight work. These wheel arrangements proved unsatisfactory for the service required on the Canadian lines and by 1860 all were rebuilt to 4-4-0 types, as shown in this view of the ADAM BROWN taken about 1870.

These engines followed the design of Alexander Allan, a pioneer in British locomotive design, and were known as the Allan or Crewe type, Allan having served as Foreman of Locomotives at the Crewe Works; the dome is covered with a copper or brass casing and fitted with a Salter spring-balance safety valve, and another Salter safety valve is located on the thin column above the name plate, just ahead of the column supporting the whistle. The deep Allan outside frame, supporting cylinders and crosshead guides, the typical British 3-wheeled tender, and the absence of a bell all indelibly stamp this engine as an English product, even though a North American type of pilot, stack, and head light have been applied. (Courtesy of Canadian National Railways)

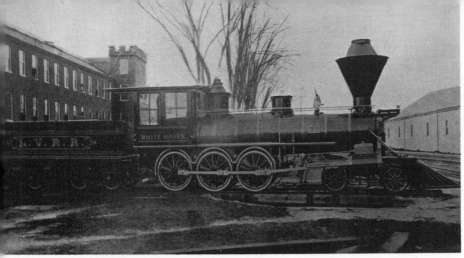

EARLY MASON. The locomotive WHITE HAVEN of the Lehigh Valley Railroad was the 132nd engine built by William Mason of Taunton, Massachusetts; in addition to her name, she bore road number 30. Out-shopped in May of 1863, she was a 4-6-0 but lacking in the refinements that generally characterized Mason's graceful engines. Her cylinders were slightly inclined and a serpentine of continuous mud guard covered her 48 inch driving wheels.

Her cylinders were 17 × 24 inches.

Her driving wheels are fitted with conventional counter-balances, placed visibly between the spokes of her drivers opposite the crank pins; to achieve a symmetrical appearance Mason engines usually had the counterweight material concealed in the hollow rims of the drivers where it served its purpose without offending the artistic senses.

The WHITE HAVEN was named after the town in Pennsylvania's Luzerne County, located 17 miles north of Penn Haven. The Lehigh Valley acquired the Penn Haven & White Haven R.R. in 1864, linking the towns named in the corporate title. At the close of 1864 the Lehigh Valley owned 53 locomotives; this number was increased to 90 by 1867, to 136 by 1869, and to 158 by 1870. Six years later the expansion and growth of business had increased the roster to 232 locomotives. (Courtesy of George Eastman House)

AN N.Y.C. BEAUTY. Engineer Sam Austin and his fireman pose for the photographer in this fine old view of the New York Central's Engine No. 285, a beautiful American type built in the road's West Albany Shops in 1867. A spread eagle screams his painted defiance from the cab panel and a waterfall cascades down the mountains in the oil painting on the headlight house.

Quite a number of American railroads built their own engines and turned out very creditable machines, maintaining extensive shops for running repairs. In 1858 the New York Central's Western Division operated repair shops at Buffalo, Niagara Falls, and Rochester, New York, those at the latter location being the largest of the three. The Rochester Shops employed 42 machinists and 6 machinist's apprentices, 5 blacksmiths and 6 helpers, 5 boilermakers and 3 helpers, 3 coppersmiths, 6 carpenters, 2 painters, a brass moulder and a pattern maker. In addition there was a sheet iron worker, a bolt cutter, a boiler cleaner, 3 flue makers, 8 locomotive wipers, 7 roundhouse men, 7 laborers, and a call boy. The Rochester Shops had two machine shop foremen, one boiler shop foreman, and a blacksmith shop foreman, making a total of 101 men and 4 foremen engaged in repairs on locomotives. Total cost for material and labor expended for repairs of locomotives on the Western Division of the N.Y.C. Railroad for the month of November, 1858, was $5,240.11, according to the report of Master Mechanic David Upton; this sum was expended on the 63 locomotives in service on the Division at that time. Wages for the month paid to engineers, firemen, and wipers amounted to $6,523.61. These figures are cited to present an idea of the cost of operating a steam railroad division in ante-bellum days. (Anderson collection, courtesy of H. M. Ghormley)

FREIGHT POWER OF THE 1860'S. This 4-6-0 was built in June, 1860, by M. W. Baldwin for the North Pennsylvania Railroad, where she was assigned road number 11 and named the WYOMING. She had large 19 × 22 inch cylinders, 50 inch drivers, and weighed 64,000 pounds. Note the two builder's plates in the skirt below the running board; one of these round plates bears the name of M. W. Baldwin and the shop number of the engine, and the other reads "Philadelphia—1860." Water for her boiler was pumped from the tender by two pumps, one under each side of her cab, powered by a rod from her rear driving wheels. Her cab windows are of unusual design, with her engineer seated in the center opening; at the base of her steam dome can be seen the crank and rod of her outside throttle rigging, and the heavy switch ropes with metal links spliced in both ends are draped under the tender behind the bushy-bearded conductor.

The North Pennsylvania R.R. was chartered in April, 1852, as the Philadelphia, Easton & Water Gap Railroad, but the name was changed to North Pennsylvania in October of the same year. The 55.60 miles of main line from Philadelphia to Bethlehem, Pa., was opened on July 7th, 1857; short branches ran from Hellertown to Shimerville and from Lansdale to Doylestown. The road also leased the Stony Creek Railroad, Lansdale to Norristown, and the Northeast Pennsylvania Railroad, Abington to Hartsville; the latter road was opened in 1873 and the Stony Creek in 1874.

In 1876 the Delaware River branch, Jenkintown to Yardleyville, was opened, connecting with the Delaware & Bound Brook R.R. to form what was known as the "New York and Philadelphia New Line," and the North Pennsylvania lines later were leased to the Reading.

PENNSY SWITCHER. The little 0-6-0 tank type pictured here is No. 216 of the Pennsylvania Railroad, a switch engine built by Baldwin in August, 1861. The little goat bore Baldwin construction number 1008 on the builder's plate affixed to the base of her steam dome, had 15 × 18 inch cylinders, 44 inch drivers, and weighed 44,800 pounds. Her water supply was carried in the tank straddling her boiler, and her sand supply was carried in metal boxes fastened to the frame, with individual hoppers for each front and rear driving wheel. The hand-hole visible in the outer stack casing permitted the removal of accumulated cinders trapped by the interior cone and netting; a continuous fender covered all three pair of drivers, preventing grime from being thrown upward onto the engine's neat finish. (Courtesy of H. L. Broadbelt collection)

NEW ENGLAND EXPORT. The Portland Locomotive Works, located in Portland, Maine, constructed the 0-4-0 tank engine shown here for the Panama Rail Road in 1865; the engine bore the name COLON, and carried shop number 136; she had 12 × 18 inch cylinders and 42 inch drivers, with her water carried in the tank slung over her boiler.

An unusual feature of this engine was the firebox door's location in the right side sheet, rather than in the conventional position in the back-head of the boiler. Built to the original gauge of 5 feet, the COLON had her throttle and reverse lever located on the left side of the boiler, and a view of the left side of this locomotive appears in Bulletin No. 80 of the Railway & Locomotive Historical Society.

Niles & Company of Cincinnati, Ohio, built a number of early engines for the road across the Isthmus of Panama, including some four-cylindered engines utilizing a bevel gear and third rail. The Portland Works turned out some eightwheelers for the Panama R.R. in 1852, the first being the NUEVA GRANADA, followed by the BOGOTA and the PANAMA; these were followed by the GORGONA, OBISPO, and MATACHIN in 1854. Other Portland 0-4-0's included the CHIRIQUI, DARIEN, and VERAGUES; a large number of Rogers 0-6-0's also saw service in the canal construction and railroad operation in Panama. Much of the early history of Panama Railroad engines was lost when disastrous fires in Colon destroyed the original records. (Courtesy of Smithsonian Institution)

PETROLEUM REGION POWER. The first real oil well in the United States was drilled at Titusville, Pennsylvania, in 1859 by Edwin L. Drake, a conductor from the New York & New Haven Railroad. Colonel Drake's well started a boom in the northwestern Pennsylvania area and the Civil War boosted the demand for the black gold that was pumped from the shallow wells along Oil Creek.

Several railroads were chartered to serve the new industry, among them the Warren & Franklin, the Farmers' R.R. Co., and the Oil Creek Railroad; the latter was chartered in 1862 and completed in 1866. In 1868 these three lines were consolidated as the Oil Creek & Allegheny River Railroad, but this road defaulted in 1874 and was operated by a Receiver until 1876, when it was reorganized as the Pittsburgh, Titusville & Buffalo Railroad. The 95-mile road started at Corry, ran south through Titusville to Oil City, then doubled back northeasterly through Oleopolis and Tidioute to Irvineton, Pennsylvania. In addition the road operated the 3-mile long Cherry Run Branch and a 25-mile long branch from Titusville northwest to Union, the latter branch having formerly been the Union & Titusville Railroad. After the 1876 reorganization, the road was operated in connection with the Allegheny Valley Railroad.

The Civil War vintage 4-4-0 depicted here is the old OIL CITY of the Oil Creek Railroad. Her inclined cylinders and valves were lubricated through the tallow cups on top of the steam chests, and this photo shows a tallow pot just behind the left tallow cup; directly above it is the whistle, mounted on its own connection to the boiler. Her safety valves are mounted in the old brass "cannon" type columns and her driving and connecting rods appear very fragile by later standards. The linen dusters worn by the men grouped near her tender were popular items of apparel in the 1860-70 period, and were often used by railroad officials to protect their suits from the dust, cinders, and grime that was then so much a part of railway travel. (Courtesy of Pennsylvania Historical & Museum Commission, Harrisburg, Pennsylvania)

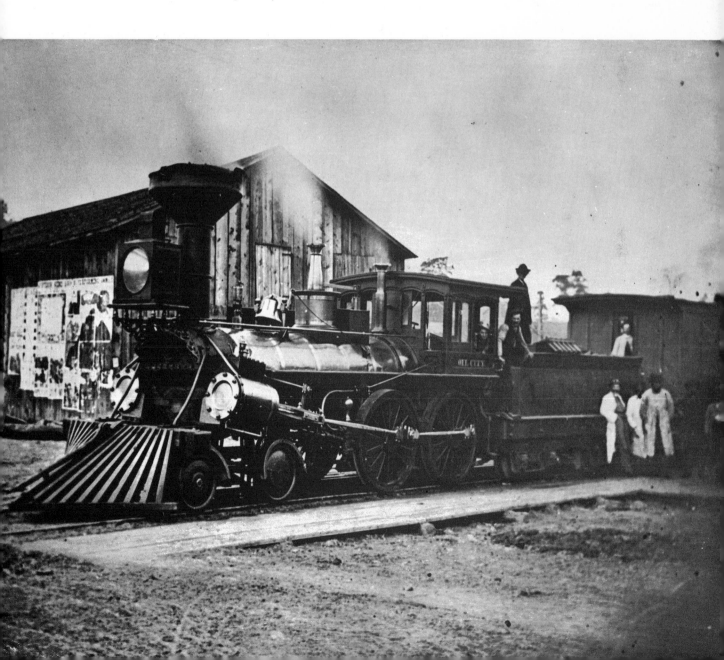

LEHIGH COAL & NAVIGATION POWER. The sturdy 4-6-0 shown here is the WAPWALLOPEN, built by Baldwin in 1865 as No. 7 of the Lehigh & Susquehanna Railroad, a property of the Lehigh Coal & Navigation Company. Her boiler extended back through the cab and the lever controlling her cylinder cocks was connected to a rod concealed inside the right handrail. The forward portion of her tender and fire pit is covered with a roof for the protection of the fireman; this device not only sheltered him from sun and rain, but probably helped shield him from the rain of hot cinders that billowed out of the funnel stack.

The Lehigh & Susquehanna was commenced in 1837 under charter of the Lehigh Coal Company and the line was opened in 1840. The main stem extended 105 miles from Phillipsburg, New Jersey, to Union Junction, Pennsylvania; branches included the Nescopec, Nanticoke, Coplay, Lemmie, Sandy Run, Everhart, and Carbon short lines and spurs. The Tresckow Railroad, Silver Brook to Audenried, Pa., was opened in 1872 and operated by the Lehigh & Susquehanna; In 1871 the L&S and its affiliated connecting lines, the Nesquehoning Valley R.R., the Tresckow R.R., and the Lehigh & Lackawanna R.R., were leased in perpetuity to the Central Railroad of New Jersey; the Nesquehoning Valley ran from Mauch Chunk to Tamanend and the Lehigh & Lackawanna ran between Bethlehem and Stroudsburg, Pa.

Note the extended "deadwood" buffers projecting from the pilot beam of the WAPWALLOPEN for coupling to the coal "jimmies" then in use; many trainmen were seriously injured with these old man-traps, which crushed fingers, hands, or arms with great impartiality. (Courtesy of H. L. Broadbelt collection)

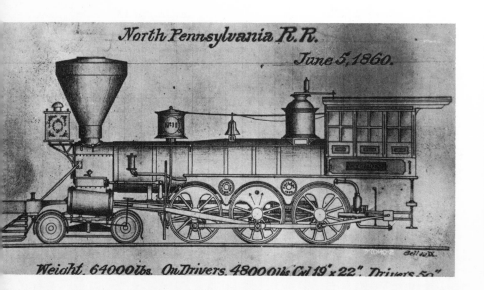

MECHANICAL ERROR. This drawing of the Baldwin 4-6-0 built for the North Pennsylvania Railroad shows the unusual curved counterbalances applied to the driving wheels, but the locomotive could never have run if actually constructed as illustrated. Note that the draughtsman has the main rod connected to the crank pin inside the connecting rod bearings; at the first revolution of the wheels the main rod would strike the side rod connecting the leading driver with the main, or middle, driver. This plate may have been turned out by or for J. Snowden Bell, author of motive power treatises; the error was detected by the keen eye of Fred Jukes, noted Northwest rail photographer, historian, and draughtsman.

ERIE MOGUL. The Erie Railway was formed in 1861 by a reorganization of the old New York & Erie Railroad, a line thrown into receivership in 1859 when it defaulted on payment of interest on its bonds. Engine 254 of the new company is shown here, a husky 2-6-0 with a roomy cab and two steam domes; the throttle valve was located in the forward dome and the rod connecting it to the throttle lever inside the cab is visible in this photo.

In 1850 the Baldwin Works had turned out four 0-8-0 type engines for the New York & Erie, the contract specifying that the front pair of drivers would be replaced with a leading truck if desired after a period of trial operation. This was a concession to Master Mechanic John Brandt of the Erie, who had advocated a 4-6-0 type.

Septimus Norris of Philadelphia had patented a 4-6-0 type in 1846 but a trial of the Norris engine in April of 1847 proved it to be rather unsatisfactory; so little weight was carried on the leading truck that the engine would not curve nor keep to the track easily. Master Mechanic Brandt adopted a modified version of the 4-6-0 with more weight carried by the leading truck, resulting in a satisfactory tenwheeler. Brandt's mechanical genius was reflected by the Erie's power designed to his specifications. (Courtesy of Erie Railroad Company)

B. & O. "GREENBACK." For many years the motive power of the Baltimore & Ohio R.R. reflected the influence of Ross Winans, the ex-New Jersey horse dealer who had come to Baltimore to sell his four-legged hayburners to the B&O in its earliest days of pre-steam operation and remained to become a designer and builder of steam locomotives. Addicted to the belief that each wheel under a locomotive should exert tractive effort, Winans' engines had neither engine nor trailing trucks; his "grasshoppers," "crabs," and "mud diggers" ruled the B&O rails and in 1848 he built his first 0-8-0 "camel," a type that was widely used on the B&O.

The 0-8-0 shown here was B&O No. 32, built in the Mount Clare shops early in 1865, one of five engines constructed to a design of Thatcher Perkins in Mount Clare. The Perkins engines were mainly built by the New Jersey Locomotive & Machine Co. and were known as "Jersey Greenbacks," but the B&O men dubbed them "fantails," since their boilers extended back through the cabs.

This rare old photo of No. 32 was taken at Weaverton Station, Baltimore, in 1871; Engineer George Hulbert leans against the rear of the cab, Fireman C. N. Coursey is at his post in the firing pit, and Conductor J. Horner and Brakeman Chas. Carter stand on the tender.

Note the flat-topped steam dome with the "buck-horn" safety valves and the water pump connected to the rear driver; the side windows of the cab were unglazed, but had canvas curtains that could be rolled down during inclement weather. This class had no apron, the fireboy straddling the opening between backhead and tender; the use of metal aprons covering this man-trap was made mandatory by the Safety Appliance laws of 1895. (Courtesy of Dr. S. R. Wood)

RAIL SPLITTER'S NAMESAKE. The long-barreled ten-wheeler shown here is No. 85 of the Delaware, Lackawanna & Western Railroad and bears the name of A. LINCOLN. A painting of the Great Emancipator decorates the sand box of the locomotive; she was built in Paterson, N.J., by Danforth, Cooke & Co. in March of 1865 and bore shop number 236, had 18 × 24 inch cylinders and 51 inch drivers.

A month later President Abraham Lincoln lay dead in a house across the street from Ford's Theatre in Washington, the victim of an assassin's pistol. The Lackawanna renamed the engine the A. J. ODELL and in 1890 she was transferred to the New York, Lackawanna & Western R.R., the leased subsidiary of the D.L. & W. that was operated as that road's Buffalo Division in western New York.

The accompanying photo shows the A. LINCOLN with an oval-shaped smokebox, cylinder cock rod concealed in the hand rail, and an outside throttle rod, the latter entering the steam dome on the right side of the dome through a packing gland. (Anderson collection, courtesy of H. M. Ghormley)

RIP VAN WINKLE REGION. One of the early lines of the upper Hudson River region was the old Rensselaer & Saratoga Railroad, incorporated in 1832 and opened between Troy and Ballston Spa, New York, in 1835. The first locomotives on the road were the CHAMPLAIN and the ERIE, the 12th and 13th engines built by Baldwin, both constructed in 1835; their service so impressed President L. G. Cannon that he wrote a testimonial letter to Baldwin regarding this pair of 4-2-0's.

The Rensselaer & Saratoga spread a network of rails into the lower valley of the Mohawk and along the southeastern tier of the Adirondacks by leasing a number of short lines, including the pioneer Saratoga & Schenectady Railroad, the Saratoga & Whitehall R.R., the Albany & Vermont (formerly Albany Northern) Railroad, the Troy, Salem & Rutland R.R., and the Glenn's Falls Railroad. In 1871 the Rensselaer & Saratoga and its leased branches were leased to the Delaware & Hudson Canal Company.

Engine No. 37 of the Rensselaer & Saratoga was built by Schenectady and named the COMMODORE VANDERBILT. A fine painting of the old Commodore decorates her headlight as she poses in front of the Tremont House for this photo taken in the days when Saratoga Springs was a popular watering place and a mecca for the pleasure-seeking cream of society. (Courtesy of Smithsonian Institution)

UP THE HUDSON. The Hudson River Railroad was chartered in 1846 and opened from New York City to East Albany in October, 1851. Three years later, in 1854, the Schenectady Locomotive Works turned out the 4-4-0 shown here for the road; the engine was named DAVID UPTON and was a typical woodburner of the era.

Connections between East Albany and Troy were made by lease of the Troy & Greenbush Railroad, a short line opened in 1845. Shrewd old Cornelius Vanderbilt obtained control of the Hudson River Railroad in the 1860's and also obtained control of the New York & Harlem Railroad, a line opened from New York City to Chatham, N.Y., in 1852. The former ferryboat operator pressured the New York Central and bought up stock in this road and in 1867, at the advanced age of 73, became president of the New York Central & Hudson River Railroad, a consolidation of the Hudson River Railroad and the New York Central; in 1873 he leased his New York & Harlem Railroad to the consolidated NYC&HR lines, control of the old Harlem road remaining in the Vanderbilt family. Cornelius Vanderbilt died in 1877, but before his passing he had established the New York Central & Hudson River as one of the leading roads of the day, and his son, William H. Vanderbilt, extended the rail empire even further. (Courtesy of Smithsonian Institution)

FREIGHT POWER OF '76. Among the standard gauge locomotives exhibited by Baldwin Locomotive Works at Philadelphia in 1876 was this handsome Consolidation type built for the Lehigh Valley R.R. as their No. 310 and named the UNITED STATES. The engine was equipped with the Bissell leading truck, carried 130 pounds working pressure steam in her wagon top boiler, and weighed 100,000 lbs. in working order. Her cylinders had a diameter of 20 inches with a 24 inch stroke and her driving wheels had a diameter of 50 ⅜ths inches; she was equipped with both a cross-head water pump and an injector for supplying her boiler with water, and while details are lacking, the injector visible through the center cab window appears to be a type called the Rue Little Giant, a product of the Rue Manufacturing Co. of Philadelphia.

The UNITED STATES is a good example of heavy duty freight power in use during the late 1870's and the photo shows her to have been tastefully finished without the gaudy ornamentation affected by some roads and builders. Lubrication for her cylinders was supplied through pipes concealed under her polished, brassbound jacket, and her exhaust nozzle was of the variable type; built to burn anthracite coal, her firebox contained 24 square feet of grate area. She had a total wheel base of 22 ft. 10 inches, and a rigid wheel base of 14 ft. 9 inches. (Courtesy of H. L. Broadbelt collection)

EXHIBITION POWER

The gallery of photographs in this chapter covers many locomotives that have appeared on display at various expositions in the United States and abroad. The engines exhibited at these affairs represented the peak of locomotive development at the time they were placed on display and the pictures in this section serve to illustrate the classic examples of the work of a variety of locomotive builders over the years.

The first large-scale display of motive power in the United States was presented at the International Centennial Exposition held in Philadelphia, Pennsylvania, from May 10th to November 10th, 1876. The Baldwin Locomotive Works exhibited eight locomotives at the Centennial of 1876, including a 2-8-0 built for the Lehigh Valley, a 4-4-0 and a 2-8-0 built for the Pennsylvania R.R., a 2-6-0 built for the Dom Pedro II Railway of Brazil, a 4-4-0 built for the Central Railroad of New Jersey, an 0-4-0 mining tank engine built to 3 ft. 6 in. gauge, and two locomotives built to 3 ft. gauge, a 2-6-0 and a 4-4-0. The Philadelphia & Reading R.R. exhibited a 4-6-0 fast freight engine and tender built for display by the apprentices in the road's Reading Shops. The Dickson Manufacturing Co. of Scranton, Pa., exhibited a pair of 4-4-0's, one large and one small, along with a 3 ft. gauge 0-4-0 mining tank engine, while the Danforth Locomotive Works displayed a standard gauge 4-4-0 passenger engine and a 3 ft. gauge 0-6-0 tanker designed for freight service.

Porter, Bell & Company of Pittsburgh exhibited a 2-4-0 passenger locomotive built to 3 ft. gauge and William Mason of Taunton, Mass., sent an 0-4-4 Fairlie passenger tank engine of the same gauge.

The Rogers Locomotive & Machine Works exhibited a 5 ft. gauge 4-4-0 mixed service engine built for the Mobile & Montgomery Railroad, while the only foreign engine displayed was an 0-6-2 tank by Dannemora Hary's Jernvay, Sweden.

The ancient Stephenson-built JOHN BULL of the Camden & Amboy, placed in service in 1831, was also on display. Outside the Maryland State Building the Baltimore & Ohio had a highly contrasting display; the old 0-4-0 "grasshopper" JOHN QUINCY ADAMS, renumbered from 1 to 6 in 1850, stood alongside the J. C. DAVIS, B&O No. 600. The ADAMS was built in 1835 and weighed about 8 tons, while the J. C. DAVIS was the road's first 2-6-0, built for the B&O at the Mount Clare Shops, Baltimore, in 1875. Named for Master of Machinery J. C. Davis, who designed and built the engine, the big Mogul won honors for being the finest and largest engine of that day; she reportedly weighed over 90,000 pounds and was designed to handle mail and express trains over the 17-mile grade of the old Third Division between Keyser and Grafton, West Virginia.

Several of the narrow gauge engines exhibited were in actual service at the Centennial Exposition, hauling passengers on the West End Passenger Railway that wound through the Exposition grounds. One of these, the Mason bogie, went to the New York & Manhattan Beach Railway after the Exposition ended.

President Chas. E. Fisher of the Railway & Locomotive Historical Society states that the Rhode Island Locomotive Works built a beautifully finished 4-4-0 and shipped it to Philadelphia for the Centennial but ordered it shipped back to Providence when they learned it was to be left out of doors and unprotected from the weather!

A previous locomotive of ornate finish had the distinction of being the only engine from the United States to be displayed at the Universal Exposition held in Paris, France, in 1867. This engine, named the AMERICA, was built by the Grant Locomotive Works and the 4-4-0 gained fame as the "Silver Engine," being lavishly jacketed and trimmed with German silver, an alloy of nickel, zinc, and copper. The AMERICA was deemed tops among the thirty-two locomotives displayed in Paris and brought home the Gold Medal, complete with a likeness of Emperor Napoleon III.

A large number of locomotives were assembled in Chicago in 1883 for display at the Exhibition of Railway Appliances. New motive power from various builders was displayed there, along with several venerable relics of earlier days of railroading. Among the latter were the British-built JOHN BULL of the Camden & Amboy and the old SAMSON from the mining road of the General Mining Association of Nova Scotia, along with the 1836 vintage Baldwin 4-2-0 that became the Chicago & North Western's PIONEER. First used on the Utica & Schenectady R.R., the ancient tea-pot was sold to the Michigan Central R.R. and then to the Galena & Chicago Union R.R. where it pulled the first train out of Chicago in October, 1848. Following the Exposition of Railway Appliances in 1883, the PIONEER appeared at the World's Columbian Exposition in Chicago in 1893, the Louisiana Purchase Exposition at St. Louis in 1904, the Chicago World's Fair of 1934, and the Chicago Railroad Fair of 1948-49.

The World's Columbian Exposition, held at Chicago in 1893, drew an outstanding collection of locomotives, old and new. The Baldwin Locomotive Works topped the list of exhibitors with 17 locomotives, three of which were shown in connection with a special exhibit of the Baltimore & Ohio Railroad. Included in the extensive Baldwin display was the new high-speed COLUMBIA, a 2-4-2 locomotive that lent its name to that class; other Baldwin power included a Decapod type built for the New York, Lake Erie & Western, a compound Consolidation built for the Norfolk & Western, a 4-6-0 single expansion freight engine for the Baltimore & Ohio Southwestern, representative single expansion American and Mogul types, a saddle-tank designed for logging railroads, three express passenger engines for the Central of New Jersey, Philadelphia & Reading, and Baltimore & Ohio operations of the "Royal Blue Line" between New York and Washington, and a compound 4-6-0 passenger engine that was shown with a train exhibited by the Pullman Car Company. Narrow gauge Baldwin power exhibited included a 30-inch gauge saddle tank for mill or furnace work, a 3-foot gauge 4-6-0 outside-framed compound for the Mexican National Railroad, and a compound 4-4-0 built to metre gauge.

Other builders exhibiting at the Columbian Exposition included Rhode Island, Brooks, Rogers, Cooke, Pittsburgh, Schenectady, Richmond, and H. K. Porter.

A Canadian Pacific 4-6-0 was exhibited at Chicago, and the JAMES TOLEMAN, a 4-4-0 with a novel boiler design, was displayed by the British firm of Hawthorne, Leslie & Company.

The locomotive engineers of the Erie Railroad exhibited a Cooke-built 4-4-0 named the E. B. THOMAS, and the New York Central & Hudson River R.R. had their noted speedster, No. 999, on display. The latter road also unveiled an operable, full-sized replica of the DE WITT CLINTON, complete with tender and cars; the original engine, an 0-4-0, had been constructed by the West Point Foundry Association and was first operated on the Mohawk & Hudson River R.R. in August of 1831.

Along with the latest examples of locomotive construction, the Columbian Exposition featured a considerable display of relics dating back to the dawn of railroading. The ancient JOHN BULL was there, along with the Reading's ROCKET and the veterans ALBION and SAMSON from the Albion Mines railway in Nova Scotia; the SAMSON was built in England by Timothy Hackworth in 1838 and the ALBION was constructed by Rayne & Burn in 1854, both being 0-6-0 types. The Nashville, Chattanooga & St. Louis sent up the rebuilt Western & Atlantic Railroad's old GENERAL of Civil War fame, and the Illinois Central shop forces at McComb, Mississippi, refurbished the ancient 0-4-0 called MISSISSIPPI and she ran to Chicago from McComb under her own power; a veteran of the Natchez & Hamburg R.R., the MISSISSIPPI was probably built by H. R. Dunham of New York in 1836. The old PIONEER of the Chicago & North Western was on display and the Baltimore & Ohio exhibited a number of engines in their large presentation of the history of land transportation. Under the direction of Major Pangborn, charged with arranging this exhibit, the B&O contributed four of their old "grasshopper" locomotives; the JOHN HANCOCK of 1835 was unchanged, saved for being renamed the THOMAS JEFFERSON, while the ANDREW JACKSON was altered to represent Phineas Davis' ATLANTIC of 1832. The JOHN QUINCY ADAMS was changed to resemble the TRAVELLER (formerly named INDIAN CHIEF) of 1833, and the MARTIN VAN BUREN was rebuilt to resemble Winans' old "crab" type of 1838, the MAZEPPA.

Railroad motive power and equipment was exhibited at many expositions following the Chicago affair of 1893. Displays were made at the Cotton States & International Exposition at Atlanta in 1895, the Tennessee Centennial Exposition at Nashville in 1897, the Pan-American Exposition held at Buffalo, New York, in 1901, and the Louisiana Purchase Exposition at St. Louis in 1904. The latter drew a sizeable display of motive power, including 12 steam locomotives of various types from the Baldwin Locomotive Works.

Smaller displays were presented at the Lewis & Clark Centennial Exposition at Portland, Oregon, in 1905-06, at the Jamestown Ter-Centennial Exposition at Norfolk, Virginia, in 1907, at the Alaska-Yukon-Pacific Exposition in Seattle in 1909, and at the Panama-Pacific International Exposition held in San Francisco in 1915.

The Fair of the Iron Horse at Halethorpe, near Baltimore, in the autumn of 1927 presented a variety of locomotives and the Chicago Railroad Fair of 1948-49 included many veteran engines as star performers.

The pages following illustrate the appearance of many of the locomotives exhibited at the various expositions, beginning with the famous Centennial Exhibition at Philadelphia in 1876.

PHILADELPHIA EXHIBIT. Baldwin Locomotive Works prepared an exhibit of eight engines for display at the Centennial International Exhibition held in Philadelphia, Pennsylvania, in 1876. The locomotives selected were chosen to illustrate the different types of engines and the practices of different railroads, both domestic and foreign. Among the larger engines displayed by the Baldwin Works were two Consolidation types, two eight-wheelers, and a Mogul type; smaller power included an 0-4-0 tank type mine engine with a gauge of 3 ft. 6 inches, and two 3 ft. gauge locomotives for service on the Centennial Narrow Gauge Railway operated on the Centennial Exhibition grounds. One of these was the 4-4-0 shown here, named the SCHUYLKILL, Baldwin Shop No. 3878. She was placed in service on May 13th, 1876, and ran until the Centennial celebration ended 156 days later. She burned anthracite coal, had 42 inch drivers, 12 × 16 inch cylinders, and weighed 42,650 pounds. Her usual train consisted of 5 cars of the eight-wheeled variety loaded with about 100 passengers per car, making a total gross train weight of about 60 tons.

The Centennial Railway was 3½ miles long and was double-tracked, making a total of 7 miles of 3 foot gauge line, and was very crooked, being curved to run near all of the principal buildings on the Exhibition grounds. The curves had a radius of 215 feet to 250 feet, and the grades ran up to 155 feet per mile, the track being laid with 35 pound iron rail. Each engine averaged about 16 trips daily, covering approximately 56 miles; each train made about 160 stops daily to load and unload passengers, and the Westinghouse air brake was applied to the equipment to handle these numerous stops, the stations being only short distances apart. (Courtesy of H. L. Broadbelt collection)

SPIRIT OF '76. The trim 4-4-0 pictured here was built by the Rogers Locomotive & Machine Works of Paterson, New Jersey, for display at the Centennial Exposition in Philadelphia, Pa., in 1876. She was typical of the Rogers eight-wheelers of the period, with a tasteful amount of brass and the fluted sand box dome, topped with a brass acorn, that became a Rogers trade-mark.

The number 76 was assigned to this engine to carry out the theme of the Centennial celebration, honoring the hundred years of American independence from 1776 to 1876. The only apparent marks that distinguished No. 76 from other run-of-the-mill Rogers locomotives was the legend lettered on her tender side walls, "Rogers Locomotive & M. Works, Paterson, N.J."

Following the Centennial, No. 76 was delivered to the Mobile & Montgomery Railroad to join a sister engine built for the road by Rogers in the same year. This sister engine was assigned road number 33 but the 76 was allowed to carry her distinctive number until the Mobile & Montgomery was absorbed by the Louisville & Nashville in 1881; she became L&N 623, later 1123, and finally 2123. This pair of 4-4-0's had 16 × 24 inch cylinders, 57 inch drivers, and weighed 69,800 pounds; both were woodburners.

The Mobile & Montgomery R.R. was a 5 foot gauge line extending between the two Alabama towns of its' corporate title; the line was formed in 1868 by a consolidation of the Mobile & Great Northern and the Alabama & Florida Railroads; when consolidated there was a gap between Mobile and Hurricane and a riverboat transfer of about 22 miles was necessary, but this section of connecting track was completed about 1872. After a foreclosure in 1874, the road emerged as the Mobile & Montgomery Railway. (Courtesy of R. E. Prince)

PENNSY CONSOLIDATION. This 2-8-0 built by the Pittsburgh Locomotive Works was one of their engines displayed in Chicago in 1883 at the Exposition of Railway Appliances. She was No. 990 of the Pennsylvania Railroad, and her specifications conformed to that road's "I" Class; the classification was established in 1867 and the "I" Class was added in 1875, indicating a 2-8-0 with 50 inch drivers and 20 × 24 inch cylinders, designed for freight service, mountain traffic and heavy trains. Class "R" was established on the Pennsylvania in 1885 to replace Class "I," the same dimensions prevailing but with an increase in boiler pressure from 125 pounds to 140 pounds; Class "S" was established in 1887 with the same specifications but lighter weight than the "R" Class.

This view of the Pittsburgh engine exhibited in 1883 is from a rare old glass plate builder's negative; unfortunately, a portion of the plate is cracked and missing, clipping the pilot of No. 990. (Courtesy of Schenectady History Center)

EXPORT EXHIBIT. This Mogul type for the Estrada de Ferro de Dom Pedro II was built by Baldwin in 1876 and displayed that year at the Philadelphia Centennial Exposition. The engine was constructed for freight service on the Dom Pedro II rail line of Brazil, was assigned road number 89, and bore the name PRINCIPE DO GRAO PARA. Her gauge was 5 feet 3 inches, and she was fitted with European style buffers, visible in this photo from a somewhat damaged glass plate negative.

Other specifications included 54 inch drivers, 18 × 24 inch cylinders, and a total weight of 80,000 pounds in working order; she had an iron boiler with plates ½ inch thick and a copper firebox ¾ths of an inch in thickness, carrying 130 pounds of working pressure. The engine had 16 square feet of grate area and burned bituminous coal.

The Imperial Government of Brazil had previously imported Baldwin locomotives for service on the Dom Pedro Segundo railway, including some 2-6-0 types built in 1862-63 that were actually a modification of the regular Baldwin 4-6-0 type; their drivers were set well back under the boiler, and the Bissell pony truck with radius bar was substituted for the regular four-wheel engine truck. The first steel tires applied to driving wheels by the Baldwin Works were fitted on locomotives delivered to the Dom Pedro II Railway in 1862; these imported steel tires had a shoulder in their inner surface, opposite the flanged side, and were shrunk onto the wheels. (Courtesy of H. L. Broadbelt collection)

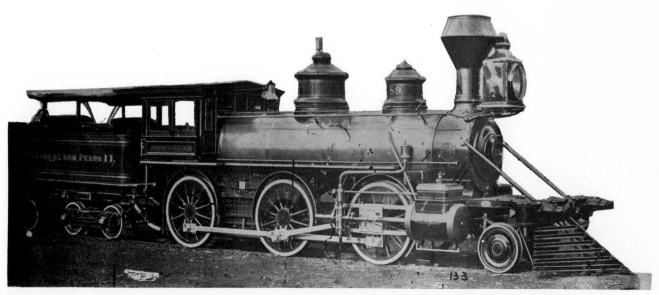

BROOKS WORKS EXHIBIT. The history of the Brooks Locomotive Works dated back to October of 1869 when President Jay Gould of the Erie Railway ordered the Dunkirk, New York, shops of that road be shut down permanently and the shop equipment moved to another location.

The Erie's Supt. of Motive Power & Machinery, Mr. H. G. Brooks, was a resident of Dunkirk and disliked the thought of the effect of the removal of the shops upon the town, the employees, and his own interests. Brooks met with Gould and proposed to lease the Erie Railway shops, to which Gould agreed; the Brooks Locomotive Works took over in November, 1869, and turned out one locomotive in that month and another one in December.

In 1883, the year the trim 0-6-0 shown here was turned out for the Exposition of Railway Appliances in Chicago, the Brooks Works purchased the shops and the twenty acres of land on which they were located from the New York, Lake Erie & Western Railway. Under the able leadership of President H. G. Brooks, the business expanded and the entire stock of the Dunkirk firm was locally owned, with each department head being an owner of the establishment.

By 1893, production at the Brooks Works was up to 25 locomotives per month and the firm had turned out 2,300 engines since it was established in late 1869.

There is reason to believe that the 0-6-0 exhibition engine depicted here became No. 96 of the Cincinnati, Washington & Baltimore Railroad. (Courtesy of Schenectady History Center)

A FAMOUS PAIR. Among the locomotives displayed at the World's Columbian Exposition in Chicago in 1893 was a husky Consolidation type built by the Rogers Locomotive

Company as No. 638 of the Illinois Central Railroad. The Belpaire-boilered freight hog captured the fancy of a young Illinois Central engineman working at the I.C. exhibit at the Exposition, and when the display ended John Luther Jones and Engine No. 638 left together; the new Rogers 2-8-0 was personally assigned to Jones and he triumphantly escorted her south to his own division.

This photo shows John L. "Casey" Jones in the cab of the exhibition engine in April, 1898, while in freight service at Hunter's Cut, Mississippi. Two years later Casey rode to eternal fame in the cab of Illinois Central's Engine 382 when his passenger train piled into the rear of a freight train at Vaughn, Mississippi. Immortalized in a ballad attributed to a Negro roundhouse worker, the saga of Casey Jones was distorted in a song that swept the country and was parodied in an unprintable bawdy version.

Casey Jones was neither the first nor last engineer to die at his post of duty, but the song and legend surrounding his demise has permanently enshrined his name on the roll of American folklore heroes. (Courtesy of Illinois Central Railroad)

CHICAGO, 1883. The Exposition of Railway Appliances drew an exhibit of 6 locomotives from the Brooks Locomotive Works of Dunkirk, New York. In addition to the 0-6-0 switcher illustrated elsewhere in this chapter, Brooks displayed a 4-4-0, a 2-6-0, and a 4-6-0 built to standard gauge, along with a narrow gauge 4-4-0 and a narrow gauge 2-6-0. The standard gauge 4-6-0, bearing shop number 907, is pictured here. The Brooks narrow gauge 4-4-0, bearing shop number 900, was sold to the Florida Southern in the fall of 1883, where she became their No. 7, the JOHN W. CHANDLER; in 1900 she was sold to the Bellaire, Zanesville & Cincinnati R.R.

Among other locomotives at the 1883 Exposition were the Hinkley-built four-cylinder balanced 4-4-0, HENRY F. SHAW; a Wootten passenger engine that burned bituminous coal with marked success; a 4-8-0 constructed for use on the Central Pacific R.R.; and four engines built by the Baldwin Locomotive works. Two of the Baldwins were standard gauge, being a 4-4-0 and a 2-8-0 constructed as part of a regular order for the Northern Pacific and probably woodburners; the other two Baldwins were narrow gauge, one being a 4-4-0 with a diamond stack for the Fulton County Narrow Gauge R.R. in Illinois and the other a straight-stacked 2-8-0 for the line of the Conglomerate Mining Company. (Courtesy of Schenectady History Center)

CHICAGO, 1883. A pioneer relic displayed at the Exposition of Railway Appliances in Chicago in 1883 was the veteran engine SAMSON, built in England in 1838 and operated by the General Mining Association of Nova Scotia. The engine, its' 4-wheeled tender, and primitive 4-wheel coach are shown here on the transfer table at the site of the 1883 Exposition; standing at the controls at far right is George Davidson, long the engineer of the SAMSON and reportedly the driver who accompanied her from England to Nova Scotia.

The SAMSON was returned to Chicago for display at the World's Columbian Exposition in 1893, after which it was stored in Baltimore by the Baltimore & Ohio R.R. for preservation; it was on exhibit at the Fair of the Iron Horse in 1927 and in 1928 was returned to the Province of Nova Scotia, where it was stored for a time in Halifax before being put on display at the New Glasgow station.

Note the fireman posed with his scoop on the front of the tender, facing the firedoor located directly beneath the stack of the return flue type boiler. (Courtesy of Smithsonian Institution)

'WAY DOWN YONDER. In 1884-85, the city of New Orleans was the site of the Cotton Centennial Exposition and an 1884 issue of the "Railroad Gazette" remarked, "The Baldwin Works have lately despatched four locomotives to the Exhibition, a Mogul engine for the Cincinnati, New Orleans & Texas Pacific; a ten-wheeler for the Central of Georgia, and two 16 × 24 in. cylinder American type engines; one being for the Morgan's Louisiana & Texas, and the other for the Jacksonville, Tampa & Key West. The Cincinnati, New Orleans & Texas Pacific Co. will also be represented by a fine passenger engine, constructed at their shops at Ludlow, Kentucky, from the designs of Mr. James Meehan, Supt. of Motive Power. The Pittsburgh Locomotive Works will contribute one specimen of each of their standard types of engines, American, Mogul and Consolidation."

The three Baldwins pictured here are believed to have been a part of the Baldwin display at New Orleans during the Cotton Centennial. The 5-foot gauge No. 5 of the Jacksonville, Tampa & Key West bore Baldwin shop number 7487 and the double-domed No. 47 of the Morgan's Louisiana & Texas bore shop number 7486; the ten-wheeler for the Central of Georgia carried road number 146 and shop number 7481, and shows an early application of outside journals and frame on her engine truck. (Courtesy of Mr. H. L. Broadbelt collection)

CHICAGO, 1893. Chicago boldly launched the World's Columbian Exposition on the vast grounds bordering Lake Michigan in 1893, in the face of the great panic that was even then casting its shadow across the face of the nation. Locomotive builders sent numerous examples of their work to the Exposition, but probably no single engine exhibited there enjoyed the widespread fame accorded old No. 999 of the New York Central & Hudson River Railroad.

The lanky American, built in the road's West Albany Shops in 1893, was sky-rocketed to fame through the efforts of Geo. H. Daniels, General Passenger Agent for the Central and a man who knew how to create publicity on a grand scale.

Daniels capitalized on the speed of old 999 and her reputed record dash of 112.5 miles per hour over a measured mile between Syracuse and Buffalo with Engineer Charlie Hogan at her throttle. hauling the crack EMPIRE STATE EXPRESS.

The speedy 4-4-0 was designed by Wm. Buchanan, a Scot who was a machinist, fireman, engineer, and shop foreman on the Central before being appointed Superintendent of Motive Power in 1881. He designed and installed a water-table firebox to provide increased heating and improved combustion in his high-stepping coal burners.

Withdrawn from active service for display at the Columbian Exposition, No. 999 drew record crowds of admirers eager to see the speed queen of the century. The engine has been preserved and is today a treasured relic of the New York Central. (Courtesy of Mr. H. M. Ghormley)

EXPOSITION NAMESAKE. Among the Baldwin exhibits at the Columbian Exposition in 1893 was a new type of locomotive designed for high speed passenger service and introducing a new wheel arrangement with a two-wheel lead truck, two pair of drivers, and a two-wheel trailing truck. This 2-4-2 type bore the name COLUMBIA and carried Baldwin construction number 13350; her name was applied to other engines of this type and while capable of fast running, the "Columbia" type was soon due to be supplanted by the 4-4-2 or "Atlantic" type, introduced in 1895.

The original COLUMBIA was a Vauclain compound and burned bituminous coal. Her cylinders had a 26 inch stroke, the high pressure cylinder having a diameter of 13 inches and the low pressure cylinder a diameter of 22 inches; the diameter of her driving wheels outside of tires was 84¼ inches and the drivers extended above her running boards under the covers visible in this photo, similar to the "splasher boxes" found on British locomotives.

Her fittings included a Janney coupler on her tender, Detroit lubricators of the sight feed variety, William Sellers & Co. injectors, Coale Muffler safety valves, and an Adams & Westlake headlight. Her driving and trailing wheel brakes were made by the American Brake Company of St. Louis, Mo., and she was fitted with Westinghouse Air Brake Company's tender and train brake equipment.

The weight of the engine in working order was 126,640 pounds and the tender weighed 78,482 pounds when full of fuel and water; their total overall length was slightly over 63 feet, and the distance from the top of the rail to the top of her stack was just over 14 feet, 4 inches. (Courtesy of H. L. Broadbelt collection)

BALDWIN HOG. This Consolidation type was built by Baldwin in March of 1893 as Norfolk & Western's No. 330, and was among the locomotives exhibited at Chicago's great Exposition held that year. The heavy 2-8-0 bore Baldwin construction number 13333, and was a Vauclain compound, with the big low-pressure cylinder mounted above the smaller high-pressure cylinder. She was equipped with the Belpaire style firebox, which extended through her cab, creating cramped quarters for her engineer and blocking his view of the fireman's side of the cab.

This 1893 engine represented the peak of development of the 2-8-0 type at that time and was a lineal descendant of the original CONSOLIDATION built by Baldwin in 1866 for the Lehigh & Mahanoy. (Courtesy of H. L. Broadbelt collection)

A TRIO OF POLISHED BALDWINS. The three locomotives pictured here are a part of the motive power exhibited at the Columbian Exposition in Chicago in 1893. Although the use of compound engines was then on the rise, the three engines illustrated were all of the old single expansion type. The 4-4-0 bore number 13400 on her cab panel, which was also her construction number; she had 18×24 inch cylinders and later became No. 16 of the Choctaw, Oklahoma & Gulf Railroad, a line later leased by the Rock Island system.

The Mogul, Baldwin's construction number 13405, was a typical 2-6-0 of the period, had 19×24 inch cylinders, and after the Exposition became No. 61 of the Lima Northern.

The 4-6-0 was built under construction number 13362 as No. 123 of the Baltimore & Ohio South Western, a proprietary road of the Baltimore & Ohio R.R. extending from Belpre, Ohio, to East St. Louis, Illinois, with branches and divisions in Ohio, Indiana, and Illinois. Both the Mogul and the Ten-wheeler had extended wagon-top boilers, and the 4-6-0 was fitted with 20×24 inch cylinders. Both engines had the link and pin coupler then in use, the 2-6-0 type being fitted with a three-slot drawhead and the 4-6-0 with one of the four-slot variety, to permit coupling to cars of varying heights; the 4-4-0, No. 13400, sported the long pilot bar coupler, and all three locomotives were equipped with air brakes, oil headlights, and cylinder relief valves. Engine 13405 was also equipped with an air-operated bell ringer. (Three photos, courtesy of H. L. Broadbelt)

WORK HORSE AND SHOW HORSE. Baldwin Locomotive Works constructed five big compound engines for the New York, Lake Erie & Western Railroad in 1891, the last one completed in December. These engines, designed for pusher service on the Susquehanna Hill, were of the Vauclain compound system, and were of the Decapod, or 2-10-0, wheel arrangement. Their specifications included a high pressure cylinder of 16 inch diameter and a low pressure cylinder of 27 inch diameter, both having a 28 inch stroke; the drivers were 50 inches in diameter, and the second and third pair of drivers were "blind," or without flanges, to allow the engines to negotiate the 5 degree curves on the Susquehanna grade. They were equipped with the Wootten firebox and a double cab, and in service they performed the work of two ordinary Consolidation type locomotives.

No. 805 was withdrawn from pusher service and displayed as a part of the Baldwin stable of engines at the Columbian Exposition in Chicago in 1893. Weighing 195,000 pounds, she was the heaviest of the locomotives Baldwin exhibited at the affair. With a 20 × 24 inch Consolidation on the point, these Decapods were capable of boosting 45 loads up the Susquehanna, where the grade ran 60 feet per mile. (Courtesy of Association of American Railroads)

BABY BALDWIN. Probably the smallest of the Baldwin locomotives displayed at the World's Columbian Exposition in Chicago, on the eve of the great panic of 1893, was this little 0-4-0 saddle tank built as No. 7 for the Wellman Iron & Steel Company. She was constructed under Baldwin shop number 13352 and was of the Baldwin design for mill or furnace and industrial work; she operated on a 30 inch gauge track. Baldwin displayed two other narrow gauge locomotives at the Exposition; one was a 3 ft. gauge 4-6-0 with outside frames, built as No. 162 for the Mexican National Railroad, and the other was a compound 4-4-0 built to a metre gauge, representative of the Baldwin engines built for export to the far corners of the globe. (Courtesy of H. L. Broadbelt collection)

ROYAL BLUE LINE. Royal Blue Line was the name given the through express service trains operated between New York City and Washington, D.C., over the tracks of the Central Railroad of New Jersey, the Philadelphia & Reading, and the Baltimore & Ohio. Scheduled running time over the 224.5 miles, including the ferry trip between New York City and Jersey City, was a flat 5 hours; including 6 regular stops, the average speed was 45 miles per hour but delays often made speeds up to 60 m.p.h. necessary. One Central of New Jersey engine, 4-4-0 No. 385, hit 97 miles per hour on one occasion prior to 1894.

The Baldwin Works exhibited three locomotives for Royal Blue Line trains at the Columbian Exposition in 1893. Shown here, they include Central R.R. of New Jersey's No. 450, a compound 4-4-0 bearing shop number 13410; Baltimore & Ohio's No. 858, a simple American type; and Philadelphia & Reading's No. 694, a compound 2-4-2 type with a Wootten firebox. The B.&O. engine bore shop number 13360 and the Reading's "Columbia" type bore shop number 13370. Each of these speed merchants had 78 inch driving wheels and could run like the wind. The Central of New Jersey's No. 450 featured a Kinsey & Frisbie chime whistle, manufactured by Manning, Maxwell & Moore of New York.

Royal Blue trains left New York City at 11:30 A.M. and departed from the Jersey City ferry terminal at 11:42 A.M., Elizabeth at 11:58 A.M., Wayne Junction at 1:20 P.M., Philadelphia at 1:35 P.M., Wilmington at 2:05 P.M., Baltimore at 3:45 P.M., and rolled into the nation's capitol at 4:30 P.M. after a speedy passage through a region of dense traffic and frequent congestion of trains. (Courtesy of H. L. Broadbelt collection)

ENGINEERS' ENGINE. The big 4-4-0 pictured here is the E. B. THOMAS, built by the Cooke Locomotive & Machine Co. for a company formed by the locomotive engineers employed on the Erie. Her construction in the Cooke plant was carried out under the supervision of Mr. J. W. Johnson, Travelling Engineer of the New York, Lake Erie & Western. A number of builders of locomotive parts and appliances donated material used in her construction, which helped to cut the cost substantially. She had 19 × 26 inch cylinders, 72 inch drivers, a 66 inch boiler, and carried 175 pounds of boiler pressure; her total weight was 67½ tons and her firebox was designed to burn hard coal. The box covering her right steam chest in this photo was a temporary housing for test equipment installed to check her efficiency during operation.

The engine was exhibited at the Chicago Columbian Exposition of 1893 by the Erie Engineers, and she drew the criticism of Angus Sinclair, editor of the technical "Locomotive Engineering" publication. Sinclair took the Erie runners to task for their apparent disregard of safety in designing the locomotive; she was fitted with the old style stub-ended rods with straps and brasses, had poor handholds, and the murderous, archaic little cast iron footpads for steps, rather than the improved safety style of gangway steps or stirrups.

Mechanically, the E. B. THOMAS reportedly turned in some fine performances on the fast trains operated between Jersey City and Chicago, where she displayed unusual speed and power. In spite of this, the days of the 4-4-0 for heavy, fast main line trains were numbered, and the crack passenger consists were soon to be highballing behind the newer Prairie, Atlantic, and Pacific types, (Courtesy of the Erie Railroad)

NORTH WESTERN VARNISH HAULER. Schenectady built Engine No. 400 for the Chicago & North Western in 1893 and she was displayed at the big exposition in Chicago. Her cab panel carried the name COLUMBUS, probably in tribute to Christopher Columbus, who discovered the New World and whose memory was honored at the Columbian Exposition held on the 400th anniversary of his famous voyage of exploration.

The COLUMBUS had 19 × 24 inch cylinders, 69 inch drivers, and weighed 129,000 pounds. Her bell was equipped with an air bell ringer, an early application of this mechanical device that became commonplace in later years; the use of mechanical bell ringers freed the engine crew from pulling the bell rope and permitted them to devote their attention to other duties. One early mechanical bell ringer was powered by a crank connected to a revolving part of the engine, so that the bell tolled constantly while the locomotive was in motion, to the distraction of those who rode her cab. Engine bells appeared in a wide variety of tone, shape, and size, and their location on the engine depended upon the whim of the builder or designer. The ornate bell stands of earlier days had given way to the plain yoke type on most roads by the turn of the century, although a few builders still topped the yoke with ornamental knob or acorn-shaped nut. (Courtesy of Schenectady History Center)

MILWAUKEE ROAD COMPOUND. Engine 830 of the Chicago, Milwaukee & St. Paul Railway was displayed for exposition visitors at the big event in Chicago in 1893. She was built by the Rhode Island Locomotive Works and was one of the three engines of the 4-6-2 wheel arrangement turned out in that year by the Rhode Island Works for fast passenger service on the Milwaukee. These engines were compounds, with 21 × 26 and 31 × 26 inch cylinders and 78 inch drivers. The locomotive weighed 143,000 pounds, of which 88,500 pounds was carried on the drivers, 36,500 pounds on the engine truck, and 18,000 pounds on the trailer wheels.

Built in March, May, and August of 1893, the three reportedly bore Rhode Island construction numbers 2880, 2913 and 2912. They proved unsatisfactory and the Milwaukee returned them to the builders. They were later purchased by Supt. of Motive Power W. E. Symons for the Plant System, the Savannah, Florida & Western Ry., which was short of motive power at the time. The Chicago, Milwaukee & St. Paul had numbered these engines 828, 829, and 830: on the Plant System they carried road numbers 104, 105, and 106. They were renumbered 287, 288 and 289 by the successor Atlantic Coast Line, and although two of them had been simpled, they still had the added trailer wheels when used out of Waycross, Georgia, in 1910, according to my friend Mr. Hugh Ghormley, veteran machinist now living in retirement in Tennessee. These trailer wheels, which had been added to carry part of the heavy weight of the locomotives, were later removed, making them 4-6-0's; they were later A.C.L. numbers 1287, 1288 and 1289. (Courtesy of Schenectady History Center)

HILL ROAD MOGUL. Engine 351 of the Great Northern Railway was built by Brooks Locomotive Works in 1893 and displayed at the Columbia Exposition in Chicago. She bore Brooks construction number 2266 and was a typical freight service 2-6-0, with 19 × 24 inch cylinders and 55 inch drivers, the engine weighing a total of 118,000 pounds. Note her bell located atop the Belpaire firebox, the forward section of her boiler carrying steam dome and sand box. Her slide valve steam chests were fitted with relief valves mounted at the forward ends and visible in this photo; these valves closed when the throttle was opened, but opened when the throttle was closed, thus permitting any steam which leaked into the chambers to escape, preventing the engine from building up pressure and perhaps straying away when left unattended. In case an engine failed to lubricate properly, a dose of valve oil could be applied to the valve by closing the throttle when the engine was running, creating a vacuum that sucked oil poured from a tallow pot into the steam chest through the open relief valve. The author of these lines has often treated a groaning valve in this manner on the little 4-8-0 type 2900 series engines of the Southern Pacific, some of which were Cooke engines dating back to 1882. (Courtesy of Schenectady History Center)

NEW HAVEN HIGH STEPPER. One of the locomotives built by the Rhode Island Locomotive Works and displayed at the Columbian Exposition in Chicago in 1893 was this compound 4-4-0, No. 254 of the New York, New Haven & Hartford Railroad. Her high pressure cylinder measured 21 × 26 inches and the low pressure cylinder was 31 × 26 inches; her driving wheels were 78 inches in diameter. Of her 125,000 pounds of total weight, 84,000 pounds were carried on her high drivers. Designed for passenger service, her drivers and also her engine truck were fitted with brakes; at the rear of her tender can be seen the hand-operated lever of the old Miller "hook" coupler, a device then supplanting the link and pin couplers in passenger service. (Courtesy of Schenectady History Center)

BROOKS TRIO. From the Dunkirk, N.Y., shops of the Brooks Locomotive Works came this trio of steamers for exhibit at the Columbian Exposition in 1893.

The American type with the roomy cab is No. 210 of the Cincinnati, Hamilton & Dayton Railroad, a busy Ohio line; she carried Brooks' construction number 2265. Although many of the locomotives exhibited at Chicago in 1893 were equipped with oil-burning headlights, the C.H. & D. engine pictured here has what appears to be a steam-driven electric generator mounted immediately behind her headlight, indicating she was equipped with the new electric light.

The pair of ten-wheelers pictured here were built by Brooks for the Lake Shore & Michigan Southern and are nearly identical; however, No. 600 was a simple engine and No. 601 was a compound, featuring the Player system of compounding. No. 600 bore shop number 2263 and No. 601 carried shop number 2268.

John Player, inventor of the Player compound system, was born at Woolrich, Kent, England in 1847 and migrated to America where he secured employment in 1873 on the Central Iowa Ry. as a machinist, rising from the ranks to become Master Mechanic of that line. From 1887 to 1890 he served as Superintendent of Motive Power on the Wisconsin Central Railroad, leaving there to assume the duties of Superintendent of Machinery on the Atchison, Topeka & Sante Fe. John Player's rise from humble immigrant and shop worker to lofty positions in the railway mechanical world is an example of the opportunities on American railroads in that era. (Courtesy of Schenectady History Center)

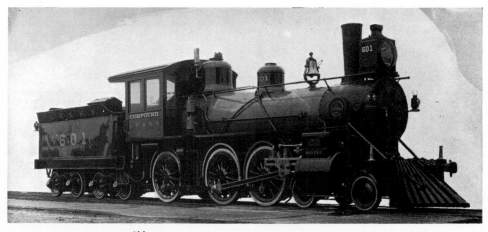

COTTON STATES EXPOSITION VISITOR. In 1895 the Cotton States & International Exposition was held in Atlanta, Georgia, and a number of locomotives were exhibited there. The veteran Western & Atlantic engine GENERAL of Civil War fame was on display, along with what was reportedly a replica of the ancient TORNADO of the Raleigh & Gaston, the latter shepherded by 90-year old Albert Johnson, a former engineer on the original TORNADO and a Master Mechanic for nearly 50 years.

Virginia's Richmond Locomotive Works displayed a new 4-4-0 built for the Seaboard Air Line Railway, along with a cross-compound 4-6-0 and a 2-8-0 built for the Southern Railway, and a cross-compound 4-6-0 built for the Chesapeake & Ohio. However, their most publicized engine in the Atlanta exhibition was Richmond Compound No. 2427, the famous "Richmond Tramp." Illustrated here, the big tenwheeler was built by the Richmond Works in 1894 and had just completed a broad sweep around the nation as a demonstration locomotive, advertising the Richmond compound product.

The "Tramp," as she was familiarly known, had made trial runs on the Pennsylvania R.R., the Rock Island lines, the Chicago, Milwaukee & St. Paul, the Chicago & Grand Trunk, the Illinois Central, and the Atchison, Topeka & Santa Fe. While the other Richmond engines at the Cotton States & International Exposition were polished to a high gloss, the noted "Richmond Tramp" was exhibited just as she came off her demonstration runs, covered with the grime of honest toil; she later became Atchison, Topeka & Santa Fe's Number 260. (Courtesy of Schenectady History Center)

TENNESSEE CENTENNIAL. The 1897 centennial celebration of the "Volunteer State" centered around the Centennial Exposition held in Nashville, the state's capital since 1812. Nashville proclaimed itself as the Athens of the South, and a reproduction of the famous Parthenon of Athens, Greece, was constructed as a part of the 1897 Centennial celebration and still stands in Centennial Park.

The classic lines of contemporary locomotives were displayed along with the classic lines of ancient architecture, one of the engines on exhibit being the Southern Railway's No. 325. The big ten-wheeler was constructed by Baldwin in April of 1897 and carried shop number 15274. She was designed by W. H. Thomas, Superintendent of Motive Power for the Southern Railway, a native of Pennsylvania who started as a shopman on the Philadelphia & Erie Railroad in 1865; in 1879 he became Master Mechanic on the Mobile & Montgomery R.R., later holding the same position on the Louisville & Nashville, the Chesapeake & Ohio, and from 1885 until 1894 he served as Superintendent of Motive Power on the East Tennessee, Virginia & Georgia Ry., becoming Asst. Supt. of Motive Power for the Southern in September of 1894. When R. D. Wade resigned in early 1896 as Supt. of Motive Power for the road, Wm. Thomas was appointed as his successor. (Courtesy of H. L. Broadbelt collection)

EUROPEAN DISPLAY. International trade was stimulated at an exposition held in Paris, France, in 1900, and the Baldwin Locomotive Works exhibited two engines at the affair. One of these was a 2-6-0 freight engine built for the Great Northern Railway of England and the other was a 4-4-2 passenger engine constructed for the French State Railways.

The Chemins du Fer Etat, or French State Railways, also had a Baldwin locomotive on display as a part of their exhibit at the Paris Exposition. Shown here, the Etat No. 2805 was a compound American type designed for French passenger service and bore the name MONTLIEU; note the European style buffers and tank steps. This engine bore Baldwin Shop No. 17360.

The locomotives exhibited by Baldwin were constructed on regular orders and went into active service on their respective roads when the Exposition closed. (Courtesy of H. L. Broadbelt collection)

L. & N. EXHIBIT. Engine No. 500 of the Louisville & Nashville Railroad was built new by Baldwin in 1897 and was displayed that year at the Tennessee Centennial Exposition held in Nashville. The trim ten-wheeler with clerestory cab and flanged stack bore Baldwin's construction number 15271; she was the L&N's first number 500, the only class G-6 engine on their roster. Other road numbers assigned to this locomotive included 200, 290, and 390; when new she had 18½ × 26 inch cylinders, 68 inch drivers, weighed 133,000 pounds, and carried 170 pounds of working pressure. In 1924 she was rebuilt with a new boiler, and her cylinders changed to 20 × 26 inches, 69 inch drivers, 200 pounds of boiler pressure, and a total weight of 166,000 pounds. She rendered faithful service on the L&N until finally retired in 1937. (Courtesy of H. L. Broadbelt collection)

FOR JOHN BULL BY BALDWIN. The Mogul freight or "goods" engine shown here was built by Baldwin in January, 1900, for the Great Northern Railway of England and bore road number 1200; her Baldwin construction number was 17359. Although her basic design was that of an ordinary American-built 2-6-0, the British influence shows in her lines, including the single dome placed well forward on her boiler and the sand boxes concealed under her running board skirts. After completion the 1200 was shipped to France and placed on display at the Paris Exposition of 1900; when the affair ended the Mogul was shipped to England and placed in service on the Great Northern Ry. for whom she had been constructed.

Perhaps as a result of the Baldwin exhibit at the Paris Exposition, large orders were received in 1900 by the American firm for locomotives for a number of foreign lines, including the Paris-Orleans Railway of France, the Belgian State Railway, the Finland State Railway, the Egyptian State Railway, and the Chinese Eastern Railroad. In the previous year, 1899, Baldwin had acquired contracts for a considerable number of locomotives for English railroads, including twenty engines for the Great Northern Ry., thirty for the Midland Railway, and twenty for the Great Central Railway. (Courtesy of H. L. Broadbelt collection)

TIMBER CRUISER. Baldwin proudly displayed this 2-6-2 Prairie type at the Lewis & Clark Centennial Exposition held in Portland, Oregon, during 1905-06. The squat woodburner, with low drivers and a bulky boiler, was named the SEQUOIA after the giant evergreen trees common to California's redwood regions, and she bore Baldwin's Shop No. 25503.

The 2-6-2 type was generally suited for main line logging road work, having a short wheelbase with much of the weight carried on the drivers to produce a maximum tractive effort and the trailing truck enabled them to operate readily in either direction over light rails and rough track. (Courtesy of H. L. Broadbelt collection)

NORTHWEST DISPLAY. The Alaska-Yukon-Pacific Exposition was held in Seattle, Washington, in 1909, bringing added fame to the key city to the Klondike gold rush of 1898. Although the railroad equipment exhibited there did not reach the scope of displays such as those featured at Chicago in 1893 and at St. Louis in 1904, several builders did send samples of their work to the Puget Sound city's Exposition.

The American Locomotive Company exhibited two locomotives and a rotary snow plow, the latter being No. 12 of the Chicago, Milwaukee & Puget Sound Railway; lettered "Rotary Snow Shovel," the rotary was powered by a locomotive type boiler with Belpaire firebox and was designed to cut a swath 12 feet 6 inches wide.

The locomotive exhibit consisted of a 2-6-2 side tank engine designed for logging service and an 0-4-0 saddle tank engine for mine, quarry, or industrial use. The 0-4-0T, bearing Alco lettering and the number 1, was a product of the Dickson works and was built in April of 1909; the 2-6-2T carried Alco lettering and on her cab panel carried number 46000. The 0-4-0T was built to 3 ft. gauge, while the 2-6-2T was built to standard gauge and during the Exposition she was sold to the 6-mile standard gauge Craig Mountain Ry. Co. of Winchester, Idaho, serving there until she was scrapped in 1950. She had slide valves, a diminutive diamond stack, weighed 113,500 pounds loaded, carried 1,200 gallons of water in her side tanks, and the bunker behind her cab held 1 cord of wood. Her straight boiler carried 170 pounds of working pressure and the top of her stack stood 13 feet, 3½ inches above the rail. The little saddletank 0-4-0 weighed 35,000 lbs., carried 165 lbs. boiler pressure, and featured solid cast steel frames. (Courtesy of Schenectady History Center)

PANAMA-PACIFIC POWER. San Francisco, California, was the site of the Panama-Pacific Exposition, held in 1915 for the dual purpose of celebrating the opening of the Panama Canal and the 400th anniversary of the discovery of the Pacific Ocean.

Among the railroad exhibits displayed there was this 0-4-0 saddle-tank, a product of the American Locomotive Company. The neatly-finished tanker was constructed in the ALCO-Cooke Works in September, 1914, and bore Shop No. 53124.

Engines of this type were popular for industrial use, switching in the close confines of factories and on the light rails of quarries and similar operations, as well as being used on construction projects where rail transportation was involved. (Courtesy of Schenectady History Center)

BALDWIN ODDITY. This unusual item of rolling stock was built by Baldwin in July, 1861, as No. 217 of the Pennsylvania Railroad, Shop No. 1005, as nearly as can be determined. Historians disagree on this data, and Edwin P. Alexander, in his pictorial history of the Pennsylvania R.R., states the engine was a Baldwin of 1851 vintage rebuilt in 1862. A roster of Pennsylvania R.R. motive power published by the Railway & Locomotive Historical Society lists P.R.R. No. 217 as a Baldwin of July, 1861, and shows Shop No. 1005, but lists the wheel arrangement as an 0-6-0.

This photo from the Baldwin negative collection owned by Mr. Herbert L. Broadbelt shows what appears to be a new piece of equipment, fresh from the factory, bearing Baldwin builder's number 1005 on the circular brass plate in the skirt of the mud guard. The 217 was a combined locomotive-coach affair, probably designed for official use by P.R.R. brass hats. The engine section is a 4-4-0 type locomotive with water tanks mounted on the sides of her boiler above the running boards; her coach body and the engine cab are incorporated under one solid roof section, and the paneled coach body is supported on an extension of the engine frame with a four-wheel truck under the rear portion. Fuel for this novel little engine was carried within the forward section of the coach body.

Record of several similar locomotive-coach combinations used on American railroads exists, including the SHAKOPEE of the Minnesota Valley Railroad and the NOVELTY, a 2-2-0 type built by Baldwin in 1860 and reportedly sold by the Pennsylvania to the Pittsburgh, Fort Wayne & Chicago Railroad.

ODD ONES

From the day when the first steam-powered wheel rolled along a rail, man was tempted to improve the locomotive. In the years of infancy the locomotive was a primitive machine and a great many of its refinements were the results of trial and error problems arising in the course of normal operations.

Skilled mechanics and talented engineers nursed the iron baby into adolescence, revising original crude devices and perfecting new attachments. Competitive trials in England weeded out inferior designs early in the game and the best of British motive power strongly influenced locomotive designers and builders in the United States.

As in any business, however, there was always a lunatic fringe and this element gave birth to some weird and wondrous contraptions. It is the aim of this chapter to present a graphic view of many of the deviations from the accepted standard designs of engines of yesteryear. Not all of the locomotives gathered here were without some merit; a number of engines of odd design did offer certain advantages over those that followed the regular style of construction in their era, but often these advantages were of such a minor nature that builders felt it impractical to incorporate the innovations and inventions into their machines.

Builders reasoned, and rightfully so, that the increased cost of installing and maintaining some of these novel features would not be offset by any advantages that they might produce, but it is to the credit of railway officials and locomotive construction firms that a large number of engines of radical departure from customary practice were actually built and given a fair trial to prove their worth.

A number of practical ideas thus experimented with were found to fulfill the expectancy of their inventors and not a few of them were incorporated into standard designs. Other engines of freak design proved to be complete failures and were scrapped or rebuilt into conventional locomotives.

In addition to the locomotives, a wondrous assortment of appurtenances showered upon the railroad world. The cab for the protection of the crew from the elements, the advent of the bell and whistle for warning and signaling, and the headlight that sprung from a blazing fire on a car pushed ahead of the engine were the results of ingenuity and common sense. The development of reversing gear and improved designs of valve motion, boiler and frame construction, and a host of other features followed the spreading use of the steam locomotive. The field was a fertile one, and practical railroad men as well as dreamy-eyed inventors hatched up many improvements; the problem of braking trains started when the first car was set in motion, and ran the gamut from sprags thrust through the spokes of the wheels to the electro-pneumatic air brake, not forgetting the continuous-chain brake that once achieved some popularity by permitting the engineer to apply the brakes on the cars of his train by engaging a drum on the locomotive to wind up the chain attached to each car's brake rigging.

By the process of trial and elimination, the best of these devices were adapted to the needs of the business and became a part of railroading; some perfectly sound innovations, such as the "bear-trap" cinder catchers used on the Colorado & Southern locomotives, never achieved widespread use but served their purpose nevertheless.

Locomotive design and appliances were not the only subjects of dispute and contention as the railroads struggled toward maturity. The great controversy over the various gauges of track raged for a number of years; narrow gauge, broad gauge, and numerous "in-between" gauges all had their champions who could expound at great length on the advantages to be derived from their own chosen width of track.

Through the medium of the camera it is possible to present some of the innovations and oddities that trundled forth on the railroads of America, a few to survive in various forms and others to fall dismally by the trackside.

BALDWIN'S 1000th LOCOMOTIVE. A great many sweeping changes in the look of American railroading had taken place from the November day in 1832 when Matthias W. Baldwin's first locomotive was given her trial run and the February day in 1861 when the 2-4-0 tank type bearing No. 1000 on her builder's plate rolled out of the Philadelphia factory. "OLD IRONSIDES," the first Baldwin locomotive, was modeled on the English "Planet" class and included such primitive items as a wooden frame and steam joints made of canvas and red lead when she went into service on the Philadelphia, Germantown & Norristown Railroad's six miles of track. Actually this was not the first steam locomotive constructed by Baldwin, for he had completed a miniature locomotive for Mr. Franklin Peale, proprietor of the Philadelphia Museum, that was placed in operation inside the Museum on April 25th, 1831, pulling two small cars with seats for four passengers on a circular track of pine rails faced with hoop iron.

OLD IRONSIDES was not an unqualified success, for her pumps failed to supply the boiler and her driving wheel slipped on the axle, derailing her on one occasion; in addition, her light weight did not permit her to pull the required tonnage on the grades of the road. Although her defects were remedied. Mr. Baldwin had trouble in collecting the sum agreed on by her purchasers and is reported to have emphatically stated "That is our last locomotive!"

Happily, such was not the case and the 2-2-0 type, weighing 5 tons, of the 1830's had grown to 27 ton giants of 0-8-0 and 4-6-0 types by 1860. The 1000th locomotive was built as No. 212 of the Pennsylvania Railroad, with 10 × 18 inch cylinders and 56 inch drivers and a weight of 42,850 pounds. (Courtesy of H. L. Broadbelt collection)

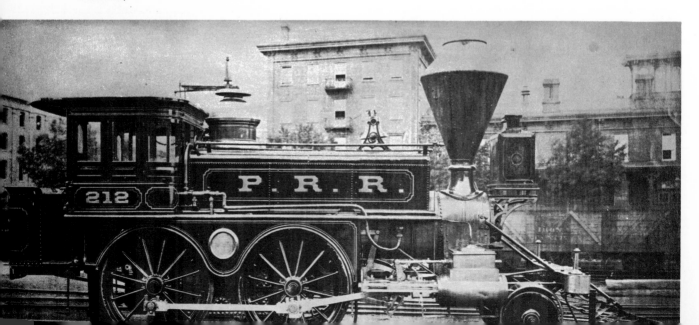

IMPORTED INGENUITY. In 1843 a 37-year old Englishman named Thomas Russell Crampton was serving under the noted Daniel Gooch on the Great Western Railway of England when he designed the first of the engines that bore the Crampton name. Crampton sought to provide a speedy locomotive with a low center of gravity and his engine featured a single pair of large drivers located behind the boiler, which was slung low by current standards. Tulk & Ley, at their Lowca Works, Whitehaven, built the first two Crampton patent 4-2-0 engines in 1846 for the British-owned Liege & Namur Railway of Belgium; these two, named LIEGE and NAMUR, had 7-foot drivers and proved so satisfactory that others of the type were built for service in England, Scotland, France, and Germany.

President Stevens of America's Camden & Amboy R.R. saw the Crampton engines at work in England and upon returning home he aided Isaac Dripps in designing a similar engine with 8-foot drivers. The first of this type was the Camden & Amboy's No. 28, the JOHN STEVENS; she was a 6-2-0 built by Norris Brothers of Philadelphia in 1849.

Although she lacked adhesion and was slow to start a train, she ran like the wind when under way but was a bit careless about remaining on the rails. Over Isaac Dripps' objection, several other Cramptons were built for the Camden & Amboy and one of these, No. 30, is shown here. She was built by Norris in 1850 and has a more substantial cab than that shown in drawings of the first engine, it merely having a roof supported by four posts; the spaces between the spokes of the drivers were filled with wood, giving the wheel a solid appearance, but the ungainly proportions of the engine render it devoid of grace and beauty inherent in other engines of the period. (Courtesy of H. L. Broadbelt collection)

MARCH OF PROGRESS. Engine No. 30 of the Mine Hill Railroad was built by Baldwin in 1860, Shop No. 972, and featured several unusual designs. Mr. Wilder, superintendent of the road, wanted an engine to operate on steep grades with a fairly constant level of water and this hump-backed boiler was designed to fulfill his desires. The top boiler sheets sloped upward from both ends of the boiler, creating a hump in the center, and the steam dome was mounted at the highest point of this hump.

The strange device at the base of the stack is a feed-water heater, the large casing containing a vertical flue and a number of smaller tubes, all surrounded by water. Exhaust steam passed through the large flue and hot gasses from the smokebox passed through the smaller flues, heating the water in the casing as they passed. This device was patented jointly by Master Mechanic David Clark of the Mine Hill Railroad and Matthias Baldwin in 1854.

Engine 30 was also equipped with a variable cut-off, with two valves in each steam chest. A similar device had been introduced by Ethan Rogers of the Cuyahoga Works of Cleveland, Ohio, and Baldwin adopted the general design, using a partition plate between upper and lower valves; in addition to the regular reverse lever, a second lever to control the variable cut-off was placed in the cab and both reach rods can be seen in this photo. The variable cut-off gear enabled the engineer to work steam expansively, resulting in a saving in fuel consumption and boiler water.

The engine had a supplementary outside frame, commonly called the "ankle rail," and carried her supply of sand in boxes placed before and behind her eight driving wheels. (Courtesy of H. L. Broadbelt collection)

CENTRAL OF NEW JERSEY TANKER. Baldwin turned out this 2-4-4 double-ender tank locomotive in June of 1871 as the No. 125 of the Central Railroad of New Jersey. The firm later specialized in several variations of this type of locomotive, featuring designs for switching, local freight, and local passenger service. In addition to the style shown here, with the tank mounted on an extension of the frame and carried on a four-wheel truck, the Baldwin plant turned out engines of similar design with an additional water supply carried in a saddle-tank hung over the boiler. Note that No. 125 has no sanders, and also sports an unusual metal buffer on either side of the drawhead on her pilot beam.

A similar locomotive, No. 1 of the Camden & Atlantic Railroad which bore the name JOHN LUCAS, was placed in service in March, 1878, and rendered very satisfactory service. In a testimonial letter written in September, 1880, Supt. F. A. Lister of the Camden & Atlantic reports that the JOHN LUCAS was in use on a run between Atco and Camden, including six turnaround trips between Camden and Haddonfield and one round trip from Camden to Lakeside, for a daily stint of 143 miles, and that the engine was in service day and night, with two engine crews alternating on her. She burned an average of 3,984 pounds of coal per day and when hauling two passenger cars her 650 gallons of water would last for about twenty miles. With one car, her crew had wound her up to a top speed of 55 miles per hour on a non-stop run. (Courtesy of H. L. Broadbelt collection)

MASON MYTHOLOGY. William Mason built this unusual locomotive in March, 1871, under shop number 438. Named the JANUS, after the two-faced Roman deity, the 0-6-6-0 was a Fairlie double-ender with 42 inch drivers and 16×24 inch cylinders. She was used on the Boston & Worcester R.R. and on the Western Railroad of Massachusetts before being sold to the Lehigh Valley R.R. in 1874; the Lehigh Valley assigned her number 164 but retained her name. In 1877 she was reported demolished in a collision with the engine TUSCARORA, and her boiler was then used as a stationary plant at Perth Amboy, New Jersey.

The idea for this type of engine may have originated with Horatio Allen's 2-2-2-2 type of the early 1830's, used in South Carolina; the Allen engine had a central firebox, a two-barreled boiler, and two smokeboxes and stacks or chimney pipes.

Allen's idea was taken up by John Cockerill of Seraing, Belgium, who improved the design by using pivoted driving bogies.

Robert Fairlie further improved upon the type and while they were uncommon in the United States, many Fairlie double-enders of British manufacture saw service in Mexico and in other foreign countries. (Anderson collection, courtesy of Mr. H. M. Ghormley)

BALDWIN SINGLE. This little 4-2-0 tank engine was built by the Baldwin Works in June, 1868, for the Rocky River Railroad, a standard gauge Ohio short line. The locomotive was named the ROCKPORT, and altho little data seems to be available on her, she was designed to operate in either direction and carried a pilot on either end; the odd shape of her jacket may be due to a water supply tank carried under the belly of her boiler, with the cap to the filler pipe located in the left running board above the forward portion of her fender.

The Rocky River Railroad was organized on February 20, 1867, and the road opened in 1868; it ran from Cleveland to Rocky River, Ohio, a distance of 5.53 miles, and carried passengers over a track laid with 30 pound rail. (Courtesy of H. L. Broadbelt collection)

GRADE CLIMBER. The Madison & Indianapolis R.R., organized in 1842, opened its' 96 miles of track between the two Indiana cities named in the corporate title in 1847; in 1862 it was sold under foreclosure and reorganized as the Indianapolis & Madison Railroad. In 1866 this road was consolidated with the Jeffersonville Railroad, a pike that was originally chartered in 1846 as the Ohio & Indianapolis R.R.; the Jeffersonville R.R. completed a line from Jeffersonville, opposite Louisville, Ky., to Columbus, Indiana, in 1853, connecting there with the Madison & Indianapolis Railroad.

The M&I track, leaving the bank of the Ohio River at Madison, climbed to North Madison by means of an inclined plane; the grade rose 310 feet to the mile, and was 7,012 feet long. To navigate this ladder-like incline, Baldwin built an 0-8-0 locomotive in 1846-47, named the M. G. BRIGHT. This engine was powered by a set of conventional cylinders measuring $15\frac{1}{2} \times 20$ inches; a second set of cylinders, 17×18 inches, were placed vertically near the middle of the boiler, and these were connected to drive a cog-wheel that could be raised or lowered to engage a rack-rail placed between the regular rails. The 42 inch drivers moved the engine during normal operations and the cog-wheel was used in addition when the engine was used on the inclined plane. The locomotive was designed by Andrew Cathcart, Master Mechanic of the Madison & Indianapolis. In 1850 Baldwin built a similar engine for the line, named the JOHN BROUGH. In 1858 Master Mechanic Reuben Wells designed the big 0-10-0 pictured here to run on this grade without using the rack-rail. Her 44 inch drivers were powered by 20×24 inch cylinders, and she weighed 112,000 pounds; her water supply was carried in cylindrical tanks on either side of the boiler, holding 1,800 gallons.

This big hill-climber was named the REUBEN WELLS, in honor of her designer, and was used regularly for 28 years, and was in part-time service for an additional 10 years, then retired and was preserved at Purdue University; the WELLS was replaced by the W. J. BRIGHT, a lighter engine of the same type.

The Indianapolis & Madison R.R. and the Jefferson R.R. consolidated in 1866, forming the Jeffersonville, Madison & Indianapolis Railroad, now a part of the Pennsylvania Railroad lines. (Courtesy of the Pennsylvania Railroad)

UGLY DUCKLING. This little Rogers 2-4-2 saddletank was No. 36 of the New York & New Haven Railroad, and was probably built in the 1860's. She is an early example of what later became the traditional design for many suburban runs, a small locomotive of the tank type with a pilot on both front and rear to facilitate operation in either direction without the necessity of turning the engine at the end of her run.

The general design of this engine gives her an awkward and rather unlovely appearance; her driving wheels and saddle tank are seemingly out of proportion to her cab, and her sand box is perched upon the tank almost as an afterthought, resulting in a decided lack of symmetry. The tank is extended forward to such an extent that it covers most of the smokebox, adding to her ungainly appearance, but her drivers hint that she could hit up a lively gait. (Courtesy of the New Haven Railroad)

LOCOMOTIVE INCOGNITO. While steam locomotives were pounding along to glory across the American countryside, a number of their sister engines were engaged in the more prosaic task of trundling passengers along the rails of city and suburban lines. Disguised under a wide variety of outer body styles, the steam dummy was a familiar sight on the street railways of many American cities.

Engine No. 1 of the Denver & Swansea was named the GOV. GILPIN and was constructed by the Baldwin Works in 1874. While some early street railway engines had vertical boilers contained in one end of the car with passengers carried in a compartment to the rear, the GOV. GILPIN had a horizontal boiler and was actually an 0-4-0 locomotive with saddle water tank, enclosed in a coach body, and was used to draw separate passenger cars.

Some dummy engines were used to handle freight cars in congested areas where railroad tracks ran down the middle of city streets. The Memphis & Charleston Railroad received a steam dummy, the MAYOR FLIPPIN, from Baldwin in 1876 and this engine handled as many as 10 cars on the steep Washington Street grade in Memphis,

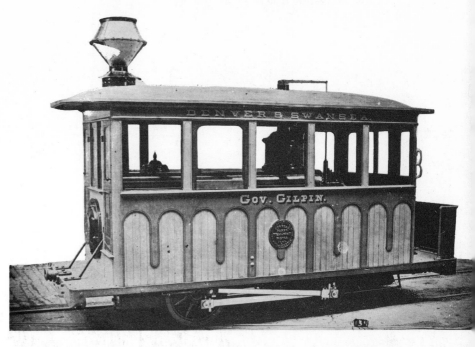

Tennessee. The MAYOR FLIPPIN was fitted with a patent exhaust chamber to muffle her stack noise, and the device proved quite effective; Master Mechanic H. N. Burford wrote the Baldwin Works a testimonial in 1878 which stated, in part, "The patent exhaust is a success without a doubt. As the engine passes by horses in the streets they do not notice it any more than they do a wagon. Our track runs through one of the most active business streets in the city." (Courtesy of H. L. Broadbelt collection)

METROPOLITAN MOTIVE POWER. In the fall of 1875 the Baldwin Works turned out their first steam street car. The novel machine, combining motive power and passenger accomodations, was completed in November of '75 and after a trial on a Philadelphia street railway it was shipped to New York City and ran there from December of 1875 until June of 1876 when it was returned to Philadelphia. While in service on the Atlantic Avenue Railway of Brooklyn the car frequently hauled a trailer and on open stretches was clocked at speeds of 16 to 18 miles per hour. After her return to Philadelphia, she was operated on the Market Street Railway, hauling crowds of Centennial visitors with fair success.

After nearly a year of operation the mechanical defects in the experimental car became apparent; the leading axle, a crank type with inside connections that drove the car, was subject to breakage and the boiler and machinery racked the light wooden horse-car type body. To remedy these defects the car was rebuilt with outside-connected driving wheels in the manner of regular locomotives, and a stout iron frame was installed to support the weight of boiler and machinery.

The reconstructed model served well, but the self-propelled steam street car did not achieve the popularity of the street cars drawn by steam dummy type locomotives. (Courtesy of D. L. Stearns)

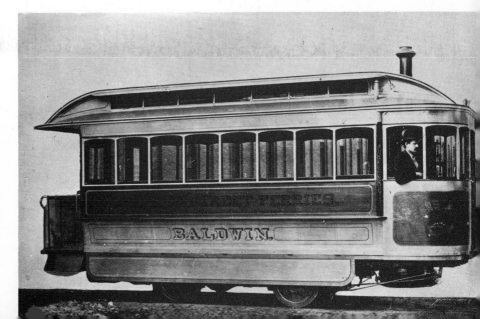

SHORT SHORT LINE. The Little Laurel Fork & Sand Hill Railroad operated in the western reaches of West Virginia, not far east of Parkersburg on the Ohio River; built to standard gauge with 56 pound rail, the main line extended for 5 miles between Volcano and Laurel Fork Junction (later Volcano Junction), where it connected with the Baltimore & Ohio. A branch 2 miles long ran from Mt. Farm Junction to Coal Bank, West Virginia.

Guiding spirits of the road when it was placed in operation in the early 1870's were the Stiles family; W. A.

Stiles of Philadelphia was a director and H. A. Stiles of the same city was treasurer, while W. C. Stiles, Jr., served as president with offices located in Volcano. Superintendent D. C. Mudge of Volcano had charge of operations of the line's two locomotives, one passenger coach, and four flat cars, the total rolling stock of the road in 1876.

Engine No. 2 of the Laurel Fork & Sand Hill was a Baldwin 0-6-0 named the MAJ. W. R. STERLING. The accompanying photo shows the trim little engine with a "Mother Hubbard" cab,

leaving her fireman exposed to the elements as he bailed coal on her open deck. This type of cab was usually applied to engines with the wide Wootten style of firebox and there seems to be no good reason why it was used in place of a conventional cab on the MAJOR STERLING. The fact that the engine bore road number 2 is emphasized by the application of that number to both front and rear sand boxes, another rather unusual application. (Courtesy of H. L. Broadbelt collection)

DUMMY LINE. The Willamette Bridge Railway Company of Portland, Oregon, was the proud owner of Engine No. 4, a Baldwin steam dummy built in 1890 under shop number 10683. This dummy was a 2-6-0 saddletank steam locomotive enclosed in a coach body and operated on a 42 inch gauge track.

The steam dummy was encased in the coach body on the theory that horses were accustomed to the sight of horse cars previously in use and therefore would not be frightened if the locomotive was thus disguised. The frequent runaways caused by the stack exhaust were abated by use of patented exhaust mufflers but the

smoke from the engines caused considerable complaining by city residents; the smoke problem was practically eliminated by the use of of coke or anthracite coal for fuel.

Steam dummy operation was not without its perils; Engineer John A. Hans, thirty years of age, was fatally scalded when his steam dummy on the Portland & Vancouver line jumped the track on a curve on the morning of April 4th, 1893. Fireman Edward Laing, later a locomotive engineer for many years on the Southern Pacific, rode the dummy into the ditch without injury; excessive speed was generally blamed for the wreck, perhaps the result of a broken throttle.

Long after the steam dummies of a number of street railway lines in the West had been forced out of town by the advent of electric street cars, the little dinkies continued to lead a useful life by finding employment on logging railroads in the big woods. (Courtesy of H. L. Broadbelt collection)

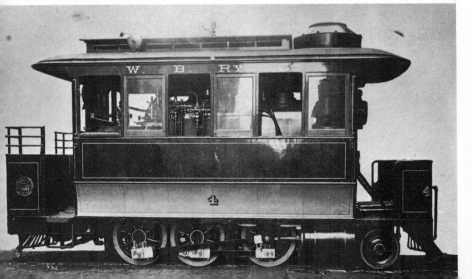

NEW HAMPSHIRE NOVELTY. It has been said that the majority of oldtime Master Mechanics did not sleep well until they had tried their hand at an improved front end, and this photo of the ANSON S. MARSHALL of the Concord Railroad illustrates one of the ingenious devices applied by the road's shop forces.

The freak stack shown here apparently incorporated a cinder catcher in its odd design, with a hopper for returning the trapped cinders back into the smokebox. According to Dr. S. R. Wood, this patent stack was a failure, as were so many other experimental improved smokebox innovations. The Toledo, Peoria & Western tried an experimental front end with dual stacks, and many other odd devices bloomed and faded as mechanical officers across the nation labored to improve draft and steaming qualities of their engines.

The ANSON S. MARSHALL was built in the Concord Railroad's shops in Concord, New Hampshire, in 1873 and bore road number 10; she later became No. 710 of the Boston & Maine and was scrapped in 1908.

BALDWIN'S FIRST NARROW GAUGE. The little 0-4-0 shown here was named the KANAWHA and was out-shopped by Baldwin in August of 1868 for the Averill Coal & Oil Company of West Virginia. She was built for their short line and had a gauge of 3 feet 6 inches; this engine is reportedly the first narrow gauge locomotive constructed by the Baldwin Locomotive Works. The small diameter of her boiler and her tall, slim stack tend to emphasize the large cab, giving her a rather ungainly appearance; her steam dome was located inside the cab and her whistle was piped out through the front wall of the cab.

Note that in the absence of a track to fit her gauge she has been rolled out of the Baldwin factory with her wheels on the right side running on the cobblestoned surface of the street to pose for this builder's view.

Baldwin constructed three locomotives of the same gauge for the Uniao Valenciana Railway of Brazil in 1869, designed for general passenger and freight service. In 1871 the Baldwin Works built the first 3-foot gauge engines used on the Denver & Rio Grande Railway in Colorado; these included the MONTEZUMA, CORTEZ, UTE, and DEL NORTE, all 2-4-0 types, and the TABI-WACHI, SHOU-WA-NO, OURAY, ARKANSAS, and HUERFANO, all 2-6-0 types. (Courtesy of H. L. Broadbelt collection)

OLD PEG LEG. An unusual method of transportation on the American scene was the monorail, a device that was tried in several locations in the United States but never proved to be very practical. The monorail engine here is the COL. A. I. WILCOX, number 2 of the Bradford & Foster Brook Railway in Pennsylvania's McKean County. Chartered in October of 1877, the monorail was completed from Bradford to the wicked oil boom village of Tarport by January of 1878; it was eventually extended from Bradford to Gilmore, about 4 miles. Meandering up Foster Brook Valley, the line closely paralleled the Olean, Bradford & Warren R.R. from Bradford to a point near Derrick City, and in a row over an attempt by the latter road to block the monorail by building a spur across it, the O.B.&W. tried to have the monorail's charter revoked on the grounds that it was not a railroad in the accepted sense of the term. The monorail continued to serve such places as Tarport, Foster Brook, Babcock Mills, and Harrisburg Run. One of its engines blew up on January 28th, 1879, killing six people; the explosion was laid to low water in the boiler.

Baldwin built the COL. WILCOX in 1878, shop number 4370; along with other monorailers in 1879, these Baldwins were adapted to the system devised by General Roy Stone and that of W. W. Riley. The Pacific Foundry in San Francisco built a monorail engine in 1876 for the Sonoma Valley Prismoidal Railway on the design of Mr. Crew of Opelika, Alabama. The greatest drawback to these monorails was the grade crossing problem, which was never satisfactorily resolved.

As shown in the photo, the COL. WILCOX balanced herself on a single rail atop an elevated wooden structure and was held upright by a set of outriggers on either side of her frame; these outriggers had a set of rollers bearing upon a base timber on each side of the track. (Courtesy of H. L. Broadbelt collection)

BOYNTON'S BICYCLE. Inventor Boynton's odd monorail locomotive ranks high up on the scale of freakish innovations in the motive power field. As shown in this photo of CYCLE No. 1, the locomotive had but a single driver, centered under the belly of the boiler; this wheel and the two trailing wheels under the tender ran on a single rail. To keep the contraption upright, two sets of rollers straddled an overhead wooden stringer suspended from timber trestling; one set of these supports was mounted on a frame that also served as the bell bracket and the second set was mounted near the rear of the extended cab roof that covered the tender. A conventional set of cylinders under the smokebox supplied the power for the single driver.

The strange design was tried out on the Boynton Bicycle Railway Company's experimental track but proved a dismal failure. (Courtesy of Mr. R. Rush)

CHICAGO NOVELTY. Brooks Locomotive Works built this odd 4-4-0 for the Chicago Locomotive Improvement Company as their No. 60. Data is scant regarding this engine. but she appears to have been constructed with an experimental boiler that probably included a set of return flues; instead of being placed in the normal position on the smokebox, her capped stack emerges from the boiler directly over the crown sheet and just forward of her cab. The pipe extending between the smokebox and the shell of the boiler below the base of the stack probably carried exhaust steam from her cylinders.

Whatever benefit in steaming qualities this arrangement produced is doubtful, since the innovation did not spread, but the unusual location of the stack must have had one beneficial effect as far as her crew was concerned —the stack is of such height and close proximity to the cab that trailing smoke and exhaust steam would not tend to obscure the enginemen's vision when the engine was "drifting" with a light throttle opening. (Courtesy of Schenectady History Center)

PIPE DREAM. The novel stack on this locomotive featured a cinder catcher embodied in a design that appears to have been influenced by a pipe-smoker!

The engine thus equipped is the EAGLE of the Boston, Lowell & Nashua Railroad, a 4-4-0 whose fine lines were not especially enhanced by the ornamented funnel of rather grotesque design.

The advent of the extension front end, with its incorporated features for cinder retention and removal, put an end to much of the tinkering with new designs in stacks, but the EAGLE carried a stack with a practical feature that was to later appear on the engines of the Colorado & Southern. This feature was the pipe leading from the bowl of her stack through which the trapped cinders were conveyed to the roadbed. While the "bear-trap" stacks on the Colorado & Southern locomotives delivered their cinders to the outside of the rail by means of a pipe leading down the left side of the smokebox and forward of the left cylinder, the cinder drain pipe on the EAGLE curves back under the belly of her boiler and evidently discharges the cinders between the rails. (Courtesy of Mr. Phil Blackmarr)

BALLAST SCORCHER. Baldwin's 5,000 locomotive was built for the Delaware & Bound Brook Railroad and was completed in April, 1880. An odd 4-2-2 type with a boiler and firebox designed by John E. Wootten for burning fine anthracite, she was constructed to meet the requirements of the parent Philadelphia & Reading Railway for a fast passenger engine to cover the distance between New York and Philadelphia in two hours. Assigned road number 507, she turned in some very speedy runs but was returned to Baldwin when the Bound Brook became involved in financial difficulties.

The engine was re-sold to the Eames Vacuum Brake Company and was named the LOVETT EAMES. She was shipped to England to demonstrate the Eames brake system in 1881 and later passed into the hands of England's Great Northern Railway; she was eventually scrapped but her bell was used as the time bell at the Hornsby engine sheds and has been preserved.

Built with 18 × 24 inch cylinders, she had a 78 inch driver fitted with a tire 3 inches thick, and was fitted with Allen pattern valves. A novel feature of the engine was a device patented by Wm. P. Henszey of the Baldwin Works; by means of a steam cylinder, fulcrums, and equalizing beams, her engineer could increase her adhesion in starting by throwing added weight onto her driving wheels. This weight on the drivers could be decreased at the discretion of her engineer when she had attained the proper rate of speed. Note the brakes applied to both driver and trailing truck. (Courtesy of H. L. Broadbelt collection)

PERAMBULATING ADVERTISEMENT. Under construction number 1379 the Hinkley Locomotive Works turned out this unusual 4-4-0 in 1880 and she was used by her designer, H. F. Shaw, to demonstrate his revolutionary idea of locomotive concept. Named the HENRY F. SHAW, this engine was known as Shaw's Balanced Locomotive and was an experimental 4-cylinder locomotive but was not a compound. Her cylinders were arranged in pairs, set side by side, with one steam chest for each pair of cylinders; two sets of main rods were connected to crank pins diametrically opposed and supported by a bearing in the outside frame. Her drivers were 63 inches in diameter and Angus Sinclair stated her power plant was the equivalent of a conventional engine with 16 × 24 inch cylinders; the SHAW weighed 74,000 pounds in working order. The drivers were not counterbalanced, the arrangement of the rods and crank pins serving instead.

The legend on the tender reads: "No counterbalanced drivers, ergo, no hammer blows and no nosing around. Steam is the motor of balance as applied to the reciprocating parts"; the inscription on the outside frame states: "Drivers without counterbalance. A single movement of valve with duplex action."

According to reports the HENRY F. SHAW performed satisfactorily but the design was not accepted and the engine was sold to the Philadelphia & Sea Isle, according to the *Railway Gazette* of 1893, and passed into oblivion. (Courtesy of Smithsonian Institution)

DOUBLE-BARRELED MUZZLE LOADER. This view from the Baldwin Locomotive Works negatives in the H. L. Broadbelt collection shows the backhead of a boiler equipped with the Wootten firebox. Note the two fire doors to enable the fireman to distribute the coal over the wide grate area and into the back corners of the firebox. This photo graphically illustrates the design of the Wootten style of locomotive boiler, with the firebox located above the engine frames to permit a wider grate area than was possible with the old style of narrow firebox located inside the frames.

Steps and running boards give access to the doors in the back of the cab, and the "one-lung" Westinghouse air compressor is hung at top center of the backhead of the boiler. Also visible is the drawbar for coupling the engine to the tender and the cross-braced supports that carried the rear of the boiler. (Courtesy of H. L. Broadbelt collection)

DETROIT DELUSION. The quest for speed prompted locomotive engineer Eugene Fontaine, of Detroit, Michigan, to patent the unusual locomotive pictured here. It was Fontaine's contention that the speed of an engine could be increased by use of a series of wheels operated on a friction principle and producing the same effect as gearing; the cylinders of his locomotive connected to a set of drivers mounted on a frame above the boiler, their tread contacting the rim of a smaller friction wheel mounted within the periphery of the pair of drivers running on the actual rails. The upper set of drivers were 72 inches in diameter, the friction wheels measured 56 inches, and the drivers on which they were mounted measured 70 inches; an air-operated system of levers could raise or lower the upper set of drivers, thus increasing or decreasing the friction they exerted.

Fontaine Engine Company's No. 1 was built by the Grant Locomotive Works in March, 1881, shop number 1491, based on the patent granted to Fontaine in July of 1880. A sister engine, No. 2, was built under Grant's shop number 1503 in June of 1881. The view here shows No. 2 upon arrival in St. Thomas, Ontario, in July of 1881 when the engine was being tried out on the Canada Southern R.R.; Engineer Ike Deyell stands in the gangway and Fireman George Westfall is seated in the cab.

Dubbed "Fontaine's Folly," the odd engines gave rise to much heated debate as to their merits. The consensus of opinion was that nothing advantageous was gained by Fontaine's invention and the engines were rebuilt by the Rome Works around 1884 and ended up as conventional 4-4-0's on the Wheeling & Lake Erie. (Courtesy of Dr. S. R. Wood)

MULTI-WHEELED FREAK. Inventor Holman's strange creation was constructed by Baldwin in their Philadelphia Works and was assigned road number 10 on the South Jersey Railroad. Her unique design led her to be termed the "Holman Absurdity." Depending upon what level you counted her "driving wheels," No. 10 could have been termed a 4-4-0, a 4-8-0, or a 4-12-0! The freakish arrangement of friction-driven wheels powered by her two pair of main drivers necessitated the high placement of her cylinders, with a resulting high-wheeled engine truck, the latter equipped with brakes. Holman apparently was inspired by the friction drive principle that led Eugene Fontaine to construct his "Folly," shown elsewhere in this chapter, and with a similar lack of success. (Courtesy of H. L. Broadbelt collection)

OFFICIAL CHARIOT. Although not a locomotive in the common sense of the word, this novel piece of equipment is an engine propelled by steam and capable of moving under its own power, thus fitting Webster's definition.

The VIGILANTE, bearing No. 1, was the first of these unique items built by Baldwin; constructed in 1881, the "steam car" was designed to take the place of the old manually-propelled hand car used for inspection purposes by roadmasters and other railway officers. The VIGILANTE was standard gauge, had 4 × 10 inch cylinders, 24 inch wheels, and was powered by a vertical boiler; in working order the car weighed 5,110 pounds. It could seat four observers comfortably in the forward section, while one man seated behind the boiler could act as both engineer and fireman.

Other cars of this type were later built, including the 1893 model constructed for the Missouri, Kansas & Texas. Lettered "Inspection Car" and bearing the number 2, the Katy version of the old "Irish Mail" had dual controls and sported such accessories as a bell, whistle, headlight, diamond stack, and steam jam brakes. The car had a fuel bunker behind the vertical boiler and water was carried in the tank concealed behind the front seats; the forward seats offered a fine, unobstructed view of the track, but scant protection from the elements. Probably the prudent roadmaster touring his domain slowed down for blind curves, as the odds would appear to be in favor of any stray cow or mule that might be deposited in his lap. (Courtesy of H. L. Broadbelt collection)

INSPECTION ENGINE. The inspection locomotive was once a common sight on many of America's larger railway systems, carrying officials over the lines on their rounds of business and supervision of the properties. Perhaps the idea for the design had its origin in the "camel" type locomotives, whose cabs mounted atop the boiler afforded an excellent view of the track and of roadside structures. The customary inspection locomotive consisted of a light engine with a coach body similar to that shown here on the Erie Railroad's No. 1, a 4-4-0 of rather utilitarian and austere design. Seats ranged along the sides of the boiler in the forward section of the engine's elongated cab structure provided the road's officers with a comfortable post from which to observe the condition of the line over which they passed.

One of the more ornate inspection engines was the Lehigh Valley's No. 300, a tall-stacked 4-2-4 named the DOROTHY and constructed in the road's Wilkes-Barre Shops in 1884. (Courtesy of the Erie Railroad)

McCLOUD RIVER DOUBLE-ENDER. Baldwin's answer to the articulated Beyer-Garratt locomotives and the double-enders designed by Robert Fairlie was this pair of Siamese twins, similar to the tank engines permanently coupled in pairs as devised by Lange and Livesey in Europe. Built in 1900 for the McCloud River Railroad's steep grades in the Shasta region pine forests of California, this pair of Vauclain compounds bore builder's numbers 17684 and 17685 and carried road number 6 on the McCloud roster. The unique piece of motive power was actually two 0-6-0 tank engines coupled at the firebox ends, with a set of dual controls for throttles and reverse gear; the crank type throttles could be operated separately or locked together as a single unit, while the two reverse levers were connected to operate as a single unit only. One engineer operated both locomotives, but two firemen were required to keep up steam in the separate boilers of this woodburner. Parts of the engines were interchangeable and the builders claimed the unit could move maximum loads over light rails on a poor roadbed with sharp curves; in addition, the units could be separated if desired, providing two separate locomotives. Built to standard gauge, the dimensions included 11½ (high pressure) and 19 (low pressure) × 20 inch cylinders, 40 inch drivers, and a total weight on all drivers of 161,400 pounds. The boilers carried 200 lbs. working pressure, and each carried 1,200 gallons of water in the tank, with a fuel bunker located on the left running board of each unit. The McCloud River later separated these twins and renumbered them 5 and 6; No. 5 was later sold to the Lystul-Lawson Logging Co. and No. 6 was sold to the Atkinson Construction Co., both units having been converted to oil burners. (Courtesy of H. L. Broadbelt collection)

MECHANICAL HYBRID. This odd locomotive is No. 21 of the Elmira, Cortland & Northern Railroad, a New York State line absorbed by the Lehigh Valley around 1905. Note the unusual arrangement of her wheels, with the engine truck located forward of the cylinders. In 1886 the Rogers Works presented a plan for a locomotive of this type, combining the stability and the weight distribution of the ten-wheeler and the 2-6-0 or Mogul type. Rogers literature states the order for this style of engine was given to "another establishment" and the Cooke Loco. Works built seven of these 4-6-0's in 1884 and four more in 1886, all for the Elmira, Cortland & Northern. Some Lehigh Valley historians believe these engines were built as Moguls and later rebuilt as shown, but the Cooke records list them as 4-6-0's. No. 21 bore Cooke shop number 1712, was built in 1886, and later became Lehigh Valley 921, renumbered 1720, and was rebuilt as a 2-6-0, probably by the Elmira, Cortland & Northern.

The steam dome was located inside the cab, with two sand boxes mounted on the boiler over the leading and main pairs of drivers; the bell was located forward of the stack on the exceptionally long smokebox, the latter sporting two sets of smoke arch braces. The engine had 20 × 24 inch cylinders, 54 inch drivers, and a long, narrow and deep firebox set inside the frames. The design of this 4-6-0 and her sisters appears to be unique in railroad history.

The Elmira, Cortland & Northern was the reorganization of the Utica, Ithaca & Elmira R.R., formed in 1871 by the consolidation of the Ithaca & Cortland R.R. and the Utica, Horseheads & Elmira. (Courtesy of Mr. H. M. Ghormley)

NOBLE EXPERIMENT. The narrow gauge North Pacific Coast Railroad Engine No. 9, a 4-4-0 built by Baldwin in 1875 and named the M. S. LATHAM, plunged through a flood-weakened bridge into California's Austin Creek on the night of February 14th, 1894, carrying six men to death. Fished out after the floodwaters subsided, the engine was rebuilt in the N.P.C. shops and assigned road number 17.

Engine 17 was later badly broken up in a collision and again entered the road's shops at Sausalito. Here Master Mechanic Bill Thomas and his master boilermaker, James McAdams, went to work on the remains and in 1900 they turned out the novel engine shown here. Numbered 21 and named the THOMAS-STETSON, in honor of Master Mechanic Thomas and the line's president, James B. Stetson, the unorthodox locomotive featured a water-tube, oil-fired boiler and a cab located at the front of the engine. The boiler had 63 tubes each 3 inches in diameter that passed through a corrugated furnace; steam was collected in the horizontal drum atop the boiler and the exhaust was carried from the cylinders under the cab to the stack located at the rear of the boiler. The THOMAS-STETSON was not an unqualified success and was scrapped in 1905, her boiler reportedly being used by a laundry firm.

Although some sources refer to the THOMAS-STETSON as the ancestor of the Southern Pacific's cab-in-front locomotives, she was not the first engine to be constructed in this fashion; Ross Winans and his son, Thomas, constructed a 4-8-0 engine named the CENTIPEDE in 1855 that housed the engineer in a cabin located on the pilot beam in front of the smokebox. This engine was used on the Baltimore & Ohio during the Civil War with the cab moved back atop the boiler in Winans' "camel-back" style. (Courtesy of Dr. S. R. Wood)

BIG TRIPLEX. The apex of the compound locomotive craze was reached in September of 1913, when the Erie Railroad placed an order with the Baldwin Locomotive Works for the triple articulated engine shown here. The locomotive was designed and constructed under patents granted to Consulting Engineer George R. Henderson of the Baldwin Works, and was a 2-8-8-8-2 type. The first of these cumbersome brutes was completed in April, 1914, and was named the MATT H. SHAY, in honor of the oldest locomotive engineer in the service of the Erie at that time. She was designed for helper service on the heavy grades of the Erie on Susquehanna Hill, but test runs were made on almost level track to determine her capabilities. On a grade of 0.09 per cent combined with a 5 degree curve, this behemoth hauled a train of 250 loaded cars weighing 17,912 tons; this drag was over 1½ miles long, the actual length of engine and cars being 1.6 miles!

The big coalburner had six cylinders of equal size all cast from the same pattern; the middle set of cylinders was operated by superheated steam directly from the boiler, in effect making them the high pressure cylinders. They exhausted into the front and rear cylinders, which in turn acted as low pressure cylinders. The exhaust from the forward set of cylinders was piped into the smokebox and discharged through the stack to create the required draught; the exhaust from the rear set of cylinders that powered the drivers located under the tender went to a feedwater heater to preheat the boiler's water supply, then was exhausted to atmosphere through the escape pipe visible at the rear of the tender. The draft gear of the rolling stock in use at the time was hardly equal to the strains the triplex locomotive would create in pulling trains, and the engine was customarily used as a pusher at the rear of freights ascending the Susquehanna grade. As a pusher the articulated MATT H. SHAY proved satisfactory to the Erie officials and two more engines of similar design and dimensions were completed by Baldwin in 1916 and place in Susquehanna Hill pusher service. (Courtesy of the Erie Railroad)

CRUDE AND COMPETENT. This classic example of a home-bred iron mule lacks many of the refinements of the products of Baldwin, Schenectady, Rogers, and other builders yet she is a locomotive in every sense of the term. The product of some logging camp's blacksmith shop, this 0-2-4 is shown at rest after dragging a very creditable train of fir logs down to a dump in Oregon's Coos County. The logs have been peeled of bark and sniped on the end, a fair indication that bull teams have brought them down a skid road to the landing where they were loaded onto the sets of 4-wheel trucks; the crude lokey, its vertical donkey boiler fired with wood, has rolled the big sticks down to the dumping ground and from here they will float to some tidewater saw mill.

The big timber region of the West Coast saw many such crude machines as the one pictured here. Some were rod engines, others powered through gearing or even chain drives, but the majority of them boasted a vertical boiler and only the rudest of frames and cab. Designed to handle heavy loads at low speed, these mechanical oxen huffed and puffed their way over sketchy track as they carted the loggers' harvest out of the woods and off to the mills. (Courtesy of Jack Slattery)

CONNECTICUT PASTORAL. Engine No. 5 of the Boston & New York Air Line Railroad poses for the photographer on the spidery heights of Lyman Viaduct in the late 1870's, with the green foliage of Connecticut's rolling hills for a backdrop. The standard gauge string of four varnished cars behind the diamond-stacked American type ran on the 50-mile short line between the terminals of New Haven and Willimantic.

The road was chartered in 1846 as the New York & Boston Rail Road Company and construction started in 1853; after consolidation with other companies the work failed to proceed as required under terms of the original charter, which expired. In 1867 the New Haven, Middletown & Willimantic R.R. was chartered to take over the original project and the road was completed on August 13th, 1873. Financial problems caused a reorganization in 1875, the road emerging as the Boston & New York Air Line Railroad. (Courtesy of Dr. S. R. Wood)

YANKEE GALLERY

This section of the album is devoted to the railroads of the North, roughly that section of the United States bounded on the north by Canada, on the east by the Atlantic Ocean, on the south by the Mason-Dixon line, and running west to the valley of the Mississippi.

Within this domain there developed a dense pattern of rail lines, large and small, and the ribbons of iron laced the coastal plains, threaded the river valleys, and braved the mountains of the Appalachian Range. And mountains there were in abundance—not the towering 12,000 to 15,000 feet ranges of the Rockies, but mountains, nevertheless, and they thrust their silent barriers skyward in the path of the westering Iron Horse.

Pioneer railroad builders tackled them with crude equipment and hacked a path for the steam locomotive through the ranges: the White Mountains of New Hampshire, the Green Mountains of Vermont, the Berkshire Hills, the Adirondacks, the Taconics, the Poconos, and the Alleghenies.

Lacking the broad farmlands of the South and the West, the North early turned to industry and as waterpower gave way to steam these industries demanded transportation and the railroads provided the means of moving raw materials and finished products. The great Pittsburgh coal seam, covering some 5,700 square miles, was one of the greatest mineral resources ever tapped by mankind, and the region yielded petroleum, iron ore, hardwoods, and other vital assets.

The great majority of American firms engaged in building steam locomotives were encompassed within this region and the fame of Yankee locomotives grew to rival that of New England's noted clipper ships. From shops in Philadelphia, Boston, Manchester, Pittsburgh, Connelsville, Dunkirk, Jersey City, Lancaster, Schenectady, and Paterson a host of engines steamed forth to blaze a trail of smoke and cinders across the nation.

A roster of the locomotive builders of the region would contain the names of men who enriched the heritage of Americans with their polished iron steeds—Matt Baldwin, the Norrises, Rogers, Cooke, Danforth, McKay and Aldus, John Souther, Coleman Sellers, John Brandt, Wm. Swinburne, H. K. Porter, William Mason, Dawson and Bailey, and a great many others.

Turn the pages of this section and from the smoke-filled roundhouses of yesteryear a cavalcade of locomotives will roll over the brightly-polished rails of memory. Proudly they steam forth, from the pine forests of Maine, the sandy dunes of Cape Cod, the vales of the Hudson and the Mohawk; over the Alleghenies and across the Western Reserve, skirting the Great Lakes and the northern banks of the Ohio, and braking to a halt at the eastern shores of the Mississippi. Pleasant journey!

PORTLAND & OGDENSBURG R.R. locomotive No. 1 was named the PRESUMPSCOT and had been built by John Souther in 1853 as No. 6, the RICHMOND, of the Portland & Kennebec R.R., being sold to the P&O in the early 1870's. The P&O was chartered in 1867 and opened between Portland, Maine, and Fabyan's, New Hampshire, on December 22, 1875. The PRESUMPSCOT was a 4-4-0 with outside frames and circular steam chests, with 14 × 20 cylinders and 60 inch drivers; known locally as "The Old Man Killer," she was scrapped in 1888. (Courtesy of George Eastman House)

VERMONT DIVISION of the Portland & Ogdensburg R.R. was a union of the Lamoille Valley, the Essex County, and the Montpelier & St. Johnsbury Railroads. Construction of the standard gauge line between Lunenburg and Johnson, Vermont, was begun in 1871, the year the Portland Locomotive Works turned out the HYDE PARK for the new line; built under Shop No. 202, the 4-4-0 was a pretty engine sporting a sunflower stack. (Courtesy of Dr. S. R. Wood)

GREEN MOUNTAIN BOY. The Hinkley Locomotive Works of Boston, Massachusetts, constructed this 4-4-0 woodburner for the old Central Vermont Railroad, where she was assigned to their Rutland Division as No. 26 and named the ETHAN ALLEN in honor of Vermont's almost legendary Revolutionary War hero, noted for his capture of Fort Ticonderoga. Note the "ankle rail" or supplementary outside frame on this engine, and the bull's-eye classification lamp mounted on the pilot beam beneath the big oil headlight.

Chartered as the Vermont Central R.R. in 1843, the road was reorganized as the Central Vermont Railroad in 1873. The main line extended 118 miles between Windsor and Burlington, Vermont, but leased lines and branches totaling 583 miles were also operated, including the Missisquoi R.R., the Sullivan County R.R., the Rutland R.R., and others. The original company leased the Vermont & Canada R.R. in 1849; this line, then under construction from Essex Junction to Rouse's Point, was opened in 1851 but the lease was a constant subject of litigation for many years thereafter.

CENTRAL VERMONT R.R. was justly proud of Engine No. 50, named the GOV. SMITH. The funnel-stacked woodburner was built in the road's shops in 1857 and was the acme of home-grown engines of that period. The 4-4-0 was a fine mechanical specimen and was ornately finished, with brass dome casings and a fancy bell stand, complete with brass eagles. The tender sported an elaborate painting and the wooden cab was an example of the joiner's fine art, with Gothic windows, one of which appears to have a decorative design etched in the glass pane. (Courtesy of Dr. S. R. Wood)

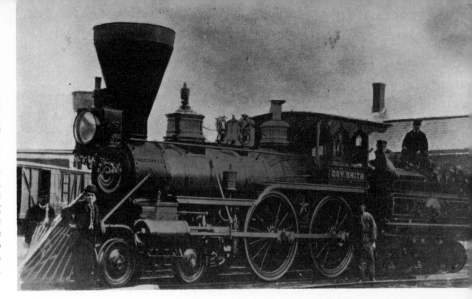

CONNECTICUT RIVER R.R. was formed in 1845 by a consolidation of the Greenfield & Northampton R.R. and the Northampton & Springfield R.R.; a standard gauge line 50 miles in length was completed from Springfield, Mass., to South Vernon, Vermont, on Jan. 1, 1849. A short branch from Chicopee to Chicopee Falls, Mass., was opened in 1845 and the Connecticut River road purchased the Easthampton-Mount Tom, Mass., branch shortly after completion in 1872. This rare view shows Connecticut River Railroad's Engine No. 2, the BRATTLEBORO, a diamond-stacked American type built in 1871. (Courtesy of Dr. S. R. Wood)

BOSTON & PROVIDENCE R.R. completed 44 miles of standard gauge line between Boston, Mass., and Providence, Rhode Island, in 1835, along with the West Roxbury and Dedham branches. The B&P later acquired the Stoughton Branch, the India Point Branch, and the Attleboro Branch Railroad. A noted engine on the Boston & Providence was the DANIEL NASON, an inside-connected 4-4-0 built in the road's Roxbury shops in 1863 under the supervision of Master Mechanic G. S. Griggs. The DANIEL NASON featured a hexagon-shaped steam dome cover and two brass "cannon" type safety valves, the bell being supported between the latter. Note the safety railing extending from cab to pilot beam, and also the odd tank trucks. (Courtesy of George Eastman House)

WHITE MOUNTAIN INTERLUDE. This 5-car string of varnish on the Portland & Ogdensburg Railroad was photographed by the Kilburn Brothers of Littleton, New Hampshire, and is halted for the occasion on a wooden trestle in the famed Crawford Notch pass.

Crawford's Notch, some 2,000 feet deep, separates the Presidential Range from the Franconia Range of the White Mountains. The Notch gives rise to the headwaters of the Saco and the Ammonoosuc rivers, the former flowing easterly into Maine and the Atlantic while the latter runs westerly to join the Coos and eventually to add its waters to the Connecticut. The timbered hills and vast granite outcroppings form a scenic backdrop which delighted travellers aboard the steam cars that threaded their way through the picturesque region.

The brass-bound woodburner of the Portland & Ogdensburg shown here is fitted with a sunflower stack, screened to catch the live sparks which erupted as the exhaust tore at her fire on the stiff grades leading through the mountain pass.

ROAD TO THE CLOUDS. The cog railway built to carry sight-seers to the summit of New Hampshire's famed Mount Washington was one of the engineering feats of its day, the rails climbing the rock-ribbed slopes on a breath-taking grade.

Locomotives with vertical boilers pushed the wooden coaches up the mountain to the great Summit House, mecca for New England tourists who came to enjoy the view from the lofty height and to thrill to the daring ascent over such spidery trestles as the noted "Jacob's Ladder," a landmark on the cog road.

In this view Engine No. 5, appropriately named the CLOUD, poses with a car loaded with happy excursionists on the log and timber trestle spanning a brawling mountain brook as she pauses for camera of the Kilburn Brothers of Littleton, New Hampshire; this firm made a series of widely-circulated stereoscopic views of the scenic wonders of the Mt. Washington Railway.

COG ROAD CLOSE-UP. This view shows one of the locomotives of the Mount Washington Railway at close range. The rack rail, laid in the center of the regular track, is visible in this photograph. Teeth in the cog wheel under the engine engaged this rack rail to enable the engine to ascend the steep grade up the boulder-strewn slopes of Mount Washington.

The 0-4-0 is posed on the flank of the ridge above the timber line, not far from the Summit House terminus of the road. (Courtesy of Douglas County Historical Society)

COG ROAD GOAL. This three story wooden frame hostelry, anchored securely atop the rocky crest of Mount Washington, was the end of the climb for the tourists who flocked to New Hampshire to ride up the scenic cog line.

Two of the vertical-boilered woodburners, each with its solitary wooden coach, are halted on the platform in this view of the Summit House. Located high above the timber line, the multi-gabled hotel was subjected to severe buffeting by the gales that howled over the barren summit in winter.

The Mount Washington Railway was chartered in 1858 but the 3.33 miles of 5 foot, 3 inch gauge track was not officially opened for traffic until July of 1869. The road cost a reported $150,000 and was operated from June to October yearly; the line is still in operation.

Mount Washington, highest peak in the northeastern United States, is located in the Presidential Range of the White Mountains, the elevation at its peak being 6,288 feet. Winds of more than 180 miles per hour have been recorded on the summit, and the mercury there has fallen to more than 50 degrees below zero.

NEW ENGLAND GRANDEUR. The highly-touted scenery of the Rockies had its New England counterpart in the White Mountains of New Hampshire, where the rails of the Portland & Ogdensburg threaded their way through Crawford Notch. This rugged stretch of mountain railroad formed the setting for the rare old photo of a Portland & Ogdensburg R.R. passenger train drawn by the eight-wheeler, SACO, posed here on Willey Brook bridge. The woodburner is followed by a mail and baggage car, a coach, and one of the open "rubberneck" tourist cars, the latter fitted with curtains that could be lashed down for protection against inclement weather.

In the 1880's the sleeping cars of the Pullman firm carried travelers directly from Syracuse, N.Y., to the noted White Mountain resort at Fabyan's, New Hampshire, over the Ogdensburgh & Lake Champlain R.R. and connecting lines; the trains of the Portland & Ogdensburg R.R. began operating between Portland, Maine, and Fabyan's, New Hampshire in December of 1875. (Courtesy of Douglas County Historical Society)

PORTLAND, SACO, & PORTSMOUTH R.R. extended 51 miles from Portland, Maine, to Portsmouth, New Hampshire. The company was chartered in 1837 and the road opened in November of 1842. After completion it was leased jointly by the Boston & Maine R.R. and the Eastern R.R. of Massachusetts, being leased exclusively to the latter in 1871. Shown here is Engine No. 12, named the BONNEBEAG, which later became Eastern R.R. of Mass. No. 86; she was built by the Portland Works under shop number 137 in 1866, had 15 × 22 inch cylinders and a rather elaborate clerestory cab. (Courtesy of George Eastman House)

BEANS AND CODFISH. The Old Colony Railroad was chartered in 1844 and completed a line from South Boston to Plymouth in November, 1845. Consolidated with the Fall River Railroad in 1854, the road operated as the Old Colony & Fall River R.R. for a number of years and acquired several other New England short lines, among them being the Cape Cod Railroad. The Cape Cod started life in 1846 as the Cape Cod Branch R.R. with authority to build from Middleboro to Sandwich, Massachusetts. It became the Cape Cod Railroad in 1854, shortly before it was extended to Hyannis. The line of iron advanced around the hook of Cape Cod, passing through Yarmouth, Harwich, and Orleans; later it ran on to Wellfleet and Truro, terminating at Provincetown on the other end of the Cape.

The photo here, from the collections of the Library of Congress, reportedly was taken in 1864 and is labelled "First R.R. Train From Boston To Orleans." (Courtesy of Library of Congress)

PORTLAND & ROCHESTER R.R. started life in 1846 when it was chartered as the York & Cumberland R.R.; the first 18 miles of standard gauge line was opened from Portland, Maine, to the Saco River in 1853. It was reorganized as the Portland & Rochester R.R. in 1867 and the 34 miles of track from the Saco River to Rochester, New Hampshire, was finished in 1871. Engine No. 3, the ROCHESTER, was built by the Portland Works in 1867 and was a pretty 4-4-0 woodburner with a sunflower stack. (Courtesy of George Eastman House)

BURLINGTON & LAMOILLE R.R. owned the MANSFIELD, an 0-6-6T built by the Mason Machine Works of Taunton, Massachusetts. The engine is shown here at William Mason's factory, ready for delivery; note the absence of a headlight, many roads preferring to apply their own favored type of lamp. In contrast with his 4-4-0 types, which had concealed counterbalances, this "bogie" has visible counterbalances in each of her drivers.

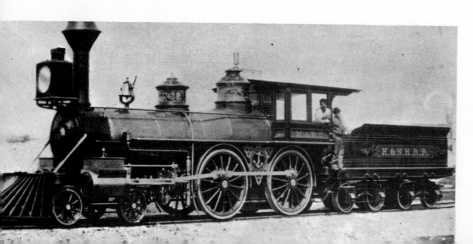

HARTFORD & NEW HAVEN R.R. was chartered in Connecticut in 1833 and the road opened between Hartford and New Haven, 36 miles, in 1839. An extension to Springfield, Mass., was chartered in 1839 and opened in December, 1844. The line consolidated with the New York & New Haven R.R. in 1872, forming the New York, New Haven & Hartford R.R. Shown here is Hartford & New Haven's No. 28, a neat 4-4-0 named the MARS. She was built by the Rhode Island Loco. Works in 1867; note the anchor in the center of her ornate builder's plate, reminiscent of the marine influence on New England's history. (Courtesy of Dr. S. R. Wood)

A PAIR OF YANKEE GENERALS. The impact of the Civil War and its leaders on the civilian population was reflected by the number of locomotives named in honor of military leaders, as witness this pair of American types on the Boston & Maine.

Boston & Maine's No. 41 was named the GEN. GRANT, honoring the Union leader who was later to become President of the United States, and her headlight bears his portrait in oils.

Boston & Maine's No. 42 was christened GEN. SHERMAN, in honor of William Tecumseh Sherman, and a very fair likeness of old "Cump" decorates No. 42's oil headlight housing. Sherman's noted sweep from Atlanta to the sea wrought havoc with railroads of the South that lay in his path, and his fire-scorched trail of destruction lent credence to the Confederate observation that "Uncle Billy" was mighty careless with matches.

The tenders of both locomotives and the cab of the GEN. SHERMAN are painted in the ornate manner of the era, presenting a colorful variety of scrolls, shields, chain link, and banners. It is lamentable that color film had not come into existence to preserve these examples of the locomotive painter's art in all of its brilliant detail. (Both photos, courtesy of Harold S. Walker)

"EDDY CLOCK." Wilson Eddy left his native state of Vermont in the early 1830's and entered the shops of the Proprietors of Locks & Canals on the Merrimac River, located in Lowell, Massachusetts. In 1840 Major Geo. W. Whistler persuaded Eddy to come to work in the Springfield shops of the Western R.R. of Massachusetts as a mechanic; he soon became a foreman and in 1850 was appointed to succeed Henry Gray as Master Mechanic. Eddy built his first locomotive, the ADDISON GILMORE, in 1850-51, followed by the WHISTLER in 1852. In the years that followed he turned out nearly 100 locomotives for his road, which, after consolidation with the Boston & Worcester R.R. in 1867, became the Boston & Albany Railroad.

In an era when many builders carried decorative effects to the extreme the Eddy engines were rather plain and unadorned but their steady dependable performance over the grades of the Berkshires earned them the nickname of "Eddy Clocks." His engines were without steam domes, the steam being taken from the upper portion of the boiler through a perforated dry pipe, with a slide valve throttle located in the "T" of the dry pipe in the smokebox. Eddy is credited with placing tallow cups inside the cab, with pipes leading to the steam chests, eliminating the dangerous practice of the fireman having to go out onto the front of the engine while in motion to oil the valves.

Wilson Eddy's son, Horace W. Eddy, succeeded him as Master Mechanic upon his retirement in 1880 and the noted old builder lived in Springfield, Mass., until his death in 1898.

Pictured here is one of his "Clocks," the ARIZONA, No. 83 of the Western R.R. of Massachusetts; she was built in 1866 for freight service and had a slot cut in her curving mud-guard through which the main rod operated.

MAINE MIDGET. New England was the home of a number of enchanting little 2-foot gauge railroads and one of these charming pikes was the Kennebec Central Railroad, 5 miles of light 25 pound rail running from Randolph, Maine, to the National Soldiers' Home located a short distance from Chelsea, the latter better known by its century-old name of Togus.

The Kennebec Central was opened in 1890 and the majority of its traffic was passengers to and from the old Soldiers' Home and cargoes of coal bound for the Home's heating plant. Four engines graced the roster of the Lilliputian road, all 0-4-4 Forney types. No. 1, a Baldwin of 1890 vintage, was named the VOLUNTEER, but No. 2, shown here, was nameless; she was built by the Portland Works, carrying shop number 621. These two tiny iron colts were replaced in the 1920's with a Bridgton & Saco River R.R. 0-4-4 and another Forney from the Sandy River & Rangeley Lakes Railroad, which served until the Kennebec Central ceased operations in 1929. (Courtesy of Dr. S. R. Wood)

B&M AMERICANS. This pair of 4-4-0's racked up many miles on the iron of the Boston & Maine Railroad. No. 308, named the ASHUELOT, was built by the Manchester Locomotive Works; the proud crew posed here with her consisted of Engineer Henry Honey, standing by her tank with long oiler in hand, and Fireman "Stub" Hastings, seated in her cab.

No. 401, the DESPATCH, is shown with a freight crew and caboose; note that her abbreviated running board ends just short of her sand pipe, giving her boiler a rather bare look.

IN THE CLEAR. The magic of the camera has recorded this nostalgic scene for posterity, preserving the look of old-time railroading in the days of the link and pin. Engine No. 10, the ONWARD, of the Boston, Hartford & Erie Railroad has pulled her consist of 10 cars and a caboose into a siding and is standing clear of the main track, simmering gently under the sun of a summer day in New England. Two freight brakemen decorate the deck of the leading car, while the skipper nonchalantly gazes up at the engine crew; soon the opposing train will ramble by, leaving a breath of coal smoke and warm oil in the fence-bordered cut, and the interlude pictured here will dissolve as the head man lines the gate and the ONWARD chuffs easily onto the main stem to resume her journey toward eternity.

Schenectady built the 4-4-0 in December of 1868, under Shop No. 526, for the little Dutchess & Columbia Railroad running between Millerton and Dutchess Junction, New York, where she bore road number 100. She was later acquired by the Boston, Hartford & Erie R.R. as their No. 10, and carried this same number when the BH&E was reorganized in 1873 as the New York & New England Railroad. The Boston, Hartford & Erie was chartered in 1863 to acquire several short lines, including the Norfolk County R.R. and the Boston & New York Central, the latter concern being formed by a consolidation of the Midland and the Southbridge & Blackstone R.R. companies. The New York & New England main line extended about 86 miles from Boston to Willimantic, Connecticut, with branches to Southbridge and Dedham and a longer branch from Brookline, Mass., to Woonsocket, Rhode Island. (Courtesy of Dr. S. R. Wood)

BLOODY BACKGROUND. The Mohawk Valley around Utica, New York, was steeped in history long before the first engine whistled through its wooded vales. Dutch and English settlers had pushed west from the Hudson in colonial days and their forts and settlements were frequently raided by French troops down from Canada during the French and Indian wars. When the Revolutionary War broke out the native Iriquois tribesmen joined with British raiding parties and the crack of the musket and the war-whoop echoed through the Oneida country; the old names linger yet in the Mohawk River's natural gateway through the Appalachians—Oriskany, Fort Stanwix, Fort Herkimer, Deerfield, German Flats, and the Palatine, a region bought with blood and tears and later linked with twin ribbons of shining rail.

Utica was the home terminal of the Utica & Black River R.R., whose Engine No. 11 is shown here. For many years No. 11 and her sisters were under the supervision of John Bailey, Master of Machinery of the Black River line. Bailey, a white-bearded patriarch who had started railroading as a locomotive fireman, lived to preside over the motive power of the Utica & Black River in the days when coal was replacing wood as fuel for the locomotives.

ATLANTIC GATEWAY. The Northern Rail Road Company of New York was chartered May 14th, 1845, and was opened between Ogdensburgh and Rouse's Point, N.Y., on October 1st, 1850, comprising a standard gauge line 118 miles in length. The pike was reorganized as the Ogdensburgh Railroad in 1858 and in 1864 became the Ogdensburgh & Lake Champlain R.R.; in 1870 it was leased to the Vermont Central and in 1901 was absorbed by the Rutland Railroad.

The road left the eastern end of Lake Ontario and cut across northern New York to the upper end of Lake Champlain, where it connected with the Portland & Ogdensburg Railroad; through connections with the Central Vermont, the Montpelier & Wells River, and the Boston, Concord & Montreal, the line attempted to siphon St. Lawrence River traffic overland to the eastern seaboard and also provided a route to the White Mountain resorts. A connection with the Rome, Watertown & Ogdensburg R.R. provided rail service from western New York and the Great Lakes region to eastern points, including through Pullman Palace Car service from Ogdensburgh to Boston in the 1880's.

The old settler depicted here is the engine ST. LAWRENCE of the Ogdensburgh & Lake Champlain Railroad, an early 4-4-0 woodburner.

BLACK RIVER LINE. One of the interesting rail lines in up-state New York was the old Utica & Black River Railroad, 87 miles of standard gauge road that started life in 1853 as the Black River & Utica Railroad. The road was opened from Utica to Boonville in 1855, was reorganized in the 1860's, and completed to the northern terminus of Philadelphia, New York, in 1873. A lease of the new Black River & Morristown R.R. in 1875 gave the Black River line a route from Utica to the St. Lawrence River valley. Also leased were the Clayton & Theresa R.R. (about 16 miles long), and the 30-mile Carthage, Watertown & Sackett's Harbor R.R.; at Watertown Junction on the latter road connections were made with the Rome, Watertown & Ogdensburgh Railroad's branch to Cape Vincent, a popular resort for the Thousand Islands tourist trade. An extension begun about 1877 connected the Black River road from Morristown into Ogdensburgh; the Utica & Black River was leased to the Rome, Watertown & Ogdensburgh R.R. in 1886 and in 1891 this lease was transferred to the New York Central & Hudson River Railroad.

The early Utica & Black River R.R. 4-4-0 shown here is the T. S. FAXTON, named for Theodore S. Faxton, a resident of Utica and a member of the road's Board of Directors.

Firemen on the old Black River earned their money the hard way, palming wood into the funnel-stacked engines as they churned north from Utica through Marcy, Stittsville, and Holland Patent to battle, the heavy grade of Remsen hill. On their return from Ogdensburgh they frequently gathered in John Collins' saloon on Water Street in Utica for liquid refreshment, free lunch, and the companionship of fellow railroad men.

ON THE OLD "HO-JACK." The Rome, Watertown & Ogdensburgh R.R. (the "h" was dropped from Ogdensburgh in later years) was formed in 1861 by consolidation of the Watertown & Rome R.R. and the Potsdam & Watertown R.R.; construction on these lines dated back to 1848, with the line from Rome to Cape Vincent, N.Y., being opened in 1852 and the line between Watertown and Potsdam opened in 1857. The road also acquired the Syracuse Northern R.R. and the property originally known as the Lake Ontario Shore Railroad. Known locally as the "Ho-Jack," the RW&O came under the control of Charles Parsons, a Maine State railroader who added the Utica & Black River R.R. to the system. In 1891, pressured by a proposed competitive line, the Rome road and the leased Utica & Black River line were leased to the Vanderbilt-controlled New York Central & Hudson River Railroad.

Engine No. 17, shown here, was originally built by the Taunton Works in 1852 for the Potsdam & Watertown R.R.; named the ANTWERP after a station on the road located between Gouveneur and Watertown, N.Y., the trim woodburner is shown here after being rebuilt in the Rome, Watertown & Ogdensburg shops. The first stationary engine in the Rome shops reportedly was the little locomotive ROXBURY of the old Watertown & Rome R.R., with the flanges removed from her drivers and her frame blocked up on a brick foundation. Many railroads over the nation used boilers from wrecked or discarded locomotives to power their shop equipment and pumping plants.

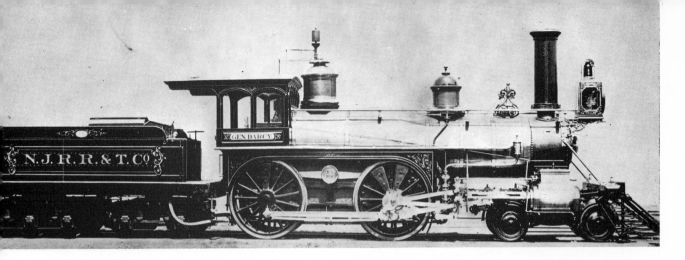

HOME-GROWN BEAUTY. The elegant 4-4-0 shown here is the GEN. DARCY of the New Jersey Rail Road & Transportation Co., built in the road's Jersey City shops under the supervision of Master Mechanic John Headden; the round brass plate between her drivers bears Shop No. 3, and the year of her construction, 1868. The engine was designed to burn anthracite coal in passenger service and had outside eccentrics and link motion to operate her valves, a form of application that gained some popularity in that era.

Chartered in 1832, the New Jersey R.R. & Transportation Co. was opened between Jersey City and New Brunswick in 1837; horses were first used for motive power on the original section between Newark and Bergen Hill and were continued in use on the temporary line over Bergen Hill until the big Bergen Cut was finished in 1838. In 1835 a "rotary steam engine" built by William Avery was tried on the line but little is known of this rotary engine, which may have been an early form of a turbine locomotive. The NEWARK, Baldwin's 16th locomotive, was placed in service on the road in December of 1835.

Connection with the Camden & Amboy R.R. in 1840 provided a through service to Philadelphia; together with a number of other companies, the road later formed a part of the United New Jersey Railroad & Canal Companies and was leased to the Pennsylvania R.R. in 1871 for a period of 999 years. (Courtesy of Smithsonian Institution)

LEHIGH VALLEY LINK. That section of the Lehigh Valley Railroad extending from Sayre, Pennsylvania, to Geneva, New York, dates back to the early 1870's and a pair of short lines reaching into the picturesque Finger Lakes region.

The Geneva & Ithaca R.R. was opened in 1871 and ran from Ithaca, at the southern end of Cayuga Lake, to Geneva, at the northern tip of Seneca Lake. The Ithaca & Athens R.R. was projected south from Ithaca to Athens, near Sayre, Pa., and was opened in 1874. Upon completion of the latter line in 1874, the two roads consolidated, forming the Geneva, Ithaca & Athens Railroad; this company defaulted in 1875 and the road was reorganized with Lehigh Valley backing, becoming the Geneva, Ithaca & Sayre Railroad.

The Baldwin Works turned out the trim little saddletanker shown here in 1871 for the Ithaca & Athens; the 2-4-0 was named the ITHACA.

The rounded saddletank applied to the ITHACA was an improvement over the square tanks applied to earlier saddletank engines; not only did it present a more graceful appearance by conforming to the contour of the boiler but it also permitted the engine crew with a better view of the track ahead. (Courtesy of H.L. Broadbelt collection)

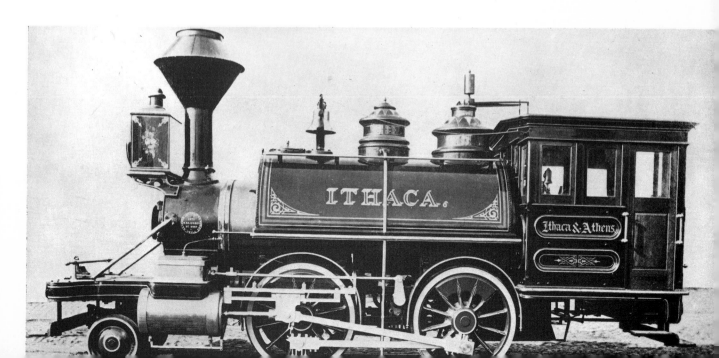

JERSEY LOWLANDER. The West Jersey Railroad was chartered in 1853, reached Woodbury in 1857 and was completed to Bridgeton in 1862. The line from Glassboro to Millville, built under a separate charter, was opened in the spring of 1860. In 1868-69 the West Jersey extending its operations down the peninsula between the Atlantic Ocean and Delaware Bay by leasing the Cape May & Millville R.R. (opened from Millville to Cape May in 1865); the Swedesboro R.R. (opened from Woodbury to Swedesboro in 1869); and the Salem R.R. (from Elmer, 26 miles south of Camden, to Salem, N.J.).

The West Jersey R.R. later became a part of the West Jersey & Seashore Railroad, affiliated in interest with the Pennsylvania System.

Engine No. 18 of the West Jersey R.R., pictured here, was a product of the Danforth Locomotive & Machine Company works of Paterson, New Jersey. Typical of the motive power of the 1870's, her sand box and tender sport elaborate scroll and painted landscapes, the one on the tender panel depicting a lofty peak overlooking a heavily-forested shore and a large body of water.

Her big oil headlight bears the names of the makers, Tanner, Walker & McAnerney; a common practice of the day was for a locomotive to leave the factory with only the headlight bracket and platform supplied, many roads preferring to install the light of their choice after the engine was delivered. Two popular makers of locomotive headlights in the mid-1870's were the Adams & Westlake Co. of Chicago and the Buffalo Steam Gauge & Lantern Co. of Rochester, New York. (Courtesy of Smithsonian Institution)

THE FAST MAIL. The comparatively level grades of the Lake Shore & Michigan Southern Railroad aided that line in building a reputation for speed that survived for many years. The Lake Shore, under the presidency of crusty old Commodore Cornelius Vanderbilt, prided itself on the "Fast Mail," a beautiful train drawn by high-stepping locomotives.

This view shows the "Fast Mail" in 1875, hauled by LS & MS engine No. 317, the J. H. DEVEREUX, with Engineer Nicholas Hartman standing in the gangway; the locomotive was new that year, built in the Lake Shore's shops in Buffalo, N.Y., and named in honor of John H. Devereux. Devereux had served as a superintendent on the U.S. Military Railroads during the Civil War under Genl. Herman Haupt, and later became General Supt. of the Cleveland & Pittsburgh, advancing to President of the Cleveland, Columbus, Cincinnati & Indianapolis Railway, holding the latter position until his death.

The mail cars are fitted with an early application of vestibules and bear ornate decorations. The head car is the GOV. BROUGH, followed by the GOV. FAIRCHILD; painted on the cars are colorful likenesses of these gubernatorial dignitaries. Near the open door of the GOV. BROUGH and just to the left of the leafy tree can be seen the wooden trackside mail crane from which the speeding train snatched the mail sacks as it hurtled along between Buffalo and Chicago.

General Supt. Chas. Paine was in charge of the Lake Shore at this time and General Master Mechanic James Sedgley ruled the motive power and enginemen from the road's main offices in Cleveland, Ohio. (Anderson collection, courtesy of Mr. H. M. Ghormley)

"BLOOM" POWER. The Lackawanna & Bloomsburg Railroad started construction in 1854 at Scranton, Pennsylvania, and was intended to tap the Wyoming Valley's rich deposits of anthracite coal; the line was opened to Rupert in 1858 and later extended through Bloomsburg to Northumberland, giving it a total length of 80 miles. In 1873 it was leased to the Delaware, Lackawanna & Western and operated as that road's Bloomsburg Division, commonly called the "Bloom."

The L & B had a very complete shop at Kingston, Pa., and began building their own locomotives there in 1871. Pictured here is the Lackawanna & Bloomsburg's second No. 2, named the CHAS. GRAHAM in honor of the Master Mechanic of the Kingston shops where she was built in 1871; first No. 2 had been a 4-4-0 built by Swinburne in 1855 and named the NANTICOKE.

The CHAS. GRAHAM was renumbered 202 by the DL&W in 1886, then rebuilt with a wide firebox in the following year and renumbered 101 in 1889. In 1905 she became No. 135 and was wrecked in November of that year; she had been converted to a "Mother Hubbard" in 1887 and her spoked engine truck wheels replaced by a set of solid ones, but she retained her rather unusual headlight bracket. (Courtesy of Dr. S. R. Wood)

GREAT WESTERN LINE. The Atlantic & Great Western Railway was formed in 1865 by a consolidation of the Meadville R.R. of Pennsylvania, the Erie & New York City R.R. of New York, and the Franklin & Warren R.R. of Ohio; the system was controlled under a series of leases by the Erie Railway and at one time was in the hands of Receiver J. H. Devereux, a veteran of United States Military R.R. operations during the Civil War. Sold under the sheriff's hammer in July of 1871, the road was reorganized as the Atlantic & Great Western Railroad.

The main stem, about 387 miles long, extended from Salamanca, N.Y., to Dayton, Ohio. It was built to a gauge of 6 feet and traffic was moved over the leased standard gauge line of the Cleveland & Mahoning R.R. between Leavittsburg and Cleveland by use of a third rail. For the 60-mile extension from Dayton to Cincinnati the road leased the use of the right-of-way of the Cincinnati, Hamilton & Dayton R.R., laying two additional rails outside of the CH&D track in what was known as a "straddle" operation; the CH&D trains ran on their own standard gauge rails while the A&GW trains straddled this standard gauge track and ran on their own 6-foot gauge track.

The Atlantic & Great Western Railroad's No. 5 was a product of Danforth, Cooke & Company of Paterson, New Jersey. (Courtesy of the Erie Railroad)

LOCAL TALENT. In 1875 the New Castle & Franklin Railroad opened 36.25 miles of 4 foot 9 inch gauge track between New Castle and Stoneboro, Pennsylvania. By 1876 the line had three locomotives, a passenger coach, one baggage car, and 15 freight cars, which provides a picture of their somewhat pastoral operations in Lawrence and Mercer counties on Pennsylvania's western border; the pleasant meanderings of the little road's trains were shepherded by Supt. A. Vandivort from the general offices in New Castle.

Engine No. 2 of the New Castle & Franklin bore the name MERCER, in honor of the county and town of the same name served by the short line. Mercer was located between New Castle and Stoneboro, about midway over the road; the home terminal of New Castle, southern end of the line, was located in the pleasant Beaver River valley.

The MERCER was built in near-by Pittsburgh by the Pittsburgh Locomotive Works in 1874. Although an 0-6-0 type, she was equipped with a wooden pilot to fit her for road service. Her boiler was supplied by a cold water pump located under her ornately-scrolled cab, and a rod from her rear driver extended to a set of guides beneath the cab to power this pump. Her steam chests show the tallow cup lubricators then common, and the only brakes she had were mounted on her rear tender truck and operated by hand. (Courtesy of Schenectady History Center)

PRIDE OF LANCASTER. One of the neglected locomotive builders of American railroad history is John Brandt, a man whose achievements have been obscured by the passage of time. Brandt operated a smith shop at Parkesburg, Pennsylvania, and around 1834 was serving as shop foreman for the Philadelphia & Columbia Railroad. He later was Master of Machinery for the Georgia R.R., filling the same post at a later date for the New York & Erie; he next became Superintendent of the New Jersey Locomotive & Machine Works in Paterson, N.J., turning out fine locomotives known in railroading circles as "Brandt engines." He returned to his home town of Lancaster, Pa., and in 1853-54 he opened the Lancaster Locomotive Works, assisted by his sons, Abe and John, Jr.; the engines built by the Brandts earned them praise from numerous sources. The plant closed in the panic of 1857 but later was reopened by Edward and James Norris.

Shown here is a Brandt engine built in January of 1857 for the Philadelphia & Columbia R.R. and named the JOHN C. BRECKINRIDGE. This view was taken after the engine had been acquired by the Pennsylvania R.R. and rebuilt with a different stack and minus the original steam dome that occupied a position about where the bell is mounted in this photo. Note the small wheel that could be moved into contact with the rear driver, a part of the Loughridge Chain Brake system.

The engine has retained Brandt's steam chests, canted outward from the saddle to permit easy access to the valve chambers; Brandt also used a front end throttle of the slide valve type, which was lubricated through a tallow cup on top of the smoke box just to the rear of the base of the stack.

His sons, John, Jr. and Abe, later served as superintendent and master mechanic, respectively, of the Oregon & California R.R. (now the Oregon Division of the Southern Pacific) while a third son, James Brandt, was employed on the road as a locomotive engineer. (Railway & Loco. Historical Society photo, courtesy of Benj. F. G. Kline, Jr.)

HOME GROWN. Engine 323 of the Lehigh Valley Railroad was built in the shops of the road in 1876 and bore the name, EMPIRE. The 4-6-0 type had 18 × 24 inch cylinders and 52 inch drivers, and was later rebuilt at the "Valley's" Sayre shops in November, 1888. (Courtesy of H. L. Broadbelt collection)

BOOM TIMES. This photograph of Civil War vintage graphically portrays a Pennsylvania oil town in the days when the earth was yielding a rich harvest of black gold. With the exception of a restless little boy and the town goat, everyone in the scene is apparently aware of the presence of the photographer who exposed this old glass plate negative and has assumed a pose of studied nonchalance for the benefit of posterity.

The polished 4-4-0 is back-dropped by the Central House, an oil field hostelry of rather imposing facade, complete with two galleries, an open porch, and a widow walk.

Although comparatively little has been written about them, the oil boom towns of Pennsylvania during the Civil War and the years immediately following were wild and tough, rivalling later notorious Western hell holes. Saloons and sporting houses flourished in many of them, thronged with oil field toughs and the lawless element that preyed on the working stiffs.

The early drillers tapped the oil deposits with primitive equipment and sent a flood of crude oil to thirsty markets by boat and by rail; soon the first pipe lines entered the region and their competition launched a number of donnybrooks between their operators and the rival railroads. (Courtesy of Pennsylvania Historical & Museum Commission, Harrisburg, Pennsylvania)

BROAD GAUGE DAYS. The Erie Railroad, chartered by the Legislature of New York in 1832 as the New York & Erie Railroad, began construction in 1836 and after a series of delays the road was opened from the Hudson River to Lake Erie on April 22nd, 1851. Although the original charter provided that the entire line was to be within the State of New York, this was later modified to permit the road to pass through a small portion of neighboring Pennsylvania.

Built in an era when the question of a general uniform gauge had not been settled, the Erie was constructed to the broad gauge of 6 feet between the rails. The rare old photo shown here was owned by Joseph Boyd and located by Julian Caster of Elmira, N.Y.; it was taken at Cameron Mills gravel pit in 1879 while the crews of the New York, Lake Erie & Western Railway were engaged in laying the Erie's second main track. Engine 199, an eight-wheeler, heads a string of ballast cars, and a steam shovel for loading them stands on the spur in the gravel pit at right.

The third rail visible within the 6-foot gauge tracks of the Erie was used by the standard gauge trains of the Lehigh Valley Railroad, the latter using a section of the Erie's trackage on the journey between Waverly and Buffalo, New York. (Courtesy of Erie Railroad Company)

WATCH FOBS. This pair of Baldwins operated on the diminutive Mt. Gretna Narrow Gauge Railway, a 2-foot gauge pike controlled by the parent Cornwall & Lebanon Railroad; the slim gauge track carried excursionists over 4 miles of scenic railroad between Mt. Gretna Port and Gov. Dick, Pennsylvania. Built in 1889, the mountain excursion line lasted until about 1916.

Engine No. 12, an eight-wheeler similar to the two pictured here, brought considerable attention to the Baldwin Locomotive Works in 1889, when a test was made to see how quickly Baldwin could construct an engine from the raw material stage. The little 2-footer for the Lebanon County line was ordered by Mr. Robert Coleman on June 22nd with the stipulation it be ready for service on July 4th. Baldwin shop forces mustered their skill and the locomotive was completed on July 2nd, in eight working days.

Note the rustic enginehouse in the background of the view of Mt. Gretna's No. 11 on the turntable; both No. 11 and No. 15, posed against the sylvan backdrop of the Pennsylvania countryside, have lagged smokeboxes, their jacketing extending to the extreme front end of their smokeboxes. (Both photos, courtesy of H. L. Broadbelt collection)

BOUND FOR PEACH BOTTOM. The 3-foot gauge Lancaster, Oxford & Southern R.R., successor to the old Peach Bottom Railroad, posed some of its equipment and crews for this photo taken at Oxford, Pennsylvania around 1894-95. The trim eightwheeler at left, coupled to two cars and headed out of the engine-house, is No. 3, built by Pittsburgh Loco. Works for the road in 1885, shop number 785; she weighed 30 tons, had 12×18 inch cylinders, and 43 inch drivers. The engine coupled on the combine at right, coming out of the car repair shops, is No. 4, a product of the Mount Savage Locomotive Works of Mt. Savage, Maryland. Bearing Mt. Savage shop number 36, she was built in 1883 for the West Virginia narrow gauge line known as the Clarksburg, Weston & Glenville R.R., later the West Virginia & Pittsburgh before being acquired by the Baltimore & Ohio.

Crew members from left to right include Engr. Morgan Spear; Fireman James McMichael, in gangway; Condr. John C. Gorsuch; Bkmn. Woodward Campbell and Frank Grayson; Peter Place; Engr. Randolph Dickey; Fireman Wm. Riney; Condr. Joseph Clark; and hostler Benton Todd. The two men seated are unidentified; the large building behind Engine 4 is the Weigal Steam Rolling Mill, still standing in Oxford.

The bucolic charm of slim-gauge operation is captured in the photo, complete even to the rail fence at far right, and the polished jackets of the engines reflect the loving care tendered by their crews. (Courtesy of Benjamin F. G. Kline, Jr.)

IN PENN'S WOODS. William Penn desired to name his American grant of land New Wales, but King Charles II of England insisted it be named in honor of Penn's father, a distinguished English admiral to whom the King was indebted financially; the Penn name was combined with a form of the Latin word "sylvanus," relating to a forest, hence Penn's woods, or Pennsylvania.

Here, agaist a backdrop of wooded hills, is Pennsylvania Railroad's Engine 118, a ten-wheeler built by Baldwin in November of 1855 and originally named the AUGHWICK. Earlier in the year Baldwin had turned out another 4-6-0 for the road, numbered 117 and named the BLACK OAK; these engines both had 19×22 inch cylinders, 48 inch drivers, and weighed 61,000 pounds.

This view reportedly shows the freight hauler after a rebuilding; note the round main and connecting rods, the early injector located below the wooden cab, and the tallow cup on the steam chest for lubricating valves and cylinder. The pipe leading from her funnel stack discharged the accumulation of cinders to the roadbed below the right end of her pilot beam. (Courtesy of H. L. Broadbelt collection)

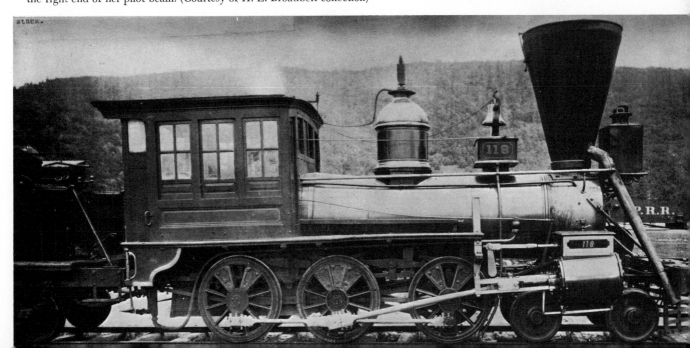

LITTLE LEHIGH CROSSING. A trio of Lehigh Valley R.R. ten-wheelers lined up for this rare shot on the 3-track bridge over the Little Lehigh River at Allentown, Pennsylvania, in 1884. The engine at left is unidentified, but a legend cast on her smokebox reads: "Rebuilt by Lehigh Valley R.R., South Easton, Pa."; middle engine is No. 323, the EMPIRE, built in 1876 and later rebuilt in 1888 at the road's Sayre shops; the engine at right is No. 317, the MINNESOTA, built by Baldwin in 1875, shop number 3802. A photo of the EMPIRE after the 1888 rebuilding can be found elsewhere in this volume.

Note the "deadwood" buffers and the link and hook style couplers on this battery of steamers, indicating use on the heavy drags of coal "jimmies" that rumbled over the Lehigh Valley's rails. (Courtesy of Mr. H. M. Ghormley)

HUSKY HOG. The Schenectady Locomotive Works, headed by President Charles G. Ellis, turned out this sturdy 2-8-0 for the Fall Brook Coal Company in 1883, and she was named the SUSQUEHANNA. The Fall Brook Coal Co. leased the Corning, Cowanesque & Antrim Railway, a 53 mile road running south from Corning, New York, to Antrim, in Tioga County, Pennsylvania. The Cowanesque Branch ran from Lawrenceville to Elkland, Pa., 11 miles. The Corning, Cowanesque & Antrim Railway was formed in 1873 by a consolidation of the Blossburg & Corning Railroad and the Wellsboro & Lawrenceville Railroad. Major commodity hauled over the line's standard and 6 foot gauge trackage was coal, but the road also operated some passenger equipment.

In 1892 the Corning, Cowanesque & Antrim was reorganized as the Fall Brook Railway and in May, 1899, the line was leased to the New York Central & Hudson River R.R. for 999 years. The Cowanesque Branch was eventually extended southwesterly from Elkland via Westfield to Ulysses, in Potter County, a total distance of about 40 miles from Cowanesque Junction on the main line between Corning and Antrim. (Courtesy of Schenectady History Center)

LEHIGH VALLEY PROTEGE. The trim 4-4-0 shown here is No. 203, the C. F. WELLES, JR., of the Pennsylvania & New York Canal & Railroad Company. The 104 miles of main stem of this road ran from Wilkes-Barre, Pennsylvania, to State Line, New York; it was chartered in 1867 and opened on September 13, 1869. The Lehigh Valley R.R. owned a controlling interest in the road and its list of officials and directorate was studded with such names as Asa Packer, Robert H. Sayre, and Wm. W. Longstreth, men who figured prominently in upper echelon affairs of the Lehigh Valley.

As indicated in the corporate title, there was a canal involved in the operations of the company but records of the 1870's indicate it was little used, except south of Wilkes-Barre.

By lease of the Waverly & State Line R.R., a short connecting road built with P&NY backing, the Pennsylvania and New York joined the Erie just north of the Pennsylvania-New York border and by utilizing a third rail operated over the Erie's broad gauge between Waverly and Elmira, providing the Lehigh Valley with a vital link to the various New York State railroads acquired to extend the Lehigh Valley north to the Great Lakes region.

When the C. F. WELLES, JR. was built by the Baldwin Locomotive Works in 1871, that Philadelphia firm of engine builders was being operated by M. Baird & Co., successors to M. W. Baldwin & Company. (Courtesy of Smithsonian Institution)

ILLINI MOGUL. Engine No. 19 of the Chicago, Danville & Vincennes Railroad was a high-wheeled 2-6-0 built by the Hinkley Locomotive Works of Boston; the clean lines of this Mogul are partly achieved by locating the body of the injector below the running board in a concealed position behind Hinkley's distinctive builder's plate.

The engineer of No. 19 is bearded in a manner reminiscent of New England sea captains. Many engineers running in cold climates sported "hair chest protectors" to shield their faces from the icy blasts of winter.

Chartered in 1865, the Chicago, Danville & Vincennes R.R. was completed in November, 1872, when the 108 miles of 4 ft. 9 inch gauge road was opened between Danville and Dolton, Illinois; Dolton, the northern terminus, was located 20 miles south of Chicago and the CD&V gained access into the Windy City by leasing the Chicago & Southern R.R. at a monthly cost of $1,866.66, payable in gold. A 24-mile branch ran from Bismarck, Illinois, east to Coal Creek, Indiana. The Chicago, Danville & Vincennes later became a vital segment of the Chicago & Eastern Illinois Railroad, serving the Illinois and Indiana coal fields. (Courtesy of Bernard Corbin)

HOOSIER HAYBURNER. The history of the Louisville, New Albany & Chicago R.R., owners of Engine No. 9, the ADMIRAL, dates back to 1847 when Indiana citizens formed the New Albany & Salem Rail Road; by 1854 the standard gauge road had reached north 288 miles from New Albany to Michigan City, Indiana, to create the first rail line between Lake Michigan and the Ohio River.

In the 1850's the noted Horace Greeley, lecturing in the cause of Temperance, boarded a train of the road at Lafayette for a trip north; scheduled for a 10:00 A.M. departure, the mixed train bearing the famous scribe pulled out around noon and rumbled across the bridge over the Wabash. It passed the site of the battle of Tippecanoe Creek and derailed its locomotive; the engine was wrestled back onto the bar iron rail and hove into Brookston at 3:00 P.M., a full 14 miles from Lafayette! Here the engine cut off from the heavy consist of wheat, hogs, cattle, lumber, and passengers and ran ahead for wood and water; it returned two hours later, coupled to the train, and proceeded about half a mile before blowing out a boiler cock and noisily expiring! The indomitable Horace completed his journey aboard an old crank-propelled handcar.

The road went under in the panic of 1857, emerged as the Louisville, New Albany & Chicago Railroad, and was again hit by hard times after the Civil War; it was sold under foreclosure in 1872 and was reorganized with the same name except the"Railroad" was changed to "Railway." After another failure in March of 1897 the line was reorganized as the Chicago, Indianapolis & Louisville Railway. It was revitalized by President John W. Barriger after World War II and proudly carries the banner of the "Monon Route." (Courtesy of Bernard Corbin)

CATSKILL TANKER. The 2-6-0 tank engine shown here was built by Danforth Locomotive & Machine Co. for the Rondout & Oswego R.R. in 1871, bearing road number 7. The Rondout & Oswego was formed in 1866 to construct a standard gauge line from Rondout, on the Hudson River's western shore, into the Catskill Mountains. In 1872 the road was reorganized as the New York, Kingston & Syracuse R.R. and extended from Rondout to Stamford, N.Y.; following a foreclosure in 1875 the road emerged as the Ulster & Delaware. In 1902 the road was consolidated with the Delaware & Otsego R.R., the Hobart Branch R.R., the Kaaterskill R.R., and the Stony Clove & Catskill Mountain R.R., but retained the Ulster & Delaware name. The line eventually became part of the New York Central system, forming their Catskill Mountain Branch.

The Coykendall family of Rondout was long connected with the Catskill line; George Coykendall served as superintendent of the road in the 1870's, while in later years the officers included President Samuel D. Coykendall, Vice-Pres. Thomas C. Coykendall, Treasurer Harry S. Coykendall, and Director Frank Coykendall. (Courtesy of Dr. S. R. Wood)

A THING OF BEAUTY. Of all the objects created by the hands of men, few so captured the fancy as did the steam locomotive. In the final stages of development the Iron Horse grew into a huge power plant that was fascinating to witness in action, but when compared with the graceful eight-wheelers of yesteryear the contrast was that of an elephant alongside a gazelle. A classic example of the lovely 4-4-0 is this diamond-stacked American built by Baldwin in April of 1870 as No. 3 of the Oil Creek & Allegheny Railroad, bearing shop number 2127.

A runner on a mid-western road in the late 1870's recounted how he and his fireboy stayed up most of one night putting a high gloss on their engine preparatory to hauling an officers' special bearing the president of the road and a group of visiting tycoons. Early the following morning they set off, running light, to the point where they were to pick up the special. About twenty miles out of town they struck a peddler's wagon loaded with goose feathers and fresh eggs; no one was injured, but their resplendent engine was a sorry spectacle indeed. The engineer recalled that he and the fireman were about the angriest crew that ever shared a cab and that most of their spare time for the next three months was spent in scraping fried eggs and scorched feathers from nooks and crannies of their pet iron steed. (Courtesy of H. L. Broadbelt collection)

BIG CHIEF'S NAMESAKE. The little Baldwin 0-4-0 tank engine pictured here bears the name PONTIAC, after the noted Ottawa Indian chieftain who died in 1769. He also lent his name to the town of Pontiac, Michigan, served by the Detroit & Milwaukee R.R. owning this tanker of 1865 vintage.

The line had its beginning in 1834 when a charter was granted to the Detroit & Pontiac Railroad; the rails from Detroit reached Royal Oak in 1838, and the first locomotive on the road, a Baldwin named the DETROIT, was built in that year. Construction carried the road through Birmingham to Pontiac, and the line west of there was built by the Detroit & Milwaukee Railway, a company formed by consolidation of the Detroit & Pontiac with the Oakland & Ottawa Railroad.

The Detroit & Milwaukee line from Pontiac to Fentonville was opened in 1855, reached Owosso in 1856, Mill Point in 1858, and entered Grand Haven, on the shores of Lake Michigan, on November 22nd, 1858; a line of lake steamers operated between Grand Haven and Milwaukee. The 189-mile line had a branch two miles long from Corunna Station, northwest of Detroit, to a coal mine, and a short branch also ran from Detroit to the nearby State Prison.

The Detroit & Milwaukee Railway was foreclosed in 1860 and reorganized as the Detroit & Milwaukee Railroad; it went into a receivership in 1875 and emerged as the Detroit, Grand Haven & Milwaukee Railroad, which in turn was leased to the Great Western Railway of Canada, now the Grand Trunk Railway. (Courtesy of H. L. Broadbelt collection)

LITTLE GIANT. The Pennsylvania short line whose main stem from Pittsburgh to Youngstown, Ohio, measured a modest 68 miles, was chartered in 1875 and opened in February, 1879. Today, the Pittsburgh & Lake Erie has expanded to cover about 221 miles and enjoys a density of traffic almost without equal in the United States. The road, controlled by the New York Central but operated by its own organization, serves a rich and highly developed industrial region, with coal a prime source of carloading. Until his recent retirement, the P&LE was under the wise guidance of President John Barriger, a man skilled in railroad management and public relations.

Engine No. 2 of the old Pittsburgh & Lake Erie was an 0-4-0 built by the Pittsburgh Locomotive Works in 1877, and is a typical example of switch engines of that era. (Courtesy of Pittsburgh & Lake Erie)

LEASED LOCOMOTIVE. The Pittsburgh ten-wheeler with the sunflower stack shown here is No. 1 of the North Wisconsin Railway. The road left the Hudson-Elroy line of the West Wisconsin Railway at Hudson Junction and was projected to Bayfield, on the southwestern shores of Lake Superior. In 1880 the North Wisconsin Rv. was consolidated with the Chicago, St. Paul & Minneapolis Ry. to form the Chicago, St. Paul, Minneapolis & Omaha Railway.

North Wisconsin Railway's No. 1 bore the name CUMBERLAND on her cab panel, a name that would seem to have no local significance for the region east of the St. Croix River and up the western slice of Wisconsin where the road operated, but a small plate affixed to her cab beneath the window holds the key; the legend cast on this plate reads, "Leased from Jacob Humbird."

Jacob Humbird was an early director of the affiliated West Wisconsin Railway and is listed as a resident of Cumberland, Illinois, which was likely the origin of the name, CUMBERLAND, applied to old Number One. (Courtesy of Schenectady History Center)

SWITCHER for Pullman Railroad, No. 4 was a 2-4-2 saddle tank built by Rhode Island Loco. Works, Providence, R.I., under Shop No. 2945. Steps on tank gave employes access to twin sand boxes, bell, and tank manhole.

MOGUL for Arcadia & Betsey River R.R. in Michigan bore road number 1 and was named HENRY STARKE. Built by Brooks Loco. Works, Dunkirk, N.Y., in 1894 under Shop No. 2431, she sported a 5-slotted link and pin drawhead and a sunflower stack.

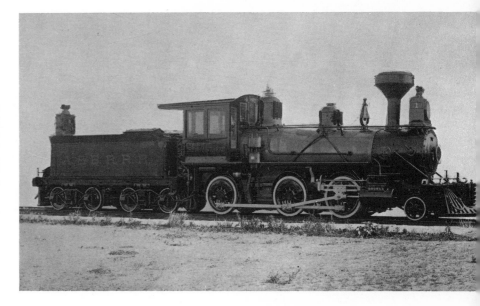

AMERICAN for the Chicago & Atlantic Railway was built by Brooks in 1883, Shop No. 904. Numbered 35, the 4-4-0 was equipped with a crosshead water pump and spoked truck wheels; her finish was neat but not gaudy, with tasteful polish and striping. (Three photos, courtesy of Schenectady History Center)

EXCURSION POWER. The gaily-decorated 4-4-0 shown here is the RUBY, Engine No. 100 of the Michigan Central Railroad, as she appeared when decked out to handle the special train of the Boston Board of Trade in May, 1870. The engine was fresh from the shops of the Manchester Locomotive Works, having been built in March, 1870, under shop number 226; she had 16 × 24 inch cylinders and 63 inch driving wheels.

The RUBY was chosen to haul the Boston Board of Trade Special on its way west from Detroit to Chicago and the road had the spanking new woodburner decked out for the occasion.

The Special was the first transcontinental train to operate across the United States after the completion of the first overland railroad, formed by completion of the Union Pacific-Central Pacific railroads on May 10, 1869.

Departing from Boston for San Francisco on May 23rd, 1870, the Special carried members of the Boston Board of Trade and a number of their wives and children, totaling 129 passengers. The equipment of the 8-car train was the finest the Pullman works could muster, and Geo. M. Pullman himself rode the train from Boston to Chicago, while his brother Albert, then General Superintendent of the Pullman works, escorted the train all the way to the Pacific Coast. The baggage car at the head of the consist contained ice closets of commodious size to assure the comfort of the Bostonians on their excursion into the wilds of the Great West, and it also contained a printing press that turned out the *Trans-Continental*, a newspaper published aboard the train as the wheels rolled westward. Next in line was the smoking car, complete with rolling barbershop, wine room, smoking room with card tables, and an office for Editor W. R. Steele of the Special's newspaper; this car was followed by two hotel cars, the REVERE and the ARLINGTON. Coupled aft of these were the PALMYRA and the MARQUETTE, a pair of fancy Pullman Palace Sleeping and Drawing-Room cars, and bringing up the rear were the commissary and dining cars ST. CLOUD and ST. CHARLES. To insure a proper Hub City atmosphere of genteel sophistication, the train carried two libraries and a pair of organs. From such decorous surroundings, the Bostonians viewed the American scene, visited the U.P. Shops in Omaha, crossed the Great American Desert, and seven days after leaving Boston arrived on the West Coast, where they ceremoniously decanted a bottle of Massachusetts Bay water into the brine of the Pacific in San Francisco Bay. En route, the tour had made a side trip from Ogden to Salt Lake City over the Utah Central, where they were entertained by Brigham Young and other Mormon dignitaries. After a hearty California welcome, the tourists visited Yosemite and the Mother Lode region, then entrained for the return trip on June 25th and on July 2nd, six weeks after having departed from the sacred home of the cod, the Board of Trade Special, also known as the "Pullman Hotel Express," rolled to a halt in Boston; thus ended the run of the nation's first transcontinental round-trip excursion, the first through train from the Atlantic to the Pacific.

MILWAUKEE "BLOOD" ENGINE. Railroaders as a group were and still are quick to apply nicknames to individuals and objects, and locomotives were no exception. For many years the engines built by the Schenectady Locomotive Works were called "McQueens," after Walter McQueen, an officer of the Schenectady firm of engine builders. The locomotives manufactured by the Manchester Locomotive Works of Manchester, New Hampshire, were commonly known as "Blood" engines, a moniker derived from the name of Aretas Blood, Superintendent of the Manchester Works.

The "Blood" engine shown here is No. 420 of the Chicago, Milwaukee & St. Paul Railroad, built in March, 1873, as Wisconsin Valley Railroad's No. 1. The Wisconsin Valley road ran between Tomah and Wausau, Wisconsin; chartered in 1856, its 88 miles were not opened until November of 1874. The 4-4-0 bore Manchester's shop number 545, and had 16×24 inch cylinders. Note the extension added to her front end, probably as a result of conversion from wood to coal; the original smokebox ended just ahead of the arch braces and the bolts holding the headlight bracket.

Arms extending from either side of the bell bracket served as supports for the handrails and are a Manchester "ear-mark," but Wm. Mason also used this style of bell bracket with a slight variation. (Courtesy of Brotherhood of Locomotive Engineers)

LAKE SHORE POWER. Earliest progenitor of the Lake Shore & Michigan Southern was the Erie & Kalamazoo R.R., which started operations on strap iron rails with animal power; the road's first engine, named the ADRIAN, was Baldwin's 80th locomotive and went into service on the 33 miles of track between Toledo and Adrian, Michigan, in June of 1837.

The Lake Shore & Michigan Southern Railway was formed in 1869 by a consolidation of the Buffalo & Erie, the Lake Shore R.R., and the Michigan Southern & Northern Indiana Railroad.

Eng. 136 of the line was named the SAXON and is shown here at the Mason Works; built in March, 1872, she bore Mason's shop number 447, had 60 inch drivers and 17×24 inch cylinders.

JOURNEY INTO YESTERDAY. The old Milwaukee & St. Paul Railway was organized in May of 1863 and on February 11th, 1874, the road changed its name to the Chicago, Milwaukee & St. Paul Railway Company. The original main line reached from Chicago to St. Paul, via Milwaukee and La Crosse, and was slightly over 409 miles long.

The photo shown here was probably taken in the mid-1870's on what appears to be an official tour of inspection over the road, with the brass hats wearing the linen dusters of that period to protect their clothing. The funnel-stacked engine, probably a woodburner, is a 4-4-0 that may be the Milwaukee's No. 132; she sports two steam domes and plenty of brass for her fireboy to polish. (Courtesy of Mr. Benj. T. Hart)

BADGER STATE BRIDGE. The big combination wood and iron truss bridge shown here is believed to have been the Milwaukee & St. Paul Railroad's span over the Wisconsin River at Kilbourn, Wisconsin, in the heart of the scenic region known as the Dells of the Wisconsin River. The Wisconsin, 430 miles long, flows through the Central Plain of the state and enters the Mississippi at Prairie du Chien; steamboats once threaded the river and offered some competition to the early rail lines.

In the freebooting days of the 1880's, the lumber barons and railroad magnets practically controlled Wisconsin through political influence, a situation that led Robert M. La Follette to battle for improved government. In the face of bitter opposition a primary election law was passed, giving the people the power to nominate candidates, and other laws were enacted which put the railroads under control of a commission of experts, all of which served to bring about political reforms. (Courtesy of Mr. Benj. T. Hart)

BROTHERHOOD EXCURSION. When the first railroad labor organizations were formed they met with considerable opposition from management and the early Brotherhood members were forced to meet in secret. As the membership increased and working agreements were placed in effect, the Brotherhoods gained favorable recognition and with the passing of the years came to be acclaimed as conservative labor organizations, generally free of the violence that marked other labor trade unions.

This old photo shows a group of members of the Brotherhood of Locomotive Firemen of North America, the occasion being an excursion of the Brotherhood over the Milwaukee road behind Engine 686.

The old-time fireman, sometimes dubbed ash-cat or tallow-pot, provided the brawn needed to keep America's trains rolling, for the art of making steam required strong muscles as well as a skilled and practiced hand. From the ranks of these artists with scoop and poker came the crops of trained engineers to man the throttles of the nation's locomotives, for the fireman's position was the travelling college where the skills of running an engine were acquired throught practical experience. (Courtesy of Mr. Benj. T. Hart)

FATHER OF WATERS. The Milwaukee rails crossed the waters of the Mississippi at La Crosse, Wisconsin, and followed along the banks of the great river to St. Paul. The bluffs of limestone and the lush foliage of summer added a pleasant touch to a trip over the road in this region.

From the train windows passengers could frequently see the picturesque river steamboats that plied between St. Louis and St. Paul as they churned the waters of the Mississippi. The brass and paint of the early locomotives could scarcely rival the grand decor of the river steamers; the sidewheeler NORTHERN LIGHT, in service on the upper Mississippi, featured oil paintings of Maiden Rock, Dayton Bluffs, and the Falls of St. Anthony in her cabins, while her paddle boxes bore a resplendent reproduction of the Aurora Borealis.

The Milwaukee train shown here may be near Turkey River Bluff. (Courtesy of Mr. Benj. T. Hart)

ONCE IN THE DEAR DEAD DAYS. In an era when life flowed at a more leisurely pace it was possible to create such picturesque scenes as the one presented here.

A funnel-stacked American type locomotive of the old Chicago, Milwaukee & St. Paul Ry. pauses with her consist on what is believed to be the covered truss spanning the Vermillion River. Two of the road's officials have descended to the rocky ledge in the foreground to pose for the wet plate of the camera artist who recorded this scene. The wooden coach bears the lettering of the Milwaukee Road while the old wooden box or conductor's car coupled behind the engine bears the initials of the Milwaukee & St. Paul, a CM & StP predecessor. The Milwaukee & St. Paul R.R., organized in 1863, absorbed a number of early roads in the Wisconsin-Minnesota region to form the nucleus of the Chicago, Milwaukee & St. Paul Railway. (Courtesy of Mr. Benj. T. Hart)

MILWAUKEE POWER. The locomotives of a number of parent short lines formed the nucleus of the motive power in use on the Chicago, Milwaukee & St. Paul Railway in the early years of that road's operation.

The upper photo shows old No. 75 of the Milwaukee & St. Paul Railroad, a 14 × 22 American built by Schenectady in 1850. Since the Milwaukee & St. Paul was not organized until 1863 it is probable that this engine came from one of the predecessor roads absorbed into the system, such as the old Milwaukee & Waukesha R.R. (later Milwaukee & Mississippi R.R.), the Southern Wisconsin R.R., or other sources. She was rebuilt in 1873; this view shows her as a woodburner with funnel stack, her footboards indicating she was probably in switching service at the time.

The lower view shows Engine 16 of the Chicago, Milwaukee & St. Paul, a two-domed 4-4-0 built by Schenectady under Shop No. 156 in June, 1856. She was originally built as the No. 16 of the La Crosse & Milwaukee R.R., a line chartered in 1852 and consolidated with the Milwaukee, Fond du Lac & Green Bay R.R. in 1854; the Milwaukee & Watertown R.R. was absorbed into this line by purchase in 1856.

No. 16 had 15 × 22 inch cylinders and 56 inch drivers, and a photo taken in 1886 while she was switching at Janesville, Wisconsin, shows that the Milwaukee had replaced her diamond stack with a slender capped stack and had extended her short smokebox. (Both photos, courtesy of A. F. Zimmerman, Brotherhood of Locomotive Engineers)

TRAIN TIME AT KILBOURN. This photo taken in the 1870's shows a train at the station of the Chicago, Milwaukee & St. Paul Railway at Kilbourn, now Wisconsin Dells, Wisconsin.

The funnel-stacked cord wood-fired engine is CM & StP No. 142, named the J. H. BENEDICT. The 4-4-0 was built by Danforth, Cooke & Company in 1869 for one of the predecessor lines which formed the Chicago, Milwaukee & St. Paul Ry., the latter corporation being formed in February, 1874.

The sign propped against the end of the neat brick depot reads "STEAMER CHAMPION LANDING." The CHAMPION was a steamboat which reportedly was in operation on the Wisconsin River in the Dells section around Kilbourn about 1874. (Courtesy of Dr. S. R. Wood)

STURDY STATION. The two-story station on the Milwaukee at Mineral Point, Wisconsin, was constructed of thick stone blocks, sturdy enough to repel a force of invaders or the onslaught of a Wisconsin winter.

The engine standing in front of the stone structure is No. 280 of the CM&StP, a 4-4-0 built by the Grant Locomotive Works in 1873. This engine had 16×24 inch cylinders and at one time reportedly bore the name BURLINGTON. The double set of rails visible in the lower right foreground mark the location of the scales used for weighing freight cars, and a portion of the Howe scale mechanism shows at the extreme right. One set of rails by-passed the scales, permitting cars to move on the track without activating the weighing equipment; the other pair, known as "live rails," were connected to the scale track by switches located a short distance from both sides of the scales and cars diverted over these "live rails" caused the scales to function. (Courtesy of Dr. S. R. Wood)

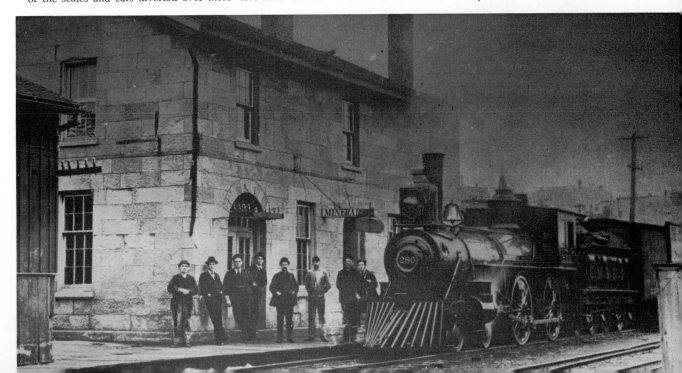

EATING THE WIND. The warm hand of summer touches the countryside and the chill of winter is forgotten; greenery edges the track and the trees are in full leaf. Truly, then, a wonderful time for railroading in days now gone beyond recall.

In the cab of the slide valve tenwheeler the runner sits relaxed yet alertly vigilant, his left hand resting lightly on the throttle. The din and racket are familiar to him—the steady drumming of the drivers on the ribbons of steel; the metallic drone of the injector; the scrape and clang of coal scoop and firedoor; and over all, the throaty music of the exhaust chanting at the stack. It is warm in the cab and the knight of the latch has his front window open; through it comes the breath of warm metal, hot valve oil, acrid coal smoke, and the nostalgic fragrance of farm meadow and woodland. Captured in the glory of its passage is the "Carolina Special," five cars of varnish trailing behind Engine 565 of the Cincinnati, New Orleans & Texas Pacific; the year is 1912 and the sparks that will kindle the holocaust of the first World War are still two years distant.

Fluid motion, surging power, and human skill are here combined in the exhilarating creation that has been termed one of man's noblest inventions. (Courtesy of Southern Railway)

DIXIE LAND

This section of the album is devoted to the rail lines of the South, covering the region from the Potomac drainage and the southern banks of the Ohio, from the eastern edge of the Mississippi and the Atlantic seaboard down to the waters of the Gulf of Mexico.

The snorting Iron Horse came early to the land of cotton and while his tracks did not cross-hatch the maps in such profusion as in the North, the role they played was fully as vital.

From Virginia's tidewater to the Blue Grass of Kentucky, from the Carolinas to the hills and valleys of Tennessee, up through the red clay and pines of Georgia, through the rich farmlands of Alabama and Mississippi, to the peninsula of Florida and the humid deltas of Louisiana, the twin ribbons of rail bound together the Old South.

This was a region with an agrarian culture, lacking the extensive manufacturing facilities of the North, yet a number of locomotive builders operated in the country south of the Mason and Dixon line. Anderson and the Tredegar Works in Richmond built creditable engines in the 1850's, as did the Virginia Locomotive & Car Manufacturing Company in Alexandria, home of the Smith & Perkins works; one of the earliest builders was the firm of Eason & Dotterer, who constructed locomotives in Charleston, South Carolina in the 1830's; other Charleston locomotive builders included Miller, McLeish, and Smith. The Covington Works in Kentucky and the Louisville Locomotive Works in the Blue Grass State also turned out locomotives, and a number of Southern roads built occasional locomotives for their own use or extensively rebuilt older engines originally purchased from Yankee firms.

Roads of the South conquered the lower reaches of the Appalachian Range, threading the Shenandoahs, the Cumberlands, the Blue Ridge, and the foothill regions to link the old colonies on the Atlantic with the interior states bordering the Father of Waters.

The holocaust of the Civil War strained the resources of railways located within the Confederacy, with heavy usage and Yankee raiders exacting toll from irreplaceable motive power. Rebel raiders made daring forays to capture badly-needed locomotives and equipment, moving their loot to Southern rails by almost superhuman effort. A lack of firm control over all rail lines in the South has been pointed out as one of the weak points in the Confederacy, yet the roads played an important role in transporting troops and supplies.

Regrettably, not many photographs of early Southern railroading have survived, and to prevent repetition of the use of photos included in the author's previous works the geographical boundaries of Dixie have been stretched a bit to include some views taken in such areas of Missouri, Arkansas, and Texas that embraced the Southern cause. All aboard for Dixie!

SOUTHLAND STEAMER. The old South Carolina Railroad & Canal Company was incorporated in 1827 and the railway pioneer, Horatio Allen, was appointed Chief Engineer in 1829. The first engine, named the BEST FRIEND OF CHARLESTON, was built by the West Point Foundry and was tried out in 1830. The line from Charleston to Hamburg, South Carolina, was completed in 1833; this 137 miles of track was then the longest continuous railroad in the world, and the road reputedly was the first railway to carry the United States mails.

The road was consolidated with the Louisville, Cincinnati & Charleston R.R. in 1844, the latter company having constructed the branch from Branchville to Columbia, S.C., in 1840.

The line was very successful in its operations, but was hard hit by the Civil War. The big 4-6-0 shown here was built for the road in 1859 by M. W. Baldwin & Co. and was named the JAS. S. CORRY. This view, taken outside the Baldwin shops in Philadelphia, shows the outside supplemental frame or "ankle rail" and the two steam domes applied to this early ten-wheeler. (Courtesy of Smithsonian Institution)

ATLANTA & CHARLOTTE AIR LINE RAIL-WAY was the successor of the Atlanta & Richmond Air Line Ry., a 5-foot gauge system extending from Atlanta, Georgia, to Charlotte, North Carolina, a distance of 265.80 miles. Engine 22 was a trim American by Baldwin. (Courtesy of the Southern Railway)

RALEIGH & GASTON RAILROAD was an old Southerner, chartered in 1836 and opened in 1838. The road extended 97 miles between Raleigh and Weldon, North Carolina, and was powered by such engines as the Baldwin-built No. 9, a 4-4-0 woodburner. (Courtesy of H. L. Broadbelt collection)

ATLANTIC & NORTH CAROLINA R.R. extended 95 miles between Morehead City and Goldsboro, North Carolina; it was chartered in 1853, began construction in 1855, and was completed in June of 1858. The road's No. 12 shown here was a 4-4-0 built by the Richmond Locomotive Works. (Courtesy of Schenectady History Center)

EASTERN SHORE POWER. The dainty American shown here is the L. SHOWELL of the Wicomico & Pocomoke Railroad, out-shopped by the Baldwin Works in March of 1868. The Wicomico & Pocomoke was a standard gauge road extending 23 miles between Berlin and Salisbury, Maryland, on the Eastern Shore region of the Old Line State. In 1870 the road boasted two locomotives, 5 passenger cars, 1 baggage, mail, and express car, and 22 freight cars; trundling along over 40-pound rail, the little pike grossed over $23,000 in the fiscal year ending in April of 1871, with a reported net income of nearly $9,000. (Courtesy of H. L. Broadbelt collection)

OFF TO TEXAS. The little 2-4-2 saddle tanker shown here is Engine No. 1 of the Rio Grande Railroad Company, and was built by the Baldwin Locomotive Works (M. Baird & Co.) in 1872, bearing Baldwin construction number 2664. Although the road's charter was dated August 12th, 1870, the Rio Grande was organized on May 22nd, 1871. Actual construction began in 1872 on the 42 inch gauge line which was intended to link Brownsville, Texas, with Port Isabel, Texas, and the first section of track, 8 miles in length, was reportedly opened on July 4th of that year. In 1873 the line was extended 14 miles further to Port Isabel, on the Gulf of Mexico; traffic was boated about 6 miles further, from Port Isabel to Brazos Santiago in the harbor of the same name. Headquarters of the slim gauge pike were located in Brownsville, Cameron County, Texas, on the Rio Grande River opposite Matamoras, Mexico. (Courtesy of H. L. Broadbelt collection)

SOUTHWEST EMPIRE. The Texas Western Railroad, chartered in 1852, died without issue but its charter was revived by the Southern Pacific (of no kin to the present S.P.) and about 10 miles of track completed about 1856, extending from Caddo Lake, Louisiana, toward Marshall, Texas. The road proposed to connect with the Memphis, El Paso & Pacific R.R., first chartered in 1853 and organized in 1856 with headquarters at Paris, Texas. One of the prime movers of the Memphis, El Paso & Pacific was Genl. John C. Fremont, a noted character in Western history; he envisioned a railway from Norfolk, Va., via Memphis, to San Diego, California, and invested heavily in the project. The franchise of the San Diego, Gila & Southern Pacific was acquired to form the western portion of the transcontinental route. About 60 miles of grade and some track had been built by the Memphis, El Paso & Pacific when the Civil War halted construction; after the War a new charter was issued, the name being changed to the Southern Transcontinental Railroad Company. The franchises and properties of the original Southern Pacific, the Southern Transcontinental, and the Memphis, El Paso & Pacific were acquired by the Texas Pacific R.R., a concern that evolved into the Texas & Pacific Railway. In addition to Fremont, the T&P properties were presided over by such notables as Thomas A. Scott and Geo. J. Gould, while Major General G. M. Dodge of Union Pacific fame was an early Chief Engineer of the Texas & Pacific Ry.

Engine No. 76 of the Texas & Pacific was constructed by the Pittsburgh Loco. Wks. about 1880 and was a neat ten-wheeler with cylinder cock operating rod concealed in her hand-rail. In 1925 the Lima Loco. Works built the first 2-10-4 locomotive for the road and this wheel arrangement was styled the "Texas" type. (Courtesy of Schenectady History Center)

GULF COAST LINK. The New Orleans Pacific Railway was established to construct about 315 miles of 5-foot gauge track from New Orleans northwesterly to Shreveport, Louisiana, there to connect with the Texas & Pacific Railway, owned and controlled by the same interests.

When the Pittsburgh Loco. Works turned out Engine No. 103 for the road about 1881, some 68 miles of track had been laid from New Orleans to Bayou Goula, in Iberville Parish. Reports of 1881 show the road had 10 locomotives, 6 passenger coaches, and 200 freight cars, operated over 56 pound rail; in addition to the main stem, proposed branches were listed as the Opelousas Branch, 25 miles, and the Baton Rouge Branch, 15 miles.

Now a part of the Texas & Pacific Ry., the original New Orleans & Pacific Railway forms the old Louisiana Division of the T&P and provides the major portion of their line in Louisiana, linking the "Crescent City" of New Orleans with the Texas towns of Fort Worth, Sweetwater, Pecos, and El Paso.

The fact that the same interests early controlled both the New Orleans Pacific Ry. and the Texas & Pacific Ry. are indicated by the similarity in design of the locomotive shown here and the preceding T&P engine, both of which are fitted with a rather uncommon design of stack and similar style of lettering, along with other features. (Courtesy of Schenectady History Center)

SOUTHERN LOGGER. The quaint little 0-4-2 pictured here is the FLORIDA, built in 1878 by Baldwin under shop number 4483 for the Messrs. Hilliard & Bailey's Lumber Railroad.

The FLORIDA represents a type used quite extensively on logging roads and on the light railways serving sugar cane estates and other plantation railways installations, as well as street railway lines.

Fully fueled and with her 332 gallon water tank filled to capacity, the FLORIDA weighed 29,250 pounds, and carried 23,150 pounds of this weight on her 37 inch drivers. The engine had 9 × 16 inch cylinders and 8.5 square feet of grate area; the total distance from the center of her leading driving wheels to the center of her trailing truck wheels was a short 10 feet, 7 inches, and this limited length of total wheelbase made is possible for her to negotiate sharp curves with a minimum of effort.

The FLORIDA, built to a gauge of 5 feet, was of the design patented by M. N. Forney in 1866. Many Forney types were built with a 4-wheel trailing truck and were operated tender-first, an arrangement that permitted the heat and smoke to be carried away from the cab, rather than into it as was the case with conventional locomotives. The Forney design also permitted wider fireboxes and larger grate areas, with the firebox being located above the frame and behind the rear driving wheels. (Courtesy of H. L. Broadbelt collection)

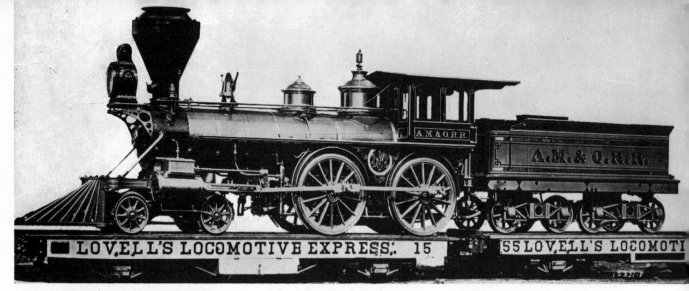

PIONEER PIGGY-BACK. The difference in gauges of track provided a number of problems in the earlier days of railroading, many lines in the North being built to the present standard gauge while many roads in the South were built to a gauge of 5 feet. Even in the northern region, the gauges of various roads might vary by several inches, and to permit interchange of equipment between some of these lines the "compromise cars" came into being. These cars were fitted with wheels of extra width to allow them to operate over gauges that varied from 4 feet, 8½ inches 4 feet, 10 inches. These "compromise cars" were blamed for the terrible wreck near Angola, New York, in 1867, on the Buffalo & Erie R.R. (later the Lake Shore & Michigan Southern). The "New York Express," with Engr. Charlie Carscadin at the throttle, was reportedly derailed at the frog of a switch at Angola; the derailed car plunged off Big Sister Creek bridge a short distance beyond, dragging another coach with it. The crash and the fire that swept the wooden cars claimed nearly 50 lives.

Transporting locomotives built in the North to the 5-foot gauge lines of the South was solved as shown in this photo. The special cars of Lovell's Locomotive Express service are delivering a 4-4-0 built by Wm. Mason in Taunton, Mass., to the Atlantic, Mississippi & Ohio R.R.; this road extended from Norfolk, Va., to Bristol, Tenn., and was formed by the consolidation of three older lines in 1870. William A. Mahone, former Confederate general and famed as the "Hero of the Crater" during the struggle for Petersburg, formed the AM&O from the old Norfolk & Petersburg R.R., the South Side R.R., and the Virginia & Tennessee R.R.; Mahone's wife was named Ophelia and wags said the AM&O initials stood for "All Mine & Ophelia's." (Courtesy of Norfolk & Western Railway)

GEORGIA NARROW GAUGE. A typical example of the 3 foot gauge 4-4-0 locomotives constructed by Baldwin is No. 2 of the Northeastern Railroad of Georgia, named the J. W. NICHOLSON.

The Northeastern of Georgia was opened in September of 1876, with 39 miles of narrow gauge track laid with 35 pound rails, and extended from Athens to Lula, Georgia. It served as a connecting link between the Athens Branch of the Georgia Railroad at Athens and the rails of the Atlanta & Charlotte Air-Line Railway at Lula, Georgia. Headquarters of the slim gauge pike were located in Athens, Clarke County, Georgia; A. K. Childs served as president of the road, and its operations were under the direction of Supt. James M. Edwards. (Courtesy of H. L. Broadbelt collection)

JUG TAVERN ROUTE. The Gainesville, Jefferson & Southern Railroad was incorporated in 1872 and by 1884 had constructed a 3-foot gauge road from Gainesville to Monroe, Georgia. In 1884 the line acquired the wide-gauge Walton Railroad, a 10-mile line running south from Monroe to Social Circle; after acquisition, the Walton road was converted to narrow gauge and a branch of the Gainesville line was constructed from Bellmont to Jefferson.

The Gainesville, Jefferson & Southern advertised itself as "The Jug Tavern Route," featuring a jug emblem suggestive of Georgia corn liquor and hospitality; in reality, Jug Tavern was a station whose name was later changed to Winder.

Operated as a separate company by the controlling Georgia Railroad & Banking Co., the Gainesville, Jefferson & Southern fell upon hard times and passed into a receivership in 1897. In 1904 the line was sold under the sheriff's hammer; the portion from Monroe north, including the Jefferson branch, became the Gainesville Midland Railway, eventually passing into the hands of the Seaboard Air Line. The 10 miles between Monroe and Social Circle was organized as the Monroe Railroad, restored to standard gauge, and ended up as a part of the Georgia Railroad.

The trim Mogul of the Gainesville, Jefferson & Southern R.R. pictured here was a 3-foot gauge engine turned out by the Pittsburgh Locomotive Works in 1883 and bore road number 3. She was later sold, becoming No. 8 of the Mount Airy & Eastern Railway, a slim-gauge pike running from Mount Airy, North Carolina, to Kibler, Virginia, and reportedly went from that road to the Norfolk & Western's tie plant at Radford, Virginia. She carried Pittsburgh's construction number 706. (Courtesy of Schenectady History Center)

UP FROM EGYPT. The little 3 foot gauge Mogul seen here is No. 6, the SPARTA, of the Cairo & St. Louis Railroad, whose slim gauge trackage extended 146 miles from Cairo to East St. Louis, Illinois. Because of its warm climate and rich soil, the Mississippi embayment region around Cairo, in the southwestern tip of Illinois, was called "Egypt" after the fertile land around the delta of the Nile. The Cairo & St. Louis R.R. was chartered in February, 1865, but the road was not completed until March 1, 1875. Entrance into the East St. Louis terminal was made over 4 miles of the standard gauge East St. Louis & Carondelet R.R. tracks, a third rail being laid to permit passage of the narrow gauge equipment.

The twin-domed 2-6-0 was built by Baldwin in 1872, Shop No. 3093, and was named SPARTA in honor of the town in Randolph County served by the road. Note that her headlight bracket supports no lamp in this builder's photo, many roads preferring to furnish their own choice of oil lamps.

After a foreclosure in 1881, the road was reorganized as the St. Louis & Cairo R.R. in 1882 and in 1886 was leased to the Mobile & Ohio Railroad Company, later becoming a part of the Gulf, Mobile & Ohio. (Courtesy of H. L. Broadbelt collection)

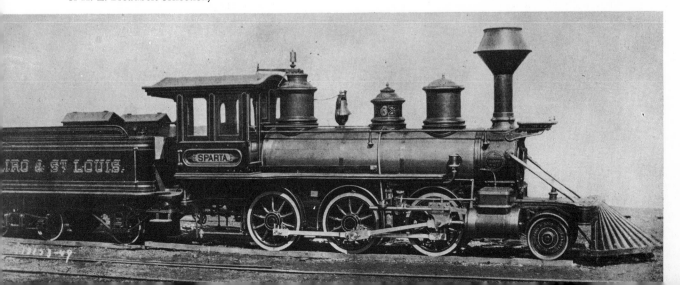

BLUE GRASS SWITCHER. Brooks Locomotive Works of Dunkirk, N.Y., turned out this pretty 0-6-0 for the Kentucky Central Railroad in 1883, under Construction No. 948. She had 17 × 24 inch cylinders, 49 inch drivers, and weighed 75,000 pounds; a sister engine, Kentucky Central No. 28, was built in the same year to identical specifications. When the road was acquired by the Louisville & Nashville in 1891 these two goats became L&N No's 331 and 332, later renumbered 1031 and 1032 in 1897.

The history of the Kentucky Central dates back to the old Covington & Lexington R.R., chartered in the gold rush days of 1849 and completed from Covington, opposite Cincinnati, to Paris, Kentucky, in 1856. Entrance to Lexington, in the heart of the famous Blue Grass region, was made over the Maysville & Lexington R.R., opened in 1859, and this last-named pike opened a line from Paris to the Ohio River village of Maysville in the early 1870's. The Covington & Lexington road followed up the valley of the Licking River toward Paris, junction point with the M&L whose line ran southwest to Lexington and northeast to Maysville, cutting across the North Fork of the Licking River. Paris is located in Bourbon County, a name made famous by the bottled variety of spirits long associated with Kentucky and as much a part of the state's heritage as race horses, moon-shine whiskey, and "My Old Kentucky Home." The Kentucky Central acquired the C&L and the M&L after these roads were sold under foreclosure and assumed the name of Kentucky Central R.R. in 1865, later reorganized in 1876 and after a receivership became Kentucky Central Railway in 1886 and was acquired by the Louisville & Nashville. (Courtesy of Schenectady History Center)

IRON MOUNTAIN AMERICAN. Grant Locomotive Works built this 4-4-0 for the 5-foot gauge St. Louis & Iron Mountain Railroad in January of 1874, construction number 1278; she had 17 × 24 inch cylinders, 63 inch drivers, and was the last locomotive built for the St. Louis & Iron Mountain R.R., that line being reorganized as the St. Louis, Iron Mountain & Southern Railway in May of 1874. The engine was named the H. G. MARQUAND in honor of Henry G. Marquand of New York City, a director and vice-president of the road in the 1870's.

The engine carried the same number under the St. Louis, Iron Mountain & Southern, and in 1877 was involved in derailment, turning over with Engineer Bill Coyne. In June, 1879, she was converted to standard gauge and renumbered 232; in 1884 she was renumbered 378, and in December, 1905, was renumbered 8707.

The original St. Louis & Iron Mountain R.R. was chartered in 1851 and opened for traffic from St. Louis to Pilot Knob, Mo., in 1858; in 1874 this line, along with the Cairo & Fulton R.R. in Missouri and Arkansas, was incorporated into the new St. Louis, Iron Mountain & Southern. The property then consisted of 195 miles of broad gauge track from St. Louis to Belmont, Mo., opposite Columbus, Kentucky; 414 miles of track from Bismark, Mo., to Texarkana; 71 miles from Poplar Bluff to Bird's Point on the Mississippi; and a short 3.75 mile branch between Mineral Point and Potosi. (Anderson collection, courtesy of H. M. Ghormley)

PLANT SYSTEM. Henry Plant's collection of railroads in the southeastern section of the United States, widely known as the Plant System of Railways, included the former Jacksonville, Tampa & Key West Railway, a Florida pike that began operations between Jacksonville and Palatka in March of 1884. Hard hit by yellow fever in 1888 and by severe freezes in 1895 and 1897 that nearly wiped out the citrus growers, the JT&KW, in receivership since the panic of 1893, was sold to the Plant Investment Co. in 1899. In 1902, the Savannah, Florida & Western Railway (Plant System) was consolidated with the Atlantic Coast Line Railroad and formed an important part of that line in the South.

The Plant System woodburner pictured here is No. 603 of the Savannah, Florida & Western Ry., built as No. 3 of the Jacksonville, Tampa & Key West in 1883. Bearing Baldwin's Shop No. 7090, the 4-4-0 had 16 × 24 inch cylinders and 67 inch drivers. After the Plant System merged with the Coast Line, she was renumbered as Atlantic Coast Line R.R. No. 562. Her first service was under the banner of the Florida Construction Company, a temporary organization set up when Jacksonville contractors John Taliaferro and D. H. Ambler began actual construction of the Jacksonville, Tampa & Key West Railway in 1883. (Courtesy of Engr. Lester L. Leavitt)

DOWN YONDER IN ARKANSAW. Arkansas, formerly called Arkansaw, may have had its origin in the French phrase "arc en sang," or "bloody bow." In the turbulent pioneer days the widespread use of Jim Bowie's long-bladed knife in the region gave that weapon its nickname of the "Arkansas toothpick." Up in the far northwest corner of the state lies Benton County, home of the trim little 4-4-0 shown here. She was built by the Pittsburgh Locomotive Works, Shop No. 748, in 1884 as the No. 2 of the Bentonville Railway Co., a six-mile short line extending between the Arkansas towns of Bentonville and Rogers, the latter a junction point with the St. Louis & San Francisco lines.

The Arkansas & Oklahoma R.R. was incorporated in April, 1898, and taking over the Bentonville road they extended it about 18 miles west to Gravette. Around 1900-01 the Frisco got control of the road and it was extended to Grove, Indian Territory (now Oklahoma). The passage of time saw railroad expansion reach its zenith and wane, with many branch roads being abandoned; such was the case of the Rogers-Grove line, and today it has returned to its original Bentonville Ry. proportions, being a Frisco branch from Rogers to Bentonville, the original terminals of the road. (Courtesy of Schenectady History Center)

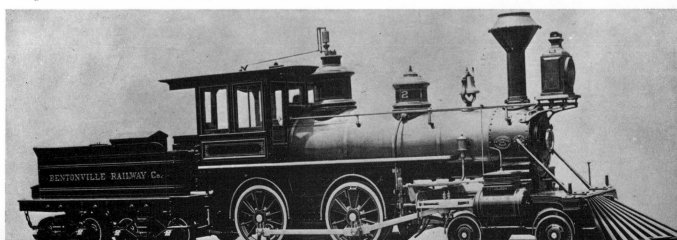

RAT HOLE DIVISION HOG. The Cincinnati, New Orleans & Texas Pacific Railway, now controlled by the Southern Railway, was chartered in 1881 and leased the municipally-built Cincinnati Southern Railway; the latter road, extending 335.92 miles from Cincinnati, Ohio, to Chattanooga, Tennessee, was constructed by the city of Cincinnati and was completed early in 1880. Difficult engineering problems in Tennessee's hill country were encountered and the line originally had 27 tunnels, resulting in the road being dubbed the "Rat Hole Division." The CNO&TP formed the upper portion of the old "Queen and Crescent Route"; the middle section of this route was formed by the Alabama Great Southern, extending from Chattanooga to Meridian, Mississippi, while the lower segment from Meridian to New Orleans was formed by the New Orleans & Northeastern Railroad. In addition to the numerous tunnels, the "Queen and Crescent Route" featured what was reportedly the second highest bridge and the second longest curve on any main line in the country; the bridge, 311 feet high, carried the CNO&TP over the Kentucky River, while the curve on the NO&NE sweeps around Lake Pontchartrain for nine miles.

The slim-barreled Consolidation pictured here was built for the CNO&TP by Schenectady in 1902, bearing shop number 25588. She had 20 × 24 inch cylinders, 52 inch drivers, and carried 180 pounds of boiler pressure; she later became Southern Railway's No. 6122 and was scrapped in 1922. (Courtesy of Mr. H. M. Ghormley)

SAD MISSION. The decorated engine shown here is Southern Railway's No. 1088, a tenwheeler and sister to the famed Engine 1102 that went to Glory in the "Wreck of Old 97." This photo was taken at Goldsboro, North Carolina, on December 5th, 1908, after she had completed a sorrowful trip pulling the funeral train bearing the body of Engineer Fred Holt, who had been murdered at the Durham coal chute on December 3rd.

A volunteer crew donated their services for the funeral run, first taking the remains to Spencer in order that the murdered engineer's sick wife could view him, then proceeding to Goldsboro for the last rites.

The white-clad runner standing by the pilot is Engineer L. A. Atkisson, who served for over 54 years. (Courtesy of R. B. Carneal)

SOUTHERN SHOWPIECES. Engine 115 of the Alabama Great Southern was built by Pittsburgh Locomotive Works under shop number 1452 and was exhibited new at the World's Columbian Exposition in 1893. She was later rebuilt as a simple engine in the Birmingham shops and her 3 inch tires were replaced with 4 inch tires, giving her 74 inch drivers that reportedly were the highest driving wheels entering Chattanooga. Her number was changed to 174. Mr. Hugh Ghormley, retired after many years of service with the CNO&TP and other roads in the South, recalls riding this engine as a young man from Chattanooga to Birmingham and return with Engineer Henry W. Elliot, Sr., a fine runner and a perfect gentleman.

The big Vauclain 4-6-0 was the Baldwin Locomotive Works exhibit at the Cotton States & International Exposition held in Atlanta, Georgia, in 1895. In honor of the host city, she bore the name ATLANTA on her cab panel; the number 14420, shown on her sand box and her smokebox number plate, is her Baldwin construction number. (Upper photo, courtesy of Mr. H. M. Ghormley; lower photo, courtesy of H. L. Broadbelt collection)

MINNESOTA MEMORIES. The first locomotive to operate in Minnesota was the WILLIAM CROOKS, a 4-4-0 built by the New Jersey Locomotive & Machine Co. of Paterson, New Jersey. The CROOKS arrived at St. Paul in September of 1861 aboard a barge towed by the Mississippi River steamboat ALHAMBRA; she was named in honor of Col. Wm. Crooks, Chief Engineer of the Minnesota & Pacific Railroad. Engineer Wm. Grubb of the Milwaukee & Prairie du Chien Railway put the CROOKS in running order for her trial trips, after which she spent the winter stored in a shed. Early in 1862 the Minnesota & Pacific R.R. was reorganized as the St. Paul & Pacific R.R. and the approximately 10 miles of track between St. Paul and St. Anthony was laid, with scheduled service beginning on July 2nd of that year. The road was extended to East St. Cloud in 1866 and a new westward extension from St. Anthony via Litchfield and Willmar to Breckinridge was completed in 1871; in 1878 this extension reached Pembina, on the Canadian boundary. The St. Paul & Pacific was acquired by the St. Paul, Minneapolis & Manitoba, which in turn became a part of James J. Hill's Great Northern Railway.

The lovely woodburner pictured here is the C.N. PARKER, JR. of the old St. Paul & Pacific Railroad. The 4-4-0 was built by the Pittsburgh Locomotive Works in 1870 and was named in honor of Mr. Charles N. Parker, Jr., the Master Mechanic in charge of the road's shops in St. Paul, Minnesota (Courtesy of Schenectady History Center)

WESTWARD HO!

West of the Mississippi lies the land of the long miles, a land where the Iron Horse was late in coming. It is a vast land, a place of limitless plain and jutting mountain, eternal snow and blistering heat, bone-dry desert and rushing torrent. Yet it was a rich land, a treasure-house of mineral wealth and natural resources; gold, silver, copper, and oil lay beneath the bosom of the earth, while the surface supported forests of a size beyond belief, endless reaches of grazing land, grain fields, and fertile valleys awaiting the plow.

Roughly, this section of the album covers that region west of the Mississippi to the blue waters of the Pacific, from the Canadian line to the Mexican border. Railroading was a well-established business in the East before the first locomotives braved the wilderness of the West. Indian war parties blocked the routes, killing survey parties and harrassing construction gangs; natural barriers blockaded the way West with the obstacles ranging from the peaks of the Rockies to the waterless reaches of the Great American Desert.

Against this backdrop the railroad was destined to play a vital role in that great saga that has come to be known as the winning of the West. The storm clouds of the Civil War were gathering as the first ribbons of rail began to invade the West and it was not until 1869 that the final spike was hammered home in the Utah sagebrush, linking the Atlantic with the Pacific. The American West was still the home of the buffalo hunter and Indian, cowboy and settler, miner and freighter, the last great frontier.

Railroading in this vast expanse was a rugged game, loaded with thrills and excitement that frequently surpassed the wildest adventures the prosaic railroads of the East could offer. Train robbery flourished, spectacular runaways smoked down the mountain grades, and forest fire, flood, and avalanche were commonplace.

The Iron Horse helped civilize this raw country and from out of the West came a fresh generation of Empire Builders—the "Big Four," Huntington, Stanford, Crocker, and Hopkins; James J. Hill; Cyrus K. Holliday of the Santa Fe and Ben Holladay, the stagecoach king who turned from flesh-and-blood horses to the iron breed. Here Henry Villard's fortunes rose and fell, leaving the Northern Pacific as a memorial to his vision, and here Edward Harriman lifted the Union Pacific to new heights.

The region is rich in rail lore, much of which has but recently started to appear to print, and a wealth remains untouched. The saga of steam railroading in the West is now history, but so new that the paint has scarcely dried and the cinders have barely ceased to rattle on the car tops. Let us not linger here, but mount the iron mustang and highball toward the Pacific.

FRONTIER SWITCHER. The American West was still wild and woolly when the Rogers Locomotive & Machine Works turned out this balloon-stacked 0-6-0 in December, 1873, under Shop No. 2367.

The little goat with her four-wheeled tender was built as No. 6 of the Midland Pacific Railway, a standard gauge line with its home terminal at Nebraska City, Nebraska, on the western side of the Mississippi River south of Omaha and Plattsmouth. By 1871 the road had been opened west across Otoe County to Lincoln, 58 miles, and in 1874 it was extended northwesterly to Seward for a total of 83 miles. Ambitious goals projected by the Midland Pacific included extending the road to Fort Kearney or a connection with the Union Pacific, and a branch off the main stem in Otoe County to run to the State Line and ". . . the general direction of Fort Riley, Kansas." Hard times fell upon the road and following a foreclosure it was reorganized as the Nebraska Railway, later becoming a part of the Chicago, Burlington & Quincy.

The aura of the frontier when old No. 6 was placed in service can best be recalled by noting that it was not until three years later that Custer and his blue-clad troopers galloped to their death on the Little Big Horn.

IRON RANGER. Headed by Charlemagne Tower, the Minnesota Iron Company succeeded in gaining control of a paper-work corporation incorporated in 1874 as the Duluth & Iron Range Railroad and Tower's son, Charlemange, Jr., was installed as President in 1883.

Construction was started at Two Harbors on Lake Superior in 1883 and the road was completed to Soudan, Minnesota, in mid-summer of 1884. On July 31st, 1884, the first train of Minnesota iron ore from the famous Vermilion Range was shipped over the road from the Breitung Mine near Tower to the newly-completed ore dock at Two Harbors; this train of 5 wooden ore cars of 20-ton capacity was handled by Engine No. 8, a Baldwin 2-8-0 of 1883 vintage. The engineer of this first train of Minnesota iron ore was Thomas Owens, who later rose to Superintendent and then Vice President of the line. In 1886 the line connecting Two Harbors with Duluth was completed; prior to this, motive power had to be barged to Two Harbors.

At the start of operations in 1884 the D. & I.R. had one Mogul, two 0-4-0's, six Consolidations, and a pair of eight-wheelers; the latter two, both built by Baldwin in 1884, were numbered 1 and 2.

Duluth & Iron Range Railroad's No. 1 is shown here with a mixed train at Tower Junction, Minnesota, in the 1880's; her derby-hatted engineer, train crew, and admirers bravely face the camera as the winter sun throws bright reflections from the snow blanketing the hills of the ore region. (Lake County Historical Society photo, courtesy of Franklin King)

ORE HAULER. Engine 66 of the Duluth & Iron Range Railroad was one of an order of ten 4-8-0 type freight haulers built by Schenectady in 1893; these locomotives, assigned road numbers 60 to 69, bore Schenectady construction numbers 4041 through 4049 and the last engine, No. 69, bore construction number 4145. One of these engines, probably No. 60, was exhibited by Schenectady at the Columbian Exposition in Chicago in 1893.

The Duluth & Iron Range was reportedly the first road in the United States to have air brakes and the Master Car Builders' approved automatic couplers on all of its equipment.

In 1930 the old Duluth & Iron Range was leased by the Duluth, Missabe & Northern, a road organized by the Merritt interests in 1891 to serve their iron deposits in the Mesabi, vastly greater than the Vermilion Range ore beds tapped by the Duluth & Iron Range. These two roads emerged as the Duluth, Missabe & Iron Range Railway and 180-car ore drags became commonplace, the steel cars having a capacity of 70 tons each; this was a far cry from the first Iron Range ore train of 5 wooden 20-ton cars that clattered into Two Harbors in 1884.

Sleek-boilered No. 66, pictured here with wooden ore cars around 1900, had 22×26 inch cylinders and 54 inch drivers; she and her nine sisters could handle trains of 80 wooden cars of ore but required helper engines to move these loads over the heaviest grades on the Iron Range. (Courtesy of Franklin A. King)

POWER FROM PITTSBURGH. The Pittsburgh Locomotive Works, located in Allegheny City, Pennsylvania, was organized in August of 1865 and operated under their own name until the firm became a part of the American Locomotive Company in 1901. In 1889 a program of renovation was begun, old buildings being replaced and better shop facilities erected with the goal of a shop capacity capable of turning out one complete locomotive each working day in the year.

In addition to regular freight and passenger engines, Pittsburgh turned out a creditable line of lighter power designed for shop, mill, mine, furnace, logging, and plantation services, along with Forney types for city and interurban railways.

A typical Pittsburgh engine of 1883 is the No. 76 of the Burlington, Cedar Rapids & Northern, bearing shop number 699. The ten-wheeler had an extended smokebox and a wrought iron bull-nose coupler, the latter extending out over her oak stave pilot far enough to permit the use of the standard link and pin coupler of that era rather than the long, heavy, and cumbersome pilot bar coupling rod in use on many engines of the day.

The Burlington, Cedar Rapids & Northern Railway was the descendant of the Burlington, Cedar Rapids & Minnesota Railroad of 1868, with 218 miles of track between Burlington and Plymouth, Iowa, and 149 miles of branch lines including the Milwaukee, Pacific, and Muscatine Divisions.

A. L. Mohler, one-time president and general manager of the Oregon Railroad & Navigation Co. who rose to fame with the Union Pacific, served on the Iowa road from 1871 until 1882 as auditor, pioneer agent, chief clerk and general freight agent. (Courtesy of Schenectady History Center)

PISTON VALVE PIONEER. The pretty eightwheeler shown here is No. 42 of the old Milwaukee & St. Paul Railway. She was built in the company's shops in 1854 and was named the D. A. OLIN.

In 1868 the engine was rebuilt with piston valves as shown in this photograph, one of the earliest pictures recording this style of valve applied to outside-connected engines. The polished brass casings covering the heads of these piston valves can be seen inside the cylinders in the saddle beneath the smokebox.

It was not until after the introduction of the Walschaert valve gear that the piston valves began to supplant the old style of slide valves mounted in rectangular steam chests.

STRIKING SILHOUETTE. Eight diamond-stacked locomotives of the Northern Pacific stand suspended between earth and sky after having successfully crossed the road's bridge over the Missouri River at Bismarck, Dakota Territory. Northern Pacific trains were in operation west of this point for some time before the bridge was completed, crossing the Missouri over tracks laid on the ice in the winter months and being ferried across by steamer after the spring thaw and breakup.

In the fall of 1882 the steel bridge across the Missouri was finished and the Northern Pacific's engineering department decided to subject it to the acid test. Eight of the road's heaviest 4-4-0's were sent out onto the main span, blanketing the track on the bridge from one end of the structure to the other. The bridge held, and the engines rolled safely across and onto the long timbered trestle approach.

One cannot help but wonder what thoughts passed through the minds of the engine crews as their locomotives clanked out onto the new bridge during this initial test.

This photo is probably one of a series of the event taken by F. Jay Haynes, official Northern Pacific photographer whose studio on wheels covered the N.P. from Minnesota to the Pacific (Courtesy of R. V. Nixon)

MOUNTAIN RAT HOLE. This chilly scene shows the mouth of the Northern Pacific Railroad's famous Mullan tunnel with a group of officials and workmen gathered around the entrance to the bore. The photo was taken on January 5th, 1882, and shows the difficult terrain the N.P. encountered in Montana, Idaho, and Washington. After comparatively easy going across the sweeping plains of the Dakota region and eastern Montana, the road found that construction through the various ranges of the Rockies and the Cascades was a tough and costly job, with tunnels to be drilled and numerous mountain streams to be bridged. (Courtesy of Montana Historical Society)

STAMPEDE PASS. The original route of the Northern Pacific between Puget Sound and the Great Lakes region was formed by trackage leading south from Tacoma, Washington Territory, to Portland, Oregon, thence over the iron of the Oregon Railway & Navigation Company up the south bank of the Columbia River to a connection with Northern Pacific rails near the mouth of the Walla Walla River. From this point, Wallula, the N.P. trains ran over their own iron to the road's eastern terminus; this route was opened in 1883, but construction was soon started on a more direct route west from Ainsworth to Puget Sound, via Yakima and Ellensburg.

The lofty Cascade Mountains barred the path of this direct line and the Northern Pacific mustered its forces to thrust the road through them. To carry the new line over the great range the famous switchback was started in 1886 and completed on June 1, 1887; the pass through which the rails crossed the Cascades became known as Stampede Pass from an incident involving a construction gang. The tunnel replacing the switchback was holed through on May 3, 1888, and both switchback and tunnel represented difficult pieces of construction.

To handle work trains on the steep grades of the old switchback the Northern Pacific ordered two Baldwin 2-10-0's, reportedly the heaviest engines in the world when completed in 1886; they bore road numbers 500 and 501, with shop numbers 8168 and 8169.

This rare old view shows the 501 with a track-laying machine and cars of rail and ties as N.P. crews rush the construction of the switchback while the spring sun melts the remnants of the deep snowdrifts that blocked the pass in winter. (Davidson photo from L. L. Stein, Jr., courtesy of D. L. Stearns)

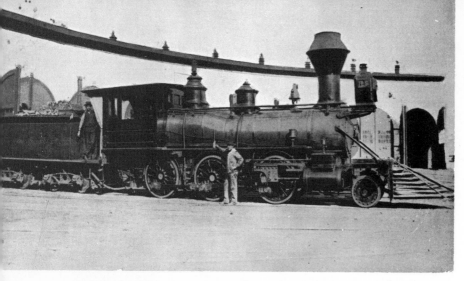

FLATLAND FREIGHT HAULER. The husky Mogul pictured here is No. 125 of the Atchison, Topeka & Sante Fe Railroad, a line that had its origin in the Atchison & Topeka R.R. of 1859 and adopted the new name in 1863. Thrusting ribbons of iron toward the setting sun, the Sante Fe reached the Colorado State Line in December of 1872 after having constructed 360 miles of road in 9 months. Access into Pueblo, Colorado, was gained over the 148 miles of the leased Pueblo & Arkansas Valley Railroad via Granada and Las Animas.

The Mogul shown here at the Emporia, Kansas, roundhouse in 1882 was built by Taunton Machine Works under shop number 736 in May of 1880; she had 18×26 inch cylinders and $50\frac{1}{2}$ inch drivers. Her sturdy pilot armed her for combat with stray longhorns on the Kansas plains and the curtains at the gangway helped to protect her crew from the buffeting winds that often swept the prairies. Engineer J. G. McNeill is posed beside her with his oil can and Fireman Joel McGahay strikes a nonchalant stance by the water leg of her coal-filled tender. (Courtesy of Dr. S. R. Wood)

A HELPING HAND. Northern Pacific's No. 486, a sturdy Baldwin Consolidation, lends her tractive effort to the task of helping the American type coupled behind her handle the heavy consist of passenger equipment trailing off into the distance.

The firemen are both posed in the cab windows in this old photo taken in the days of the link and pin, but when the skipper waves a highball and the capped stacks begin to bark, these worthies will both be busily engaged on the bouncing decks of their charges as they ladle scoops of coal into the roaring inferno of each firebox. Once the varnish has topped the climb and is rolling downgrade, these sweaty tallow-pots can ease up a bit from their laborious task and grab a few minutes of hard-earned rest on the seat boxes, keeping a watchful eye on the track ahead as they enjoy the flow of cool air sweeping through the open cab windows. (Courtesy of Arthur Petersen)

SWITCHBACK POWER. Twin sisters, this pair of Decapods were built by Baldwin in 1886 for use on the Northern Pacific's famous switchback over Stampede Pass in the Cascade Mountains of Washington.

The Baldwin builder's photo shows No. 500 as she rolled out of the factory ready for delivery to the Cascade Division, where construction was proceeding under the direction of Chief Engineer John Joseph Donovan. After service with the N.P. and some Northwest short line railroads, "J. J.," as Donovan was familiarly known, became a partner in the vast Bloedel-Donovan logging and lumbering enterprises.

The view of Northern Pacific's No. 501 shows her on the turntable at the Ellensburg, Washington, roundhouse in 1892. Her original appearance has been slightly altered by the application of a rear sand box, evidently acquired from a Northern Pacific locomotive of earlier vintage.

Both photos show the large main reservoir of the air brake system, mounted vertically beneath the cab aft of the rear set of driving wheels. (Builder's photo, courtesy of H. L. Broadbelt; photo of 501, courtesy of Ronald V. Nixon)

ROVING RELIC. In 1835 the Bush Hill works of William Norris in Philadelphia, Pa., turned out a 4-2-0 locomotive named the WM. PENN for the Philadelphia & Columbia Railroad. In the report of that road issued in 1838 the cost of the WM. PENN was listed as $6,000, although the report for 1837 indicated she had been laid up for a year. The engine was still on the Philadelphia & Columbia when that road was acquired by the Pennsylvania R.R. and is included in the Pennsy's report of 1857.

Henry Frazer, writing in *Locomotive Engineering* in 1898, states the WM. PENN was in service on the Strasburg R.R. as far back as 1854, while C. H. Caruthers' article on the Philadelphia & Columbia R.R. in the August, 1906, edition of *The Railroad Gazette,* creates the impression she was sold to the Strasburg R.R. after being acquired by the Pennsylvania Railroad; at any rate, the engine evidently operated between Strasburg and Leaman Place, where the Strasburg R.R. connected with the Pennsy, until 1864-65 when she was replaced and sold to Edward S. Norris. She was rebuilt in the Norris Locomotive Works at Lancaster, Pa., in 1865, Caruthers stating her hay-stack dome and horse-shoe firebox being then replaced with a cylindrical dome and square firebox, while the original tender and old "hook motion" valve gear were retained; the solid drive wheels shown in the accompanying photo were reportedly added during this rebuilding. The auxiliary water tank mounted on her boiler may also have been added during the Norris rebuilding.

Along with a number of new Norris locomotives built in Lancaster, the WM. PENN was sold to the Western Pacific Railroad and shipped around Cape Horn to California; the Western Pacific linked Oakland with Sacramento by way of San Jose, Niles, and Stockton, by means of connections with the San Francisco Bay R.R., the San Francisco & Alameda R.R., and the San Francisco & Oakland R.R., all gathered into the Central Pacific's fold in 1870.

The Western Pacific engines bore letters rather than numbers, and the WM. PENN was assigned the letter, "J," retaining her original name; an 1868 report lists her as having 54 inch drivers and 10 × 18 inch cylinders, and her weight has been given as 24,000 pounds.

When acquired by the Central Pacific she was assigned road number 175; reports show she was out of service in 1876 but was rebuilt and placed in yard service in 1877. Henry Frazer, a former Lancaster Loco. Works apprentice and later inspector for the Westinghouse Air Brake Co. at San Francisco, states she was used for switching around the Sacramento car shops in 1881, in the boneyard in 1883, and had about $800 worth of work done on her in 1885, under the direction of A. J. Stevens, Supt. of Motive Power & Machinery. Southern Pacific's annual report show her sold to the Pacific Iron & Nail Co. on December 18th, 1885, Frazer remarking she brought a price of $1,000; he also states that the Oakland Nail Works replaced her balloon stack with a straight one of large diameter and renamed her the DUDE. He photographed her at Oakland in 1898 and said she had been fired up and moved about the yards approximately a year before, his photo showing that the solid driver had been replaced with a conventional spoked driver with counterbalances.

Small photo shows the WM. PENN in the West Oakland boneyard in 1900, at left of the old No. 1 of the Black Diamond Railroad. (Large photo, courtesy of Smithsonian Institution; small photo from Roy D. Graves collection, courtesy of the late Gil Kneiss)

SHETLAND PONY. The miniature iron colt pictured here is the J. B. HAGGIN, a Baldwin 0-4-0 saddletank built as No. 1 of the Homestake Mining Company for use on the 22-inch gauge railroad serving their rich gold mine operations at Lead, in the Black Hills of South Dakota. Built in 1879, the engine bore shop number 4669 on her unusual (for Baldwin) rectangular builder's plate and was named in honor of a large stockholder of the Homestake mine; she weighed a whopping 5 tons.

Louis LaPlant is credited with freighting the little engine from Bismarck, Dakota Territory, into the Black Hills with bull teams, the humble ox then being the prime mover of heavy freight in the region so recently the hunting grounds of the Sioux.

The Homestake claim and the neighboring Golden Star claim were sold to George Hearst, father of William Randolph Hearst, and developed into what is reportedly the greatest gold-bearing quartz operation in the Western hemisphere, having produced over $500,000,000 in gold.

The J. B. HAGGIN served the Homestake operations until replaced by a compressed air locomotive around 1900, and is now on display in a museum at Deadwood, South Dakota, loaned by the Homestake Mining Co. of Lead, South Dakota; the engine is well-preserved and is in practically its' original condition, although a sand box, a cold water pump, and a large locomotive bell have been applied since the day it left the Baldwin factory. (Courtesy of H. L. Broadbelt collection)

BUCOLIC SPLENDOR. Engine No. 100 of the Atchison, Topeka & Santa Fe bore the name, LITTLE BUTTERCUP, and it was quite appropriate when she appeared at some Kansas fair, agricultural exhibit, or similar patriotic exhibition at Atchison, Kansas, about 1885.

The Hinkley 4-4-0 of 1879 was almost obscured beneath the lavish decorations and resembles a display of the Patrons of Husbandry more than a hauler of freight and passengers.

Tall stalks of Kansas corn dwarf the young lady and her companion standing near the smokebox, while the boy seated on the pilot beam holds what appears to be a caduceus after the fashion of Mercury, the god of commerce. A stuffed Chanticleer of heroic stature crows defiance from his perch on the sand box, while bunting and garlands of fruit ornament the boiler and dome.

A country boy, the very prototype of Hamlin Garland's Son of the Middle Border, stands on the cab roof at the handles of a "foot-burner," the old-fashioned walking plow that furrowed the prairies and buried the buffalo sod for eternity. Golden ears of corn flank the sides of the tender, while a prim goddess in liberty cap stands amid an array of pumpkins or watermelons beside the staff that supports Old Glory; the shields visible around her bear such mottoes as "East" and "Union."

In an age when locomotives were frequently decorated for excursions and celebrations of varying importance, LITTLE BUTTERCUP represents the acme of railroaders' skill and ingenuity in the art of decorating an engine. (Courtesy of Dr. S. R. Wood)

SOUTHWEST STEAMER. This tall 4-8-0 handled heavy freight drags over the iron of the Atlantic & Pacific Railroad through the desolate regions of the great Southwest in the 1880's.

Bearing road number 26, she was constructed for the Atlantic & Pacific by the Rhode Island Locomotive Works in 1881, under shop number 993. She later became Santa Fe Pacific's No. 19, was next renumbered 237, and finally became Atchison, Topeka & Santa Fe's No. 637.

Her boiler extended through the lofty wooden cab, separating the engineer from the fireman, but the latter individual spent most of his time out on the open deck, bailing black diamonds into her long, narrow firebox. (Courtesy of Dr. S. R. Wood)

ARIZONA SHORT LINE. The Prescott & Eastern Railroad was incorporated under the laws of Arizona in September of 1897 and in October of 1898 the 26-mile line was opened between Mayer and P&E Junction, the latter point being located on the Santa Fe, Prescott & Phoenix Railway near Prescott. Controlled by the Santa Fe, Prescott & Phoenix, the short line connected at Mayer with the Bradshaw Mountain Railroad, a 27-mile pike under Santa Fe control that ran from Mayer to Crown King, Arizona.

The Santa Fe, Prescott & Phoenix Railway, controlled by the Atchison, Topeka & Santa Fe, was opened from Ash Fork to Phoenix in 1895 and served the rich mining districts located around the headwaters of the Hassayampa and Agua Fria rivers.

Engine No. 11 of the Prescott & Eastern was a neat 4-6-0 built by Brooks in 1898 under shop number 3073. She later was AT&SF No. 2431 and was scrapped at San Bernardino in 1927. (Courtesy of Dr. S. R. Wood)

FACING WEST. The brawny fireman in the cab of this pioneer Western tea-kettle scans the rails ahead as his Iron Horse clatters toward the land of the setting sun. This photograph shows engine No. 31 of the Atchison, Topeka & Santa Fe; she bore the name PUEBLO. Battling buffalo stampedes, Indians, prairie fires, grasshoppers, and rival railroads, the Santa Fe thrust its iron across the Southwest to earn the sobriquet of "The Railroad That Built An Empire." (Courtesy of Dr. S. R. Wood)

THE ARTICULATED. The Frenchman, Anatole Mallet, patented the articulated compound locomotive in France in 1885, but the first of the breed in the United States was built in Alco's Schenectady plant in 1904 for the Baltimore & Ohio. This 0-6-6-0 bore road number 2400 but was dubbed "Old Maud" by the boys on the B&O, a nickname probably suggested by the balky comic-strip mule of that era; she was exhibited at the Louisiana Purchase Exposition in St. Louis and then placed in helper service on the B&O's Sand Patch grade.

The first Mallet compound articulated engines built by Baldwin were three meter gauge engines for the American Railroad of Porto Rico in 1904. In 1906 the Baldwin Works turned out the first American Mallets equipped with leading and trailing trucks, these engines being placed in service on the Great Northern and used extensively in the rugged Cascades range of mountains.

Mallet's design incorporated two sets of engines under one boiler, the forward set being hinged to permit it to curve and the forward section of the single boiler rode this set of engines on a sliding plate; on curves, this feature permitted the front of the boiler to swing wide to the outside as the leading engine nosed around the arc of the curve. An exception to this design was the 2-6-6-2 type built by Baldwin for the Santa Fe in 1910-11, when an articulated boiler was used; these engines featured boilers built in two sections, each mounted rigidly on the frame over its set of engines. The boiler sections were joined by a flexible connection resembling an accordion's bellows, the device being patented by Samuel M. Vauclain.

Engine 1167 of the Santa Fe is shown here, the 2-6-6-2 being the equivalent of two of the older Mogul type locomotives under one boiler and operated by one engine crew.

The Stephenson valve gear in common use on American railroads when the Mallet made her debut was not suited to the articulated design of locomotives and the Walschaert valve gear was applied, its application gradually spreading to other types of engines as the merits of the gear became more widely known. (Courtesy of Sante Fe Railway)

PORTAGE LINE POWER. The Oregon Steam Navigation Company operated steamboats on the Columbia River and in addition operated two portage rail lines, one at the Cascades of the Columbia and the other around Celilo Falls, as obstructions in the great River of the West prevented through steamboat service. Three old locomotives built by the Vulcan Iron Works of San Francisco served as the original power at the Cascades and the O.S.N. Co. acquired a pair of 4-2-4T type engines from Danforth, Cooke & Company in 1862 to run on The Dalles-Celilo portage route.

In 1865 the Oregon Steam Navigation Co. added two American type woodburners to their portage line at the Cascades, and one of these twins is pictured here in a photo taken about 1867 by Carleton E. Watkins, pioneer West Coast photographer. She was named the S. G. REED and her sister was the J. S. RUCKEL, both being named in honor of men connected with the portage railways and boats.

Both engines were built by Danforth, Cooke & Co., had 12 × 22 inch cylinders, 55 inch drivers, and each weighed 50,000 pounds; built to a gauge of 5 feet, they were later converted to standard gauge by the successor Oregon Railway & Navigation Co., who assigned road number 3 to the J. S. RUCKEL and road number 4 to the S. G. REED.

The original portage road at the Cascades, operated by mule power, was a target of the Indians during the Yakima War in 1856 and was the scene of considerable bloodshed during a siege that lasted for several days. (Courtesy of Oregon Historical Society)

NORTHWEST PASSAGE. The Oregon Short Line R.R. was incorporated in February of 1897 as the successor to the Oregon Short Line & Utah Northern Railway, and was a key link in the Union Pacific's drive into the great Pacific Northwest. The main stem of the O.S.L. left the Union Pacific at Granger, Wyoming, and cut across southern Idaho, roughly following the Snake River drainage from Pocatello through Glenn's Ferry to Huntington, Oregon, where it joined the Oregon Railroad & Navigation Co. to provide a through route to Portland, Oregon.

The Oregon Short Line wheeled freight across vast expanses of sagebrush desert in the 1890's behind a fleet of Cooke and Rhode Island tenwheelers, such as Engines 644 and 630, doubleheading a drag in this rare old photo.

Train and engine crews took a dim view of the policy of running excess tonnage trains necessitating the use of two engines; draught gear designed to withstand the strain of one locomotive often failed when two engines heaved on it, resulting in dangerous break-in-twos. On trains not equipped with air brakes, a break-in-two often resulted in serious trouble, the detached section running away or crashing into the forward portion of the train. Many oldtime railroaders believed it was a better policy to run lighter trains at higher speeds, thus offering faster service to shippers, but the operating departments of a number of roads subscribed to the theory of holding traffic until a full tonnage drag accumulated and then running a doubleheader, saving the wages of a train crew and reducing train movements. This practice was more frequent in areas where there was little or no competition for freight traffic. (Courtesy of Arthur Petersen)

THE FACE OF HARD TIMES. The Panic of 1893 engulfed the United States and the railroads suffered along with everyone else. Even while locomotive builders were displaying their latest engines at the World's Columbian Exposition, they were laying off employees in their shops in the face of growing depression; the Baldwin Works, who had turned out 946 engines in 1890 and 772 in 1893, saw their orders drop off until only 313 engines were built by them in 1894.

Widespread unrest followed on the heels of the great economic decline and labor troubles erupted across the nation. The Pullman Strike of 1894 brought the railroads into the strife and the Government sided with management to suppress the united action of the workmen.

In April of 1894 a band of several hundred unemployed, led by Jacob S. Coxey, marched on Washington, D.C., to plead for Federal aid in remedying conditions. The idea spread and soon "General" Coxey and his band were joined by others from across the nation, the movement's members being known as Coxey's Army. Charles Kelly led a contingent from San Francisco to join in the march; in the Pacific Northwest another army moved east, commandeering trains on occasion and having a few brushes with the officers of the law.

This historic photo shows a brigade of Coxey's Army in camp on the banks of the Snake River near Huntington, Oregon, with an Oregon Short Line passenger train passing in the background.

In Washington, Coxey mounted the Capitol steps to address a gathering crowd and was arrested for having walked on the grass; his followers were disbanded and the future looked as bleak as the barren hills bordering the Snake, but the nation slowly recovered. (Courtesy of Arthur Petersen)

ROAD'S NAMESAKE. Engine No. 35 of the Atchison, Topeka & Santa Fe bore the historic name of SANTA FE, after the ancient pueblo that lent the road a part of its corporate title. This Mason 4-4-0, built in 1872 under shop number 465, was a familiar sight in the cow towns along the line in the days when wild cowboys trailed their heards of long-horned cattle up the dusty trails of the Southwest to shipping points on the Santa Fe's iron. (Courtesy of Dr. S. R. Wood)

THE FACE OF WINTER. Lower Cascade Bridge on the Central Pacific's transcontinental link over the Sierra Nevada in California provided the setting for this view of mountain railroading in the winter of 1890. A 4-6-0 fitted with A. J. Stevens' valve gear noses across the enclosed Burr type of Howe truss spanning the deep ravine and will soon plunge into the murky depths of the protective snowshed at the far end of the span.

Pretty as a Christmas greeting card, the scene is highly deceptive; the white blanket choked the cuts, blocking traffic for days on end. Communications were snarled, as the snow toppled telegraph poles, and 2,500 men were sent into the rugged mountains to shovel out the blockade that lasted seventeen days. The "Storm Kings," experienced mountain railroad men, rammed at the drifts with wedge plows coupled ahead of six to twelve locomotives before the first rotary plow came to the Big Hill in 1889. About 37 miles of snowsheds and galleries were also erected to protect the tracks from slides and snowdrifts, the latter often piling up 20 to 30 feet deep.

Chilled by the icy winds that swept through the open cabs, frequently wet and hungry, the men of the mountain lines braved danger at every curve as they sallied forth to battle with Old Man Winter in their ceaseless struggle to keep the trains rolling. (Courtesy of Southern Pacific)

WYOMING HOGS. The camera of Fred Jukes, dean emeritus of photographers of the Western rail scene, recorded this fine view of a pair of Union Pacific hogs on a cold morning in Wyoming—icicles can be seen on cab eaves and running gear, and steam exhausting from the frost cocks indicates that the injectors and piping are being heated to prevent freezing, one of the necessary precautions required when running steam locomotives in cold weather.

The two Consolidation types shown here are Union Pacific's No's. 1625 and 1635, and are representative of 80 engines of this type built by Baldwin for the U.P. in 1900-01; originally Vauclain compounds as shown here, they were later rebuilt as simple engines. The series was numbered 1620 to 1699 when built, and were later renumbered 400 to 479; the 1620 and the 1621 were built with Vanderbilt boilers, but were given conventional boilers when they were rebuilt; two engines in the series, No's. 1633 and 1673, were reportedly built as simple engines, having 23 × 30 inch cylinders instead of the 15½ and 26 × 30 inch cylinders applied to the Vauclain compounds.

This Jukes photo taken at Laramie about 1902 shows the wooden stave pilots and flanged stacks in use on the Union Pacific at that time. (Courtesy of Fred Jukes)

POCATELLO PANORAMA. The Consolidation with the diamond stack is tied onto a string of westbound freight at Pocatello, Idaho, in this early view of that noted terminal point.

The engine is No. 1270 of the Union Pacific, a 2-8-0 reportedly built by Danforth, Cooke & Co. in 1882 as Union Pacific's 2nd No. 145. She is later believed to have been sold to the subsidiary OR&N for service west of Huntington, Oregon.

There was a considerable turnover of operating crews at Pocatello in the wild old days and many boomer railroaders passed that way, working long enough to acquire a stake and to create the legendary "Pocatello night yardmaster" of rail lore.

This photo comes from the collection of Arthur Petersen, retired Union Pacific telegrapher who worked the key in Pocatello until he was recently pensioned after many years of faithful service. (Courtesy of Arthur Petersen)

DEATH RODE THE RAILS. Railroading has always been a dangerous occupation and countless numbers of railroad men have gone to their graves in the performance of their duties.

Numerous safety devices helped to cut the loss of life and limb, including block signals, automatic couplers, air brakes, slide detectors, fusible boiler plugs, and similar aids; the Hours of Service Act, limiting the time crews were allowed to be on duty, was another important factor in reducing accidents, as were the laws requiring stricter inspection and maintenance of locomotives, cars, and other equipment.

The undetected washout claimed the lives of many railroaders and is a threat still present on the iron road, especially in the barren stretches of the West where flash floods destroy the roadbed and undermine bridges. Frequently flooding streams wash away a portion of a fill, leaving the rails suspended and the bond wires intact, resulting in a "proceed" indication of the block signal leading the train into a death trap.

The two views presented here show what happens when a train encounters a trestle weakened by flood. Union Pacific's Eng. 1716, a former Oregon Railroad & Navigation Co. tenwheeler, plunged through this trestle spanning Willow Creek on the Heppner Branch in Oregon; Engineer Sam Hansen, a veteran boomer, was killed in the drop and his body pinned under his locomotive. Section Foreman Habelt, riding in the cab of the 1716, was also killed but the fireman was thrown clear of the engine into the water and miraculously escaped. (Both photos, courtesy of the late Ben W. Griffiths)

TRAGIC PLUNGE. Many a brave railroad man met his Maker when the giddy wooden trestles of yesteryear gave way and sent engines and trains hurtling into the depths of rocky canyons or rushing streams. On occasion the trestles were weakened by flood or damaged by fire, but many of them collapsed as a result of neglect, their rotting timbers weakened with age.

This photo shows the stark results of an engine tumbling from a high wooden trestle; the locomotive is No. 54 of the Pacific Great Eastern and the accident occurred in the Cariboo region of British Columbia. (Courtesy of Ernie Plant collection)

CANTARA LOOP. The rugged mountains of the West presented numerous obstacles to pioneer railroad builders and some great engineering feats resulted when the locators of early roads ran headlong into natural barriers.

When the Central Pacific's line from Redding north toward Oregon was being built the rails reached Dunsmuir in the fall of 1886 after following up the Sacramento River. The line north from Dunsmuir was laid out by Chief Engineer S. Montague, a veteran of Central Pacific construction work; to climb out of the steep canyon of the upper Sacramento, the road made a sharp horseshoe curve near Cantara, crossing the Sacramento River for the last time as it struggled up Big Canyon under the flank of snowclad Mount Shasta. Montague died in the winter of 1886 and was succeeded by William Hood, who carried the line over the rugged Siskiyous to a junction with the Oregon & California R.R. at Ashland, Oregon, in December of 1887.

This view of the Cantara curve was taken around the turn of the century and shows the private car of Gen. Mgr. Richard Koehler on a tour of inspection of the road between Dunsmir and Portland; the diamond-stacked 4-6-0 is No. 17 of the Astoria & Columbia River R.R., far from its home rails. Too heavy for the new grade of the A&CR, the 17 and three other A&CR engines were temporarily exchanged for lighter O&C engines that could operate between Portland and Astoria. The stone piers for the Sacramento River bridge were constructed by Col. James Scobie, a Scot who had charge of all masonry work on the road through northern California; his camp, moved from point to point as the hand-dressed stonework was completed, was always known as "Scobieville." (Courtesy of E. U. Gogl)

IN THE PIT. Railroading is filled with minor catastrophes, many of which pass unknown to the general public. Engines and cars derail, sideswipe, and come to grief in many other forms but unless loss of life or great damage occurs these events are seldom considered newsworthy. Indeed, frequently the officials of the road involved fail to learn of some of these minor contretemps, for the operating crews strive to clean up their own insignificant troubles and conceal them from the brass hats, thus avoiding a call on the carpet and perhaps a handful of demerit marks on their personal records.

Derailed wheels can be coaxed back onto the iron and the tell-tale flange scars on the ties hidden by the judicious application of dirt and gravel; bent grab-irons can be straightened, and split switches that have been run through can be repaired by the use of a length of pipe fitted over the handle for leverage and a track spike or monkey wrench properly placed in the switch stand.

Accidents such as the one pictured here are more embarrassing and little can be done to conceal a locomotive toppled over in a turntable pit. Failure to have the table lined for the proper track generally caused such mishaps,

although engines with leaky throttles left unattended in their stalls with cylinder cocks closed and reverse levers not placed on center occasionally wandered off into the pit.

The tenwheeler shown here is a Northern Pacific kettle that strayed into the turntable pit at the old Northern Pacific Terminal Company roundhouse in Portland, Oregon, about 1907. (Courtesy of Herbert Arey)

SHASTA SHORT LINE. Baldwin turned out this trim woodburning Prairie type under construction number 16239 in 1898 for the McCloud River Railroad in northern California's pine region. Assigned road number 4, the sturdy little log hauler reportedly survived until 1939.

This photo shows her equipped with the Sweeney air pump, a device used widely on the Southern Pacific in the mountainous regions of the West. Although designed primarily to be used in case the regular air compressor failed, engineers frequently used it as an auxiliary air pump when braking trains on long, steep grades.

The Sweeney was a simple device, consisting of a pipe tapped into the top of the steam chest and leading to the main reservoir of the air brake system; this pipe contained a stop cock, a check valve, and a safety valve.

When braking on heavy grades taxed the capacity of the small air compressors then in use, the Sweeney could be used to restore the depleted main reservoir pressure. With the throttle closed, the reverse lever was moved slightly back of center, causing the locomotive's cylinders to act as compressors and the air they compressed was pumped through the opened stop cock into the main reservoir, recharging it rapidly. A leaky stop cock could cause trouble when the engine was working steam, as the steam would pass through the leaking cock and enter the air brake system.

The operating lever from the cab, the stop cock, check valve, and safety valve of the Sweeney can be seen in this photo, on top of the steam chest and behind the lubricator pipe. (Courtesy of H. L. Broadbelt collection)

GOLDEN STATE STEAMER. The quaint little locomotive shown here ran on the Visalia Railroad, a short line 7.41 miles long, extending from Visalia to Goshen Junction in California's Tulare County. The road was opened in 1874 and passed under Southern Pacific control in 1897, being absorbed into that system in 1899.

Engine No. 2 was built by Baldwin in 1877 as an 0-4-4 tank locomotive, construction number 4102; she proved

too light and unsteady and was returned to the Baldwin factory for rebuilding. She emerged later in 1877 as as 2-4-4 tank engine under a new Baldwin construction number, 4226, as shown in the accompanying photograph. The little tea-pot served as a shop switcher at Fresno and later at Bakersfield, having been converted to a rather homely 0-4-0 with a saddle tank.

Steam for her injector came directly from the dome, as seen in this builder's view, rather than from the conventional steam turret or fountain located on top of the boiler within the cab; this turret provided steam for such adjuncts as the injectors, air compressors, steam reverse gear, etc., and on some roads was called the "niggerhead." (Courtesy of H. L. Broadbelt collection)

148

RAILS THROUGH ZION. The rails of the Oregon Short Line in Utah passed through arid lands turned into fertile farms by the perseverance and industry of the Mormons led into the Salt Lake Valley by Brigham Young. Young's acute business sense and his visions of Utah's future caused him to support the coming of the railroad, the Church of the Latter-Day Saints becoming actively involved in the construction of the pioneer lines in the State of Deseret.

The tree-shaded station grounds at Logan, Utah, provided the background for this fine view of a mixed train operating on the Oregon Short Line in 1899. The three freight cars and the wooden combination are coupled behind OSL's

engine 205, a trim little 4-4-0 with diamond stack and stave pilot. Note the old harp type switch stand at the right of the photo, a style which was commonly used with the stub switches of earlier days. (Courtesy of Arthur Petersen)

EXCURSION ROAD POWER. Although the geared Shay type locomotives built by the Lima Locomotive Works were primarily used by logging lines and a few mountainous mining roads, this pair earned their keep by hauling excursion trains loaded with passengers up the steep, crooked grades of the Mill Valley & Mt. Tamalpais Scenic Railway in California.

The open-sided passenger cars of the Mount Tamalpais line can be seen here in the middle background at Summit terminal in June of 1907.

At right is Shay No. 5, with Fireman Roy D. Graves standing by the pilot beam and Engineer Jake Johnson resting his hand on the reciprocating machinery of the little "side-winder." At left is Engine 4, with Engineer Frank Clark and Fireman Pagannini.

The Mill Valley & Mt. Tamalpais, a standard gauge scenic line 8.19 miles long, carried excursionists from Mill Valley to the summit of Mt. Tamalpais and its excessive curvature earned it the sobriquet of "The Crookedest Railway in the World"; the road was opened for service in August of 1896. (Courtesy of Roy D. Graves)

REDWOOD RAMBLER. When native Indian tribes along the coast of northern California began raiding the settlements of the white invaders, the U.S. Army established a military post about one mile north of the mouth of the Noyo River; erected in 1857, it was named Fort Bragg, in honor of Captain Braxton Bragg, a West Pointer who later became a general in the Confederate Army.

The name stuck, even after the fort was abandoned, and the village around the site became the center of extensive redwood logging and saw milling. Fore-runner of the Fort Bragg R.R. was the short Noyo & Pudding Creek R.R., a logging pike built in 1881. The Fort Bragg Redwood Company opened their redwood mill in 1885 and started construction of the Fort Bragg Railroad the same year.

Engine No. 1 on the Fort Bragg R.R. was a Baldwin 2-4-2 tanker built in 1886 and named the SEQUOIA. The second engine was the Fort Bragg's 2-Spot, another Baldwin saddletanker shown here; she was a 2-4-4T, built in 1887 under shop number 8852, and was originally a woodburner but later was converted to oil. She bore road number 2 on the successor California Western Railroad & Navigation Co., and in 1910 was sold to the Irvine Muir Lumber Company.

The California Western R.R. & Nav. Co., formed in 1905 by the parent Union Lumber Co., opened a through line between Fort Bragg and Willits, California, in 1911, connecting with the Northwestern Pacific R.R. at the latter terminal. (Courtesy of H. L. Broadbelt collection)

LONE STAR STATER. Engine No. 3 of the San Antonio & Aransas Pass was a 2-4-4 tank type constructed by the Baldwin Locomotive Works in 1885, Shop No. 7690. Named the A. BELKNAP, the engine had 49 inch drivers, 12×20 inch cylinders, and weighed 54,000 pounds. The SA&AP was incorporated in 1884 and completed a line extending from San Antonio to Houston, Texas, a distance of 238 miles; branches ran to Waco, Kerrville, Corpus Christi, Rockport, and other Texas terminals. Headquarters for the road were located in historic San Antonio, scene of the gallant defense of the Alamo by Crockett, Bowie, and other legendary American frontiersmen; the road's main office was housed in the Maverick Bank Building.

The San Antonio & Aransas Pass was reorganized in 1893 and later was absorbed by the Southern Pacific. In addition to No. 3, the A. BELKNAP, the Baldwin Works constructed five other engines for the road in 1885. These were No. 1, the SAN ANTONIO, and No. 2, the ARANSAS PASS, both 4-4-0 types; No. 4, the M. KENEDY, and No. 6, the CHAS. HUGO, both 2-6-0 types; and No. 5, the SAM MAVERICK, an 0-4-0 type. (Baldwin photo, H. L. Broadbelt collection)

ARIZONA SHORT LINE. The little United Verde & Pacific Railway was short on both mileage and width, its 26 miles of main line being built to a gauge of 3 feet. It was chartered in March of 1894 and completed on December 31st of that year; the road ran from Jerome, Arizona, to a connection with the Santa Fe, Prescott & Phoenix Railway at Jerome Junction, a station between Ash Fork and Prescott.

Engine No. 2 of the United Verde & Pacific was a 2-6-0 Baldwin with Vauclain compound cylinders, designed to handle ore traffic in the rough country around Jerome, site of extensive copper mining; built in June, 1894, the slim-gauge Mogul carried shop number 14026.

The terminal of Jerome was named in honor of a New York lawyer, Eugene Jerome, who invested in the early copper mine of Arizona's Territorial Governor F. E. Tritle; Jerome was the grandfather of Sir Winston Churchill. The rich copper deposits on Mingus Mountain were mined by the United Verde Copper Company, formed in 1893; they sold out to the big Phelps Dodge Corporation during the first World War. Prime mover in the United Verde mine and railway was Montana's Senator William A. Clark, who became interested in the mine in 1884. He served as president of the narrow gauge United Verde & Pacific Railway and reportedly invested a million dollars in developing the mine project. (Courtesy of H. L. Broadbelt collection)

WESTERN HILL CLIMBER. To provide heavier power for the hard pulls up the old Central Pacific line over the Sierra Nevada the Southern Pacific's General Master Mechanic A. J. Stevens designed and built a 4-8-0 locomotive which was completed in the road's Sacramento Shops in April, 1882. This engine, No. 229, incorporated a number of novel features including double valves, clasp driver brakes, a combustion chamber ahead of the firebox, power reverse gear, and three eccentrics on each side. Her cab roof, which included a clerestory, dropped down into a curved duck-tail overhang to shelter the fireman at work on her deck.

Designed to burn either wood or coal, the big 4-8-0 was placed in service over the Sierra Nevada and soon proved her worth. She was so successful that she was sent east to the Cooke Locomotive Works, along with Stevens' plans and some of the men who had built her. Cooke built 10 of these engines in 1882 and 15 more in 1883 with only a few minor alterations, including cylinders 20 × 30 inches instead of the 19 × 30 inch cylinders applied to No. 229. Known as the "Mastodon" type, these engines were used over the Tehachapi as well as on the Sierra Nevada run, and No. 68 is shown here at Kern City (Bakersfield), California in 1889; built under Cooke shop number 1426 in 1883, she was scrapped in 1902, but some of the 1882 series engines were worked over and continued in service on the Southern Pacific until 1950. In this old photo Fireman Bert Bell stands in the gangway, Fireman Bill Thomas is seated in the cab, and Fireman Mart Collins is standing in the spacious cab window; on the ground at left is Seth Arkills, the third man from the left is Fireman Dick Bacher, and Machinist Billy Webb is standing by the cylinder; others in the view are unidentified. (Courtesy of Southern Pacific)

SHORT LINE TRIO. Pictured opposite are three Baldwin locomotives constructed for short line logging railroad service on the West Coast, fine examples of the lighter motive power used on main line hauls between logging camps and saw mills.

Eldest of the trio is No. 1 of the Klamath Lake Railroad Co., a husky little woodburning Prairie type built under Baldwin's construction number 27686. The Klamath Lake Railroad was chartered late in 1901 and opened for service in the spring of 1903, operating 25 miles of standard gauge track from Thrall, California, to Pokegama, Oregon. The road was owned by the Pokegama Lumber Co. and connected with the Siskiyou line of the Southern Pacific at Thrall; in later years the road was acquired by the California Oregon Power Company.

The trim 4-6-0 of the Peninsular Railway Co. bore the name SOL. SIMPSON and carried road number 7. She ran out of Shelton, Washington, serving the Simpson Timber Company, and was built by Baldwin in April, 1907, under shop number 30606. Note the lower link and pin drawhead beneath her regular coupler, enabling her crew to attach a cable for logging road chores.

The third engine is a stocky Mikado built by Baldwin under shop number 38271 for the Smith-Powers Logging Company, who gave her road number 101. She handled log trains from Powers to Marshfield, Oregon, in a joint track operation with the Southern Pacific's Coos Bay branch, delivering logs from Albert Powers' logging camps to the C. A. Smith Lumber Company saw mill located on the tidewaters of Coos Bay's Isthmus Slough. (Three photos, courtesy of H. L. Broadbelt collection)

RUBBERNECK ROUTE. The crooked iron of the Mill Valley & Mt. Tamalpais Scenic Railway carried sightseers up the steep slopes of California's noted peak and the two-truck Heisler shown here was one of the locomotives that threaded the curves of the famed "double bow-knot." She bore the name, JOS. G. EASTLAND, but was known to crewmen as "The Bull." This photo shows her at Mill Valley in 1897; the town was called Eastland for a time but this name did not stick.

The engineer seated in the cab is Ernest Thomas, who later met his death aboard this engine when she turned over on August 22nd, 1900, while coming down the mountain.

The Heisler was one of the gear-driven type of locomotives most commonly found on logging roads in the West; her two cylinders were mounted V-fashion beneath the belly of the boiler just forward of the cab, driving a line shaft that transmitted power to each axle by means of gears. (Courtesy of Mr. Roy D. Graves)

PROFILE OF COURAGE. Back around the turn of the century Engine No. 26 of the St. Joseph & Grand Island, a Rogers ten-wheeler, was rambling along through the lush farmlands near Fairbury, Nebraska. Her engine crew was suddenly gripped with fear as a small child appeared on the track and the runner plugged his train, but it was evident that the speed could not be reduced in time to halt the engine before striking the child. While the engineer applied sand to the rails and hossed the old teakettle into reverse in a desperate effort to stop, the alert fireman darted out the front cab window, along the running board, and down to a precarious perch on the narrow foot-ledge fronting the bottom of the wooden stave pilot. The child stood in the track, paralyzed by the approaching engine; the fireman stood poised and motionless. At the critical moment his arm swept out, clutched the toddler, and hurled him out of the path of danger; the act that saved the child's life caused the gallant fireboy to slip from his narrow foothold and the rolling wheels passed over his legs as he fell from the pilot.

Later, when the fireman was able to get about on artificial limbs, the crew returned to the scene of his heroism and the episode was re-enacted and preserved for posterity by Photographer Chambers of Fairbury. Unable to railroad after the accident, the fireman was given a life-time job as County Clerk by the appreciative citizens of Nebraska's Jefferson County.

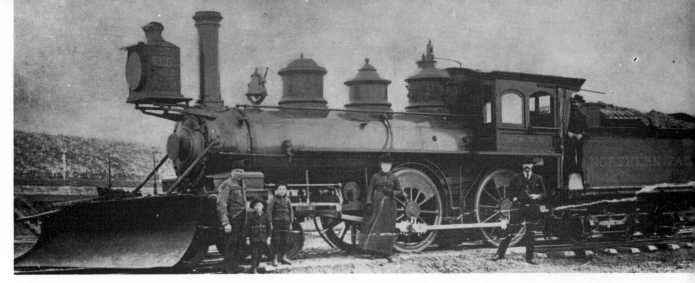

N.P. BRANCH LINE POWER. This shot of Northern Pacific's No. 36 was taken at Belmont, Washington, on May 20th, 1891. The double-domed American type sports a rakish pilot plow in this view and curtains have been applied at the gangway to protect her crew from the winds that sweep the Palouse region.

The Palouse & Lewiston Branch of the Northern Pacific left the main line at Marshall Junction, a short distance southwest of Spokane, Washington, and ran south along the eastern border of the Evergreen State, turning east to cross the Idaho boundary and enter Moscow. From here the line curved southeast to Juliaetta, then swung southwesterly to the Snake River port of Lewiston. (H. V. Banks collection, courtesy of R. V. Nixon)

A JUKES CLASSIC. Veteran rail photographer Fred Jukes shot this traditional view of a locomotive engineer oiling around at Rawlins, Wyoming, in 1905. The big ten-wheeler is Union Pacific's No. 1851, a Vauclain compound built by Baldwin in 1900; note the extended piston rods on both high and low pressure cylinders and the experimental stack. Her big 79 inch drivers set a lively pace along the U.P. trail while the coal from her Vanderbilt tender held the needle on her steam gauge at 200 pounds and sent a shower of cinders over the plains of the Great Divide Basin. Her iron path east and west of Rawlins led through stations named in the best of Western nomenclature: Medicine Bow, Bitter Creek, Green River, and Point of Rocks.

The engineer with his long-snouted oiler, probing the innards of his iron horse, was a familiar sight as long as steam ruled the rails; silhouetted by the flame of his torch at night, the intimate chore of oiling around provided a picture firmly planted in the memories of generations of wistful small boys who longed to some day follow in the footsteps of the knight of the smoky charger. Oiling around consisted of more than met the casual eye of the layman; in addition to lubricating link motion, eccentrics, and other vital spots such as driving box wedges, the circuit around the engine provided her runner with an opportunity for inspection of all her external organs, and many a serious breakdown and possible accident has been prevented by the discovery of defects during the task of "greasing the pig." (Courtesy of Fred Jukes)

NATURE'S HELPING HAND. Natural obstacles hindering the expansion of railroads included mountains, deserts, and rivers and the elements customarily presented only problems for railroaders to cope with, in the form of floods and washouts, fires, snow blockades, and sun-kinked rails.

On occasion, however, the herders of the Iron Horse were able to harness Nature and cause the elements to help rather than hinder. An example of this is depicted in the view of the Union Pacific's station of Genoa, Nebraska, taken in 1894. The prairie winds are being utilized to pump water for the U.P. engines by means of the big windmill visible above the water tank in the right background.

The 4-car passenger train standing at the station platform is headed by American type No. 574. This locomotive was reportedly the Union Pacific's original No. 7, named the IDAHO, and built by Schenectady in 1865 at a cost of $14,500. She and her sister engine No. 8, the OMAHA, both had 63 inch drivers and 16 × 24 inch cylinders. The IDAHO is shown here after a rebuilding in the U.P. shops bearing her 1882 number, 574; she was scrapped in 1896.

Engineer H. A. Riley and Fireman E. P. Rogers are posed aboard the engine, while Conductor Harry Shaffer and Brakeman W. F. McFadden stand on the platform alongside the baggage and express car. Note the old oil locomotive headlight mounted on a post to illuminate the freight dock, just to the right of the pile of assorted boxes of freight. (Courtesy of Union Pacific Railroad)

LESS THAN CARLOAD LOTS

This section of the album presents a variety of photographs dealing with railroading and the American scene. The subjects illustrated are of interest to those who delve into railroad history and equally as intriguing to those who enjoy a graphic look at yesteryear.

Since the limitations of space prevent the presentation of full chapters devoted to the following views, they are presented here under a chapter heading known in railroad operating circles as "L.C.L.," or "Less than carload lot."

Included in this cargo the reader will find a gallery of the classic engines representing the various types of wheel arrangements, based on the classification system invented by Mr. F. M. Whyte. Before Whyte's system came into use there was some confusion regarding the names applied to the various types of locomotives; the 4-4-2 type was known variously as the Atlantic, Chautauqua, Northwestern, or Central Atlantic type and the 2-8-2 was designated as both the Mikado and Calumet type.

Space has been provided for a spread of railway bridges and trestles, prosaic structures mingled with awesome spans that tax the ability of the viewer to believe they ever supported locomotives and trains, even in an era of lighter equipment. The stable character of bridges in the eastern states, where metal and masonry were more readily available, contrasts with many of the earlier spans in the western region that were thrown up with the raw materials at hand, the timbers often being cut within sight of the bridge or trestle.

Here, too, are views of locomotives built in the United States for use on the railroads of Canada, Cuba, and other countries, with views of engines serving Mexico and Panama.

Encompassed within this chapter are anecdotes of unusual occurrences along the iron highroad to adventure and glimpses into scenes of the past, snow fighting, methods of promotion, and other kindred subjects.

The pay car rolls again through these pages, along with official inspection trains, and each scene that passes in review presents to the reader some facet of railroading in the days when steam ruled the rails.

OFF TO DIXIE. From a broken glass plate negative in the Alco Collection preserved by the City of Schenectady's History Center comes this rare print of the GOV. BULLOCK, JR., a 4-4-0 built in 1871 for the Cherokee Railroad in Georgia, fresh from the plant of the Pittsburgh Locomotive Works.

The Cherokee Railroad was formed in 1871 as the successor to the Cartersville & Van Wert R.R., the latter road having done some grading on a route from Cartersville, Georgia, (on the Western & Atlantic) toward Pryor, Alabama.

The Cherokee Railroad ownership passed to the Cherokee Iron Company in 1879 and in 1881 this outfit converted the original 5-foot gauge line between Cartersville and Taylorsville to a 36-inch gauge road. The narrow gauge was extended to Cedartown and reached Esom Hill, on the Georgia-Alabama state line, in the fall of 1882. Shortly after this 46-mile road was leased to the East & West R.R. of Alabama, who extended it to Pell City, Alabama, and it was converted to standard gauge in 1889. The road became a part of the Seaboard Air Line in 1903, with the old Cherokee Railroad from Rockmart through Cedartown forming a portion of the Atlanta & Birmingham Air Line Railway, a Seaboard Air Line controlled and operated organization.

Note the privately-owned flat car of the Pittsburgh Locomotive Works, used to deliver engines built to other than standard gauge. (Courtesy of Schenectady History Center)

MUSCULAR MOUNTAIN CLIMBER. In 1882 the Brazilian Government dispatched an inquiry to the Baldwin Locomotive Works in regard to motive power for the Estrada de Ferro de Cantagallo, or Cantagallo Railway, capable of moving 40 gross tons of loaded cars up a grade of 8.3 per cent. The Cantagallo line was a succession of sharp reverse curves and because of the steep grades the road had been operating with the Fell system of a center rack-rail, but it was desired to secure locomotives which would climb the grades by ordinary adhesion. The Baldwin engineers submitted a design and received an order for three locomotives, which were shipped to the 3 ft. 7⅜ inch gauge Brazilian road in 1883. These engines were 0-6-0's with side tanks, had 39 inch drivers and 18 × 20 inch cylinders. On a trial trip made on October 17th, 1883, the Baldwin engine met the guaranteed requirements by hauling 3 freight cars loaded with ties and one passenger car up the 8.5% grade; the total weight was 40 tons, as specified. The first three locomotives rendered such satisfactory service that eight additional engines were ordered from the Baldwin Works in the following ten years; one of the later engines is illustrated here. This engine, No. 35, was a 2-6-0 side tank design bearing Baldwin shop number 7797 and was constructed in 1886. The pot on the cab roof is the muffler covering the exhaust of the vacuum brake ejector. (Courtesy of H. L. Broadbelt collection)

ONE FOR RIPLEY! Baldwin constructed this Mogul, named the OAKLAND, for the Sharpsville & Oakland R.R. in February of 1870. On May 29th, 1871, the OAKLAND was backing toward the Pennsylvania village of Sharpsville, in Mercer County, with a heavy drag of laden coal cars; Engineer Charles Greene was at the throttle and Godfrey Carnes was skippering the train. At a point about two miles from Sharpsville a young bull ran upon the track and was struck by the tender; the tender derailed and went off on the east side of the track, while the engine rolled over on the opposite side, burying her dome in the dirt about 16 feet away from the rails. A weigh-master for one of the coal mines who was riding the engine was killed.

In picking the OAKLAND up, Roadmaster A. D. Palmer had a hole dug under the buried dome and placed a jack-screw under the dome to aid in righting the locomotive; this hole was left unfilled after the wreck was cleared.

On August 12th, 1881, the same engine was backing toward Sharpsville with Robert Logan at the latch, hauling 15 cars of coal and a caboose. At the same spot where the bullock had met his death 10 years previously, a large hog ambled onto the track and went to his death under the tender truck; the tank once again derailed and went off on the east side of the track, while the OAKLAND rolled over on the opposite side and came to rest with its dome resting in the hole it had created in the wreck of 1871! The fireman of the OAKLAND was killed in the wreck.

The odd coincidence of the same engine being derailed at the same point due to striking stray livestock, and coming to rest in the exact spot both times with each wreck causing one fatality, is an occurrence rare in the annals of railroading. (Courtesy of H. L. Broadbelt collection)

CORNFIELD MEET. This unusual photograph shows the results of a collision between two locomotives of the New York Central & Hudson River Railroad near Batavia, in western New York, on February 16th, 1885; the two engines met on the Canandaigua Branch about one mile east of Batavia just as day was breaking.

The lower locomotive is No. 470, originally No. 34, and was built by Schenectady under shop number 61 in January of 1854; the eightwheeler perched atop the 470 is No. 295, built in the road's Rochester Shops in 1869. Surviving this pile-up with only superficial damages, she was renumbered 717 in 1889.

Firmly wedged and balanced in this unique position, the two engines were brought into Batavia where this shot was made by Photographer Houseknecht on the day following the accident.

In an age innocent of safety devices, such head-on collisions were all too frequent, due to such factors as overlooking orders, poor dispatching, and occasional chance-taking. Liquor was responsible for some wrecks, as was sleeping on duty, the latter occasioned by lack of proper rest in the era before the length of time an engineman could normally be kept on duty was limited to 16 hours by law.

Train collisions were so common that even around the turn of the century textbooks on locomotive management stressed that engineers faced with inevitable collisions should use every means available to check the speed of their train, if unable to halt it, before seeking personal safety by jumping off the engine. (Anderson collection, courtesy of H. M. Ghormley)

THE FORCE OF STEAM. The terrific power exerted by steam is very graphically illustrated in these two photographs taken by Fred Jukes. They show the boiler and running gear of one of the Union Pacific's 2-8-0 type Vauclain compounds after her boiler went skyward in an explosion in Wyoming. These views were taken after the remains of the engine had been loaded aboard flat cars following the explosion.

A common cause of boiler explosions was the introduction of cold water onto an overheated crown sheet; other boiler explosions could be traced to faulty design, failure of safety valves to relieve excess pressure, an excess of broken stay-bolts, and other mechanical factors.

Rigid laws governing the frequent testing and inspection of boilers and related appliances, such as steam gauges, water glasses, safety valves, gauge cocks, blow-off cocks, and fusible drop plugs or "soft plugs," did much to eliminate the frequency with which oldtime locomotive boilers blew up, usually carrying their crew to glory as they went. (Both photos, courtesy of Fred Jukes)

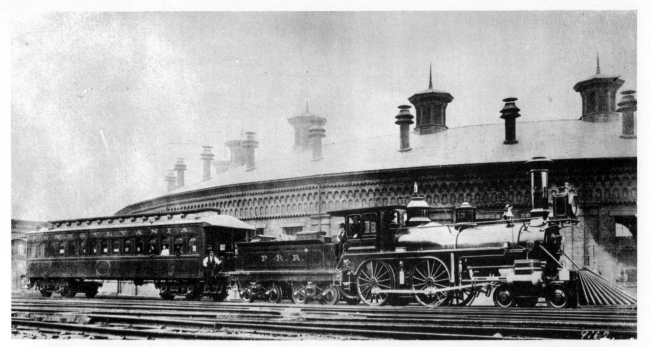

THE GREATEST GIFT. Probably the greatest contribution to the art of railroading was made in 1869 when George Westinghouse patented his air brake. Experimental trials of this brake were made in April of 1869 on the Pennsylvania Railroad's Pan Handle Division, where it was applied to the accommodation train making a daily round trip between Steubenville and Pittsburgh. In September of 1869 the Westinghouse brake was applied to Engine 360 on the Pittsburgh Division, but the device was removed, improved, and installed on Engine 45; six Pennsylvania R.R. passenger cars were fitted with Westinghouse equipment and in November the first train equipped with air brakes ran between Pittsburgh and Altoona.

So successful was the Westinghouse Atmospheric Brake, as it was then known, that by July of 1879 it had been applied to all Pennsylvania R.R. passenger locomotives; the old photo reproduced here shows P.R.R. Engine 13 and a coach with the new brake. The 4-4-0, with the Westinghouse compressor mounted between her drivers, was built in the road's Altoona Shops in 1869, replacing first number 13, a Baldwin of 1850 named the CLINTON.

The Westinghouse brake was improved and rapidly gained popularity across the country, its use spreading to many foreign countries. The air brake was a Godsend to railroad men for it brought train control to the tip of the engineer's fingers and relieved brakemen of their dangerous scramble over the swaying, ice-coated car tops to apply and release the old hand brake.

ONE-ARMED WILLIE. Hinkley Locomotive Works of Boston built the odd 4-2-2 shown here in 1887 as a demonstration engine for the Swinerton Locomotive Driving Wheeel Company. Note the unusual type of counter-balance and the early form of clasp brake, the latter having brake shoes placed before and behind the single driver.

The Swinerton experiment was not an unqualified success and the locomotive was sold to the Portland & Rochester Railroad as their No. 13, named the ONWARD. Her trailing truck was removed and another pair of drivers added, converting the odd 4-2-2 into a satisfactory 4-4-0.

RUNNERS IN THE MAKING. The momentous day in the life of a railroad fireman was the day set for his examination for promotion to the position of locomotive engineer, a day looked forward to with mingled emotions; anxiety, lest he fail the test and disgrace himself in the eyes of his mates, and happiness, for if he passed his examinations he would move over to the "three dollar side" of the cab, be relieved of the physical labor of firing, and generally be considered to have arrived at the goal of his chosen profession. Promotion practices varied on different roads, even as they do to this day. Customarily the Master Mechanic in need of additional engineers would summon the senior firemen to his sanctum and examine them as to their qualifications for the highly responsible position. Since these men had been firing under his supervision, the Old Man was generally familiar with their abilities and early examinations were often sketchy indeed.

Operating rules on early pikes were often few and simple, and if a tallow-pot could recite them and convince the Master Mechanic he could run an engine without burning her up, he was usually moved over to the right-hand side of the cab.

With the passing years, railroading became more sophisticated and stricter examinations were inaugurated on the larger lines, including such niceties as tests for color blindness and even physical examinations. Fireboys called in for promotion were often required to demonstrate their knowledge of locomotive running and repairs to the Master Mechanic; the accompanying photo shows a group of Louisville & Nashville firemen being examined at Russellville, Kentucky, in 1894. The engine is L&N No. 45, a 4-4-0 formerly numbered 302 and built in the L&N Shops in 1872. (Courtesy of Dr. S. R. Wood)

162

THE EAGLE SCREAMS! Working on the railroad produces many compensations, including such intangibles as the thrill of a fast run, pride in a time-honored profession, and the self-satisfaction of a job well done. One of the more concrete rewards and one anticipated by everyone from the "Old Man" down to the lowliest gandy dancer is the institution known as pay day, "the day the eagle screams."

To recompense railroaders for their time, knowledge, skill, and strength, the companies designated certain days for payment of wages due; as the lines lengthend, the railroad pay car came into being and a book could be written about the "money wagon" and anecdotes connected with it.

Customarily drawn behind a special engine with a picked crew, the rolling treasury on wheels made its monthly rounds over solvent roads, dispensing cold, hard cash to employes in all branches of service; some roads merely coupled the pay car to any convenient train instead of running a special. On one Western road the pay car run was held in high esteem and the engine crew was selected by the Master Mechanic; crews vied for this honor, as it gave them a chance to run over the entire Division, main stem and all branches, visiting old friends, catching up on Division gossip, and breaking the routine of their regular assignments. The ever-present danger of a holdup added zest to the pleasure of pulling the Paymaster and his golden coins.

The three engines and large crowd of employes shown here are assembled at Hussey's construction camp near Bessemer, Alabama, in 1890 on that festive occasion called pay day. Happy smiles and the comfortable feeling of hard cash bulging in pockets is the order of the day; the money will soon evaporate and when the pay train whistles into camp a month later it will be a sight to gladden the eye and spread joy among the beholders. (Courtesy of Southern Railway)

PAYDAY HUSSEY'S CAMP RR. RRR

BRASS HAT SPECIAL. An interesting phase of railroading was the movement of special trains, of which there was a wide variety. Emergency runs were made by special trains bearing fire-fighting equipment when conflagrations threatened cities, and relief trains rushed medical aid and supplies to areas stricken by floods, earthquakes, and other catastrophes. High priority was given to troop trains during the various wars, and the trains carrying the Presidents of the United States were given red carpet and kid glove treatment. Circus trains moved from town to town, following a tight schedule of performances that sometimes complicated the normal operations of rail lines.

Two noted rail excursions were the W. Seward Webb hunting party trips from Shelburne, Vermont, to the Dakotas and the Yellowstone region in 1896 and 1897; Webb, a rail magnate and a son-in-law of Wm. H. Vanderbilt, was fond of hunting and came West by special train to take trophy elk heads and game in the company of a number of sportsman friends that included English nobility and Army officers.

Railroad officials frequently traveled in special trains aboard their private cars, and one such "brass hat special" is shown here; Union Pacific's President E. E. Calvin was riding this special behind tenwheeler 1300 at Kearney, Nebraska, when Photographer M. J. Hazelrigg recorded the scene for posterity. The private chariots of top brass today are designated by the more euphonious name of "business cars" in an era when rail magnates seek a humbler role in their public image than did their flamboyant predecessors.

A DRINK FOR THE IRON HORSE. Back in the link and pin days this New Haven passenger crew posed for the photographer while engaged in watering their iron steed. The speedy eightwheeler is No. 810 of the New York, New Haven & Hartford Railroad, and her spoked engine truck wheels are equipped with brakes in addition to the cam type driver brakes.

The Westinghouse and the New York air brake systems became the two most commonly used on American railroads, but other air brake systems were tried out in the quest for improved train control. One of these was the Loughridge air brake, developed by William Loughridge of Baltimore, Maryland. In a test on the Baltimore & Ohio in February, 1876, a train of 10 coaches running about 43 miles per hour on a dry rail on level grade was halted in less than 600 feet, the time required to stop being 16 seconds. Although the Loughridge brake was used to some extent on the Baltimore & Ohio, the Cumberland & Pennsylvania, and the Western Maryland roads, it did not gain widespread acceptance. An earlier brake device was the Loughridge Chain Brake, consisting of a friction wheel that could be brought into contact with the rear driving wheel of an engine, rotating a drum and winding up a continuous brake chain applied to the cars. (Courtesy of New Haven Railroad)

VERMONT WAR VETERAN. The Schenectady-built woodburner shown here is the GENERAL WOOL and is believed to have been the Troy & Boston R.R. engine involved in Vermont's "Railroad War" of 1867. The Troy & Boston had leased the old Western Vermont R.R., later reorganized as the Bennington & Rutland R.R., and when the lease terminated the management of the Western Vermont lines became involved in litigation and secured a writ of attachment on the Troy & Boston rolling stock in Vermont.

On Wednesday, January 16th, 1867, a Vermont sheriff seized two passenger trains, a wood train, and a freight train of the Troy & Boston at North Bennington; the locomotives involved were the JOHN PAINE, I. V. BAKER, WALLINGFORD, and R. P. HART. After a minor donnybrook with agents of the local law, Master Mechanic Foster Church and some loyal Troy & Boston employes ran away with the I. V. BAKER and the R. P. HART, the latter carrying away a passenger train with it. A deputy aboard the train attempted to stop the flight but was tossed off the engine by Fireman Burr Cole at the state line.

The GENERAL WOOL and train, bound for Adams, Massachusetts, was seized at Pownal, Vermont, and the passengers sent on by sleighs. Early on the morning of the 17th, a Troy & Boston train set out from Eagle Bridge to recapture the confiscated equipment; arriving at Pownal, the raiding party found the local officers at breakfast with the rolling stock unguarded. They seized the GENERAL WOOL and her train and scurried off to safety beyond the Vermont boundary.

The engine, HILAND HALL, with a Vermont officer aboard, seized the engine D. T. VAIL at Manchester and headed for Rutland to tie up the WALLOOMSAC and a passenger train, but a telegrapher flashed a warning ahead and the Troy & Boston crew ran their train to safety over the rails of the Rutland & Washington Railroad.

RAILROAD INDUSTRY. A fact not widely known among railroad enthusiasts is the existence of the subject of this photograph taken by veteran camera artist Fred Jukes on a bitterly cold day in 1902. The steaming, smoke-belching plant is the Union Pacific Rolling Mills, located at Laramie, Wyoming.

The elevated railroad track in front of the establishment, terminating near the right side of the picture, is the high line where cars of coal were emptied to provide fuel for the hungry furnaces of the mills.

Many Union Pacific fans are unaware that the road rolled its own iron in this busy plant in Laramie and must be indebted to Mr. Jukes for preserving this scene of an unusual railroad operation more reminiscent of Pittsburgh than the windy plains of Wyoming. (Courtesy of Fred Jukes)

CONSERVATION BY RAIL. When railroads began to thread the vast reaches of the American West the mountains and prairies teemed with game animals and the rivers offered a finny horde to tempt the disciples of Isaac Walton. Specially-fitted railroad cars carried parties of hunters and anglers to remote locations to pursue their sport, and photographs reveal huge bags of game garnered by the excursionists.

By the turn of the century the inroads of unlimited hunting and angling were beginning to show up in the form of reduced numbers of fish and game and pioneer conservationists sparked a belated action to protect and propagate fish and wildlife.

In a role quite the opposite to that played in the old days of the hunting excursions, the railroads aided in the venture to restock the dwindling resources. Pictured here is the State of Oregon's Distributing Car, RAINBOW, named after the scrappy species of trout; from its' specially-equipped interior cans of young fish are being transferred to a vintage horseless carriage for transport to a stream to be released for re-stocking. The year is 1914 but the location is unknown; the car RAINBOW was used by the Oregon Game Commis-sion from 1913 until 1922, tank trucks supplanting the railroad as a means of transporting the young fry reared in State fish hatcheries. (Courtesy of Oregon Game Commission)

FORNEYS FOR THE WINDY CITY. In 1866 Matthias N. Forney patented an 0-4-4 tank locomotive, with the boiler and tender carried on a solitary frame, that was designed to operate tender foremost; British locomotive design may have influenced Forney, as four-coupled engines with a trailing "bogie" seem to have been in use in England at the time. In actual practice the Forney locomotive was found to operate about equally well when run in either direction but it did not gain any widespread degree of acceptance for American road service; however, a number of Forney types proved popular on elevated street railways.

In 1892 the Baldwin Locomotive Works completed an order of 20 of the Forney 0-4-4 tank engines for the Chicago & South Side Rapid Transit Company, an elevated street railway line more commonly known as the "Alley El"; a fine article on this road and its engines written by Mr. Fred Jukes appears in Bulletin No. 105 of the Railway & Locomotive Historical Society. The Forneys on the "Alley El" were Vauclain compounds, the low pressure cylinder being mounted above the smaller high pressure cylinder; a total of 45 of this type was built by Baldwin for the road and another engine of duplicate design but with cross-compound cylinders followed them.

When the first batch of 20 Forney type elevated engines was completed, they were hauled from Philadelphia to Chicago in a solid block, drawn by Baldwin Loco. Works Engine 82, a big Vauclain 4-6-0. This rare photo shows the solid train of engines en route to their new home on the "Alley El." (Courtesy of H. L. Broadbelt collection)

"ALLEY" ELEVATED. The Forney type 0-4-4 shown here is No. 1 of the Chicago & South Side Rapid Transit Co., the line known as the "Alley El" because its elevated tracks followed down the alley between State Street and Wabash Avenue for a considerable distance.

Built by Baldwin in March of 1892, the Vauclain compound bore shop number 12555, and was fitted with several protective devices; drip pans under the guides caught any oil or grease droppings that otherwise might have fallen on street traffic under the elevated tracks, and condensation from the cylinder cocks passed through the pipe shown in the photo and drained into the cinder pocket built under the front of the smoke box. To prevent scalding of crew and passengers in case of accidents, the boilers were fitted with check valves located inside the shell of the boiler. To avoid water from the injector overflow falling from the engine, it was piped back into the tank.

Burning coke and anthracite to insure smokeless operation, the Forneys on the "Alley El" clicked along at about 18 miles per hour on their schedules, hauling trains of 5 to 7 coaches, each equipped to seat 58 persons. (Courtesy of H. L. Broadbelt collection)

RAILS ACROSS RIVERS. As the infant rail lines of the United States expanded, the problem of bridging streams in their paths was a major one. To carry the Iron Horse across the watercourses blocking his way a wonderful and frequently awesome series of bridges were built; high or low, long or short, of timber, stone, metal, or a combination of materials, the nation's railroad bridges soon spanned every major stream in the country.

The first major bridge on the Pennsylvania Railroad was the Rockville bridge over the broad Susquehanna a few miles above Harrisburg. Work on bridge started in 1847, the stone piers being completed in late 1848; despite a tornado that wrecked six of the wooden spans of the superstructure in the spring of 1849, the bridge was completed in September of that year. The bridge was 3,670 feet long and was a single-track affair. It served until 1877, except for a short time in 1868 when fire burned out five spans.

The double-track iron truss bridge shown here was built in 1877 and had 23 spans, with a total length of 3,680 feet. The Belpaire-boilered 4-4-0 in the photo is P.R.R. No. 568, heading up the plush Pullmans of the road's crack "Pennsylvania Limited" on the New York-Chicago run.

The iron truss bridge at Rockville was replaced in 1902 by a four-track stone arch bridge, reputed to be the longest and widest of its kind in the world; it contains 48 spans, each 70 feet in length, is 52 feet wide, and carries the tracks across the river at a height of 46 feet above the normal stage of water.

WESTERN NORTH CAROLINA R.R. carried its wood-burning locomotives across Gashes Creek, some eight miles east of Asheville in North Carolina's Buncombe County, on this curved wooden trestle of slender poles with the bark left on; line is now part of the Southern Ry. (Courtesy of Southern Railway)

GREAT NORTHERN rails crossed the Two Medicine River in Montana on this towering wooden structure, erected in 1891; located in the heart of the Rockies, the bridge had 5 wooden truss spans supported by high wooden piers, in addition to trestle approaches. (Courtesy of Great Northern Ry.)

PITTSBURGH & WESTERN R.R. bridge did double duty, with slim-gauge rails on the top deck and a wagon road on the lower deck; although not positively identified, this may be the Allegheny River crossing at Parker, Pennsylvania. (Courtesy of Smithsonian Institution)

FROM THE JAWS OF HELL. One of the stirring sagas of American railroading was enacted in the pine country of Minnesota in September of 1894. The summer had been hot and dry, with many small fires smouldering over the region, but the big blow-up came on September 1st; Tommy Dunn, telegrapher at Hinckley, copied a message shortly after 1:00 PM on that day, informing him that Pokegama, nine miles south, was being destroyed by fire. A freight train and a passenger train of the Eastern Railway of Minnesota was quickly consolidated and the alarm was spread, bringing many refugees to board the train. Engineers Ed Barry and Bill Best pulled this train of salvation out of town as the depot burst into flames and moments later Hinckley was a solid mass of flames. Conductor H. D. Powers stationed Brakemen Pete McLaughlin and O. L. Beach on the rear of the tender of the leading locomotive, which was backing up, to act as lookouts; the bridge over the Grindstone River was afire as the train crossed it and north of Sandstone the crew found the high Kettle River bridge wrapped in flames, with the body of the aged bridge watchman charred near the structure. The flaming hell sweeping north behind them caused them to risk a crossing and the train rumbled across; it had gone no more than 2,000 feet beyond when the bridge began to collapse, but the 5 coaches, 3 box cars, caboose, and two engines evaded the flames and arrived safely in Superior.

Train No. 4, the "Duluth Limited" of the St. Paul & Duluth R.R., neared Hinckley bound for St. Paul and halted when it met a stream of refugees fleeing from the red death at their heels. Engineer Jim Root paused long enough to load them aboard, then backed his train toward a shallow marsh known as Skunk Lake, some 6 miles north.

There were heroes aboard that string of St. Paul & Duluth varnish—Fireman Jack McGowan doused Root with pails of water as the cab caught fire from the intense heat, while back in the coaches the colored porter, John Blair, passed out wet towels and soothed the panic-stricken passengers. The train reached Skunk Lake and those aboard found a haven of safety in the shallow slime, but the wooden coaches were burned to the trucks.

The Hinckley fire had a heroine as well as heroes; May Boyington, telegrapher at Partridge on the Eastern Minnesota road, stuck to her key until her depot began to blaze before she took refuge in a small lake nearby; Tommy Dunn, the operator at Hinckley, was not so fortunate and his body was later found about a block from the ashes of his station.

Engine No. 45 of the St. Paul & Duluth, shown here, was a Brooks 4-4-0 typical of the power on the roads of Minnesota at the time, having been built in 1887. (Courtesy of Schenectady History Center)

170

CANADIAN CELEBRATION. The arrival of the Iron Horse was the major event in the history of many towns and villages in both the United States and Canada during the great years of western expansion. The coming of the railways linked pioneer settlers with the outside world and the whistle of glossy locomotives prophesied expansion, prosperity, and a glorious future. Small wonder that enthusiastic citizens turned out to celebrate the completion of a new road serving their community.

Photographer James Morton uncapped his lens on September 13th, 1870, to record the scene at Fergus, Ontario, when the Wellington, Grey & Bruce Railway was opened. The road was chartered by the Ontario Parliament in 1869 and leased to the Great Western Railway Co. of Canada for 1,000 years. The main line from Guelph to Southampton, Ontario, was completed in 1873 and the Palmerston-Kincardine branch was finished in the summer of 1874; the 168 miles of track was operated with rolling stock furnished by the Great Western Railway, and the venerable locomotive ADAM BROWN is shown here at the Fergus celebration, flanked by uniformed bands, military companies, and a throng of happy celebrants. (Courtesy of the Smithsonian Institution)

SHADOWS OF THE FLEUR DE LIS. Poignant memories of the foothold France once established in the New World are recalled by these rare old photos of two locomotives operated in Canada. Note the "Chemin De Fer" on the tenders of this pair, French for "road of iron," or railroad. Further evidence of the French influence can be seen in the names applied to the engines, No. 18 bearing the title, LES DEUX MONTAGNES (The Two Mountains), while No. 23 was christened the LOTBINIERE. The locomotives belonged to the Quebec, Montreal, Ottawa & Occidental Railway, a line projected by the Government of the Province of Quebec in the 1870's.

Note the brakeman holding the heavy pilot bar coupler up in coupling position in the view of Engine No. 18, while a fair mademoiselle looks demurely on from the tender of LES DEUX MONTAGNES. Engine 23, the LOTBINIERE, was built by the Portland, Maine, Locomotive Works, in the 1870's. The line between Quebec and Montreal followed the original North Shore project route and was reputed to be the most feasible location for a railway between the two Canadian cities. The French influence is still felt on the rail lines of eastern Canada, with bilingual time tables presenting schedules and information in both French and English; certain Brotherhood publications contained a French language section in deference to the Canadian membership. (Both photos, courtesy of Dr. S. R. Wood)

MAPLE LEAF POWER. The Midland Railway of Canada started life in 1846 when the Port Hope, Lindsay & Beaverton Railway was chartered. Aided by municipal subscriptions, the road was opened from Port Hope, Ontario Province, to Lindsay in December of 1857 and a branch from Millbrook to Peterboro' was completed in August of 1858. In 1869 the name of the line was changed to the Midland Railway of Canada; an extension of the main line to Beavertown was formally opened in January of 1871 and the Millbrook branch was extended to Lakefield later in the year. The Orillia extension was opened in 1872 and in August of 1875 the extension to Waubashene on Lake Huron was completed.

The pretty 4-4-0 with sunflower stack shown here was built for the Midland Railway of Canada in June of 1874 by the Portland Company locomotive works, under shop number 298. She was assigned road number 15 and bore the name ADOLPH HUGEL, in honor of Adolph Hugel of Port Hope, Ontario, who served as president and general manager of the prosperous 129-mile long road. (Courtesy of George Eastman House)

KEYSTONE STATE POWER FOR CANADA. Pennsylvania's Pittsburgh Locomotive Works turned out Engine No. 49 of the Canadian Pacific Railway in 1882 under shop number 558; the trim American was one of an order of five built by Pittsburgh for the C.P.R. in that year, the engines being assigned road numbers 45 to 49, inclusive.

Note the injector located between the drivers and the boiler check valve at the waist of the boiler; the introduction of cold water in such close proximity to the flue sheet was deemed responsible for excessive contraction and leaking flues. In American practice the boiler checks were located near the smokebox to avoid this, introducing the water at a point as far as possible from the firebox in order to permit it to become heated before it circulated to the hotter evaporating surfaces around the combustion chamber.

A number of American builders, including the Portland Works, Rogers, Danforth, Hinkley, Baldwin, and Rhode Island, constructed locomotives for the Canadian Pacific. Other early C.P.R. engines came from Dubs & Co. of Glasgow, Scotland, and from the Canadian Locomotive & Engine Co. of Kingston, Ontario. Starting in 1883 the Canadian Pacific built many fine engines in their DeLorimier Avenue shops in Montreal, later moving to the new Angus Shops in the same city around 1905. (Courtesy of Schenectady History Center)

BORDER ROAD. The Grand Trunk Railway of Canada was chartered in 1851 and completed between Portland, Maine, and Montreal, Canada, in 1853. The road reached Toronto in 1856 and in 1858 the end of track reached Sarnia, Ontario Province. From Port Huron, Michigan, across the St. Clair River from Sarnia, the Grand Trunk gained entrance into Detroit over the Chicago, Detroit & Canada Grand Junction Railroad, a 59.37 mile standard gauge road opened in 1859. A noted feature of the Grand Trunk line was the great Victoria Tubular Bridge spanning the St. Lawrence River between St. Lambert and Montreal; the structure was 9,155 feet long, and completely enclosed with sheet iron, forming a metal tube in which crews and passengers alike were nearly asphyxiated from the time the span was opened in 1854 until a vent slot was cut in top of the entire length of the tube around 1860.

It was in a baggage car on the Grand Trunk line between Port Huron and Detroit that a youthful news butcher improvised a rolling laboratory and lost his job when his chemicals started a minor fire; the lad became an expert telegrapher, holding the key at Stratford Junction, Ontario, Canada, in 1863 and then booming around the country as a telegrapher. He achieved later fame as an inventor and the former news butch, Thomas Alva Edison, became known the world over as the "Wizard of Menlo Park," with more than 1,200 U.S. patents acquired by him.

Engine 286 of the Grand Trunk Railway was built by Schenectady, Shop No. 937, in November, 1873. She had 66 inch drivers and 17 × 24 inch cylinders. Engr. Eugene Fontaine ran this engine for several years after the failure of his single-driver engines in 1882, the so-called "Fontaine's Folly" locomotives. (Anderson collection, courtesy of Mr. H. M. Ghormley)

BIG HILL POWER. A tough chunk of mountain railroading was that section of the Canadian Pacific Railway's transcontinental line known as the Big Hill, 14 miles of track between Laggan and Field over the summit of the continental divide; the grade on this line ran up to 4.7 per cent, demanding husky engines and iron-nerved crews in the days of the hand brake.

Baldwin built the No. 312, shown here, for the C.P.R. in 1884, under shop number 7434; her sisters, No's 313, 314, and 315, were used in helper service on the Field hill.

Engine 314 was involved in a tragedy on the Big Hill in January of 1889 when descending the steep grade from Hector to Field, B.C., west of the summit station of Stephen. Her crew lost control of their 14-car train, all loads, and through a misunderstanding the switchtender at the last of the three safety switches west of Hector let the runaway train proceed down the main line instead of heading up the stub safety incline track. Engineer Jack Spencer jumped off and escaped with minor injuries; Conductor Bob Nelson and Brakeman Brown unloaded safely from the rear car when the 314 and her train left the rails. Fireman Charlie Fidler was climbing up onto the tender when the big hog hit a rock bluff and was so badly injured that he died on his way to the hospital several hours after the wreck; Brakeman Phelan, clubbing hand brakes near the head end of the runaway freight, was killed instantly when the flying cars crushed him.

Superintendent John Niblock hurried to the scene with a wrecking train from Medicine Hat and the 314 was fished out of the canyon and was soon back in service; she blew up on Field Hill in 1895, killing Engineer Wheatler and his fireman. The famous spiral tunnels of the C.P.R. eliminated much of the dangerous steep grade of the Big Hill. (Courtesy of H. L. Broadbelt collection)

PACIFIC GATEWAY. The camera of Fred Jukes, dean of Western rail photographers, captured this memorable scene in the rugged canyon of the Fraser River in British Columbia. A freight train on the Canadian Pacific toils along under the flank of majestic mountains while the Fraser brawls down its rocky bed; across the stream is line of the Canadian National and high above it the grade of the wagon road. The Fraser was an historic route to the western ocean long before the Canadian Pacific iron threaded its canyon, a waterway traversed by explorers and the brigades of the Hudson's Bay Company.

It is fitting that the grandeur of Canada's magnificent scenery should be represented by Fred Jukes, for that veteran lensman and railroad devotee was born in the town of Emerson, Manitoba, and his first recollection of a locomotive is that of a Canadian Pacific engine at Portage la Prairie. By a coincidence, the first passenger train on James J. Hill's St. Paul, Minneapolis & Manitoba R.R. rolled across the boundary between Minnesota and Manitoba at Emerson on Mr. Jukes' natal day, December 2nd, 1877. In speaking of the momentous occasion, Mr. Jukes says the arrival of the first train didn't mean a thing to him at the time, humorously adding, ". . . by the same token, it probably meant about half that much to the St. P.M.&M. that another little Canadian was whistling his way into daylight at the same time."

Generations of railroad enthusiasts yet unborn must ever be grateful to Fred Jukes for his artistry and imagination with a camera has left an undying record of Western railroading to delight the eye and revive nostalgic memories. (Courtesy of Fred Jukes)

SOUTH OF THE BORDER. In the days of the boomer the railroads of Mexico and other South American countries were often a haven for railroad men who, for a variety of reasons, found it desirable to leave the States for a time. Unemployment, the "black list," or simply the lure of adventure sent many railroaders below the Border; some found the life good and took root, only to be forced out later during revolutions. Others had to flee to avoid prosecution by law when they became involved in accidents resulting in fatalities.

One American engineer who ran a locomotive below the Border sent back the photo reproduced here. This inside-connected passenger engine was built by Dubs & Company of Glasgow, Scotland, around 1891 for the Mexican Railway Co., Ltd., a road incorporated in 1864 as the Imperial Mexican Railway Co., Ltd., and constructed east from Mexico City to Vera Cruz, a distance of 264 miles. A branch 28 miles long was opened between Ometusco and Pachuca in 1890 and a 29-mile branch also connected Apizaco with Puebla. A roster of equipment issued in 1905 listed 82 locomotives on the road; the British influence is reflected by a list of luggage and goods brake vans, and a unique item in the rolling stock inventory was 43 pulque cars. The Dubs & Co. 4-4-0 shown here had 6 foot drivers and 18×26 inch cylinders, 175 pounds boiler pressure, and was fitted with both a steam brake and Westinghouse automatic air brake; her 6-wheeled tank carried 2,200 gallons of water and 4 tons of coal.

When Engineer Jimmy Corbett was discharged from a southern road in the U.S., he hired out in Mexico as a runner; he found the native firemen irresponsible and sent back to the States for his colored fireman with whom he had worked before being discharged. They ran in Mexico until forced to leave during the Madero-Diaz revolution. (Courtesy of William Batman)

RAILROADS ON PAPER. Engravers and printers must have enjoyed a lucrative trade in the field of railroad stocks and bonds, turning out reams of ornate work for roads which were actually built and for others that were but the visions of promoters. (Right, courtesy of Texas & New Orleans R.R.; Left, courtesy of the Union Pacific R.R.)

SEA TO SHINING SEA. The Panama Railroad can claim the honor of being the shortest rail line linking the waters of the Atlantic with those of the Pacific, although it might fail to fall into the "transcontinental" category since it spans an isthmus rather than a continent.

Construction of the road was started by Americans in May of 1850 and the ends of track met on January 27th, 1855; the final rails of the 47.60 mile line were laid at midnight in a tropical downpour. Actual construction had been hampered by jungle, swamps, and disease; pioneer construction supervisors had worked waist-deep in water in alongside native laborers for miles before the first through train could run from Aspinwall (Colon) to Panama City's suburb, Playa Prieta, the Pacific terminus. Brigands raided the road to such an extent that the railway company was forced to establish a troop of rangers to clean out the swarms of robbers who preyed upon it.

The Panama Railroad was sold in 1879 to the French company engaged in building the canal but returned to American ownership in 1903 when the United States Government took over both the Panama Railroad and the unfinished Panama Canal.

The accompanying photo shows Panama R.R. engine No. 51, named the LE MANS in honor of the French city and rail terminal that is the capital of the Department of Sarthe in France's Maine Province; the 5-foot gauge American type was built by Cooke in 1883, Shop No. 1529, and is shown here with a passenger train at Frijoles station. (Courtesy of Smithsonian Institution)

PEARL OF THE ANTILLES. The rich islands of the Greater Antilles form a bulwark between the Atlantic Ocean and the Caribbean Sea, and the star of their crown is Cuba. Under Spanish domination, Cuba's fertile soil yielded vast quantities of cane and the production of sugar was a major business on the island. Great plantations were developed and soon the locomotive appeared on the scene, transporting raw cane to the sugar mills and hauling the finished product to various shipping ports.

The quaint little 0-4-0 shown here was built by Rogers Locomotive & Machine Works in 1880 for export to Cuba, bearing construction number 2687. Named the MANUELITO, she bore road number 2 and was destined for service in Santa Clara Province, on Cuba's north coast. The lettering on her diminutive tender stands for Ferro Carril del Oeste de Sagua la Grande, or Railroad of the West of Sagua la Grande; the town of Sagua la Grande lies north of Santa Clara and Cienfuegos and east of Matanzas and Cardenas.

Although Cuba's climate is hot and humid, with an average mean temperature of 75 degrees in Havana, tropical rains often sweep the island during the wet season; this combination of sun and rainfall probably account for the canopy which covers the tender of the MANUELITO. (Courtesy of Mr. H. M. Ghormley)

COLLECTOR'S ENIGMA. The search for old locomotive photographs can be frustrating as well as rewarding for the lover of engines who seeks to establish the lineage of each locomotive whose likeness he obtains. A careful search for clues often leads to a complete case history of a particular locomotive, from erecting shop to boneyard, even though it may take years before all of the details are unearthed.

Occasionally a photo turns up to baffle the researcher, and the one reproduced here is a fair example. The Smithsonian Institution obtained this view from the Chicago Historical Society with the notation that it was a logging railroad scene near Pike's Peak, Colorado; contacts with Colorado rail historians have failed to identify any such operation.

The engine is a trim Baldwin 2-6-0 and bears the name, GENERAL SHERIDAN, on her cab panel; she carries road number 4, but is posed at such an angle that her builder's plate is obscured, preventing the observer from obtaining her construction number and date of birth. Unfortunate, too, is the fact that the lettering on her tank is not clear enough for positive identification. However, such obstacles lend zest to the search and a sense of satisfaction prevails when the questions are answered and the problems solved. (Courtesy of Smithsonian Institution)

BLIZZARD OF '88. Winter frequently strikes a heavy blow at rail traffic, especially on roads threading the mountains of the west and the sweeping northern plains, but the great blizzard of 1888 swept the nation and many eastern lines were hard hit. Tales and recollections spawned by the heavy snowfall of that year became legion, and the "Blizzard of '88" became a milestone in railroad reminiscing.

The four views shown here present a graphic idea of the effects of the great snowfall of 1888. These photos show the blockade on the Philadelphia, Wilmington & Baltimore R.R. in the vicinity of Oxford, Pennsylvania, and the crews sent out to dig through the drifts in an effort to clear the line. Traffic was halted for days following the blizzard, and even the trains of the mighty Pennsylvania R.R. were stalled by drifts that buried the tracks. Many eastern roads were caught with limited snow-fighting equipment and armies of laborers had to be recruited to shovel out the drifts that blocked the lines. (Four photos, courtesy of Benjamin F. G. Kline, Jr.)

LITTLE-KNOWN BUILDER'S PRODUCT. The saddle-tank 0-4-0 shown here is the JOHN F. DRAVO of the Pittsburgh & Connellsville Gas, Coal & Coke Company. She was turned out about 1871 by the Pittsburgh & McKeesport Car Co., of McKeesport, Pennsylvania, a firm well-known for the construction of railroad cars but not widely known for the construction of locomotives.

Although referred to in old contemporary accounts as the "Pittsburgh & McKeesport Car & Locomotive Works," the lettering on the builder's plate of the JOHN F. DRAVO shows only the initials "P. & McK. Car Co." Other data on the builder's plate includes the following: "Designed by J. A. Lantz (?) No. 5 McKeesport, Pa."

Fire destroyed the Pittsburgh & McKeesport Works on October 2, 1877, and the *Railroad Gazette* reported early in 1878 that the stockholders had voted not to rebuild the factory. While in the business of constructing locomotives, the firm seems to have specialized in light engines for shifting and industrial use, and in steam dummy locomotives, although the engine built for the Buffalo Valley R.R. reportedly weighed 22 tons. (Courtesy of Schenectady History Center)

THE CLASSIC AMERICAN. The 4-4-0 type locomotive was so widely used in the United States that it became known as the American type and for many years ruled as the standard engine on the nation's rail lines, serving in both passenger and freight service. The 4-wheel leading truck guided the engine on the sharp curves common to the American roads and the general flexibility of the design made it suited for the light and often uneven track over which it operated.

Chief Engineer Henry R. Campbell of the Germantown Railroad secured the patent for the first American 4-4-0 on February 5th, 1836, and James Brooks of Philadelphia started construction of a 4-4-0 for Campbell in March of 1836; this engine was completed on May 8th, 1837. The Campbell eight-wheeler was a success but it lacked equalizing beams between the drivers and the Philadelphia firm of Eastwick & Harrison soon began to construct 4-4-0 types fitted with equalizing beams.

The first Baldwin 4-4-0 was built in 1845 for the South Carolina Railroad, Baldwin having purchased the Campbell patent along with Eastwick & Harrison's rights to the equalizing beams.

Shown here is a lovely American built by Baldwin in 1871 as No. 6 of the infant Northern Pacific Railroad; the two-domed eight-wheeler reportedly arrived in St. Paul, Minnesota, on February 15th of that year. (Courtesy of Northern Pacific Railway)

SIX WHEELS CONNECTED. The 0-6-0 type, with three pair of driving wheels but lacking engine and trailing truck wheels, appeared quite early on the British railways, but the sharp curvatures encountered on American lines rendered the type rather impractical. In 1842 Matthias W. Baldwin patented a locomotive with six drivers, the two front pair being carried in a flexible truck which permitted enough lateral motion to enable the 0-6-0 to pass readily around curves having a short radius. The first Baldwin engine of this design was completed in December of 1842 and shipped to the Georgia Railroad & Banking Company; the engine worked well and larger locomotives built on this pattern followed.

The 0-6-0 type was widely used in the 1845-60 period for road service, but increased speeds and heavier engines led railroaders to favor locomotives equipped with engine trucks and the old 0-6-0 or six-wheels-connected type was generally relegated to yard service or transfer work, where speed was no object and the total weight of the engine on the driving wheels for tractive effort was an asset.

The 0-6-0 illustrated here is No. 4 of the Niles & New Lisbon Railroad, a 35.60-mile Ohio line linking the cities named in its corporate title; the 0-6-0 was built by Baldwin in 1870 and the application of a pilot instead of a footboard indicates she may have been used in road service.

In 1872 the Niles & New Lisbon was consolidated with the Cleveland & Mahoning R.R. and the Liberty & Vienna R.R. under the name of Cleveland & Mahoning Valley Railroad, and was operated under lease by the Atlantic & Great Western. (Courtesy of H. L. Broadbelt collection)

THE VERSATILE TENWHEELER. The ten-wheeled engine, with a 4-wheel leading truck and 6 drivers connected, was apparently first patented by Septimus Norris of Philadelphia in 1846 and the first Norris ten-wheeler was tried out in April of 1847. The trial runs proved that the engine would not track around curves as readily as expected, a fault attributed to the fact that too much weight was carried on her three pair of drivers and not enough weight on her leading truck.

Master Mechanic John Brandt of the New York & Erie next improved the 4-6-0 type by increasing the weight supported by the lead truck and in 1852 the Baldwin Works secured a contract for a number of heavy freight locomotives for the Pennsylvania R.R., the design to utilize three pair of connected drivers; the first engines of this order were constructed as 2-6-0 types, but the weight on the single truck proved too great and the rest of the locomotives were constructed as 4-6-0's.

The popularity of the 4-6-0 soon spread and the engines were widely used in freight and passenger service. When trains became heavier, the old American type frequently proved too light for heavy passenger service and their place was taken by 4-6-0 types with high drivers.

An early example of a Baldwin ten-wheeler is shown here, being Engine 48 of the Northern Central Railroad, built in March of 1862. (Courtesy of Smithsonian Institution)

MOGUL TYPE. The origin of the 2-6-0 or Mogul type has apparently been lost in the passage of time, altho some evidence exists that the American builders Harrison, Winans & Eastwick constructed a 2-6-0 locomotive in their works in St. Petersburg, Russia, as early as 1844. James Millholland's "Pawnee" class engines on the Philadelphia & Reading in the early 1850's were 2-6-0's, but the leading wheels were fastened in the frame behind the cylinders, as were similar engines built for the Pennsylvania Railroad by Smith & Perkins of Alexandria, Virginia. In 1860 the Baldwin Works turned out several 2-6-0 locomotives for the Louisville & Nashville that featured the Bissell leading truck, followed by one or two similar types for the Dom Pedro II Ry. of Brazil; in the following decade, the true Mogul type began to appear, coming from such builders as New Jersey Locomotive & Machine Co., Rogers Locomotive & Machine Works, and Baldwin Locomotive Works.

In the true Mogul type, the single pair of leading truck wheels was equalized with the leading set of drivers, providing three-point suspension for the engine; the 2-6-0 carried most of its weight on the driving wheels and still curved readily, making it ideal for heavy freight service. The type probably received its name from the moguls of India, since both personified power. While a number of high-drivered Moguls were built for passenger service, the type was mostly used in freight duty and was well adapted to combination service; shown here is the BEAVER, a classic 2-6-0 used on the Beaver Creek & Cumberland River Coal Co. road, fresh from the Pittsburgh Loco. Works, Shop No. 618. (Courtesy of Schenectady History Center)

FIRST OF HER BREED. The 2-8-0 type pictured here was built by Baldwin in July of 1866, and was the first locomotive of this design turned out by the Philadelphia builders. Her plans and specifications were laid out by Master Mechanic Alexander Mitchell of the Mahanoy Division of the Lehigh Valley Railroad and the engine was lettered for the subsidiary Lehigh & Mahanoy R.R. and assigned road number 63.

Mitchell designed this engine for service on the Mahanoy plane, a stiff pull with a rise of 133 feet per mile. The locomotive had four pair of 48 inch drivers connected and a Bissell pony truck ahead of the cylinders; this truck was equalized with her front set of drivers. The engine weighed 90,000 pounds in working order, with 80,000 pounds of this total weight being carried on her driving wheels; her cylinders measured 20 × 24 inches.

The engine was named the CONSOLIDATION and lent her name to the 2-8-0 type of wheel arrangement; the belief prevailed for many years that she was given this name because she embodied a consolidation of the better features of several earlier types of locomotives, but it would appear this belief was in error and that her name reflected the consolidation of the Lehigh & Mahanoy R.R. with the Lehigh Valley R.R., a merger that took place about the time she was built.

The 2-8-0 or Consolidation type proved to be one of the most popular freight designs and the type was continued for many years, their car-handling capabilities earning them the nickname of "hogs" among many railroaders. (Courtesy of Smithsonian Institution)

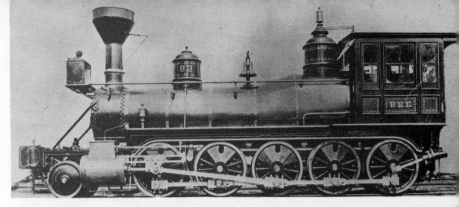

FIRST DECAPOD. In 1867 the Norris locomotive works at Lancaster, Pennsylvania, built two locomotives of the 2-10-0, or Decapod type, which were reportedly the first of that wheel arrangement ever constructed. These monsters were built for the Lehigh Valley R.R. and were designed by that road's Master Mechanic Alex. Mitchell.

Engine No. 81 was named the ANT and her sister, No. 82, was named the BEE; the latter is shown here. They had 20 × 26 inch cylinders, 48 inch drivers, and weighed 97,000 pounds each. The curves of the Lehigh Valley limited their use, due to their long wheelbase and resulting rigidity, and both were later rebuilt.

The BEE had her rear pair of drivers removed and a trailing truck applied, giving her a 2-8-2 wheel arrangement, and is still later reportedly rebuilt into a 2-8-0 type. The ANT was converted into a 4-8-0 type in her rebuilding, and both locomotives were reported in service as late as 1894.

MASTODON TYPE was more familiarly known as the twelve wheeler or 4-8-0 type. The CENTIPEDE, an experimental engine of this wheel arrangement, was built by Ross Winans in 1856, and in 1882 Master Mechanic Philip Hofecker of the Beaver Meadow Division of the Lehigh Valley designed a 4-8-0 named the CHAMPION, which was constructed in the Lehigh's Weatherly Shops.

The Central Pacific constructed a

4-8-0 in their Sacramento Shops in 1882 and followed her with a fleet of similar engines from Cooke and Schenectady, including a number of compounds.

A good example of the development of the 4-8-0 is the husky No. 4 of the Central Railroad Company of Pennsylvania, pictured here as she rolled out of the shops of the Schenectady Locomotive Works. (Courtesy of Schenectady History Center)

COLUMBIA TYPE. The first of this type was exhibited at the Columbian Exposition in Chicago in 1893 and this gave the 2-4-2 type its name. The original COLUMBIA was a Vauclain compound, as was a similar type built for the Philadelphia & Reading.

The type was designed for high speed passenger service but it never achieved widespread popularity. The 2-4-2 shown here was constructed by Baldwin in 1895 for the Chicago, Burlington & Quincy, and was designed to handle a train of six cars

between Chicago and Galesburg at an average speed of nearly 55 miles per hour. Her specifications included 84¼ inch drivers and 19 × 26 inch cylinders, with inboard piston valves.

Designed to burn bituminous coal, No. 590 had a combustion chamber ahead of her firebox but this proved unsatisfactory and a new firebox was supplied in 1897. In 1905 the engine was rebuilt into a 4-4-2 or Atlantic type. Note the European style tank with the three sets of wheels placed in a rigid frame. This engine bore Baldwin Shop No. 14410 and was classed as an N-1 on the Burlington. (Anderson Collection, courtesy of Hugh Ghormley)

THE HIGH-STEPPING ATLANTIC. The 4-4-2 locomotive is designated under the Whyte classification as the Atlantic type, since the Baldwin Works constructed the prototype for the Atlantic Coast Line in early 1895. The type was generally favored for high speed passenger service; the firebox was located behind the rear drivers, permitting a large combustion area for a big boiler, and the boiler was carried lower than on the preceding types of locomotives, thus giving a lower center of gravity. An added advantage was the location of the cab at a safe distance from the drivers, offering protection to the engine crew in case a rod should break while running at speed; this safety factor was sacrificed by some roads using Mother Hubbard cabs hung astride the boiler directly over the drivers.

The Atlantic was also known as the Chautauqua type, a designation that never gained popularity; the Northwestern or Central Atlantic was once used to designate 4-4-2 engines with supplemental frames carried outside of the trailing wheels.

Shown here is Atlantic No. 405 of the Chicago, Milwaukee & St. Paul, built by Baldwin under shop number 16316 in November of 1898; she was a compound with 13 × 26 and 22 × 26 inch cylinders and had 78 inch drivers; originally CM&StP No. 872, she was renumbered 405 in 1899, became No. 905 in 1901, and was later numbered 3005 and 22. This photo shows the high-wheeler at the coal chutes with Engr. C. E. Mills in the gangway and John Bunce in the cab; note the unusual dome housing for her headlight. (Courtesy of A. F. Zimmerman, Brotherhood of Loco. Engrs.)

MIKADO TYPE. The 2-8-2 wheel arrangement was selected by the Baldwin Works in 1897 to meet the requirements for an order of freight engines for the Nippon Railway of Japan. The engines were designed to burn a very poor grade of coal and required a large firebox with ample grate area. An engine was chosen that embodied the good features of the conventional 2-8-0 or Consolidation type, and a rear truck was added for stability and to help carry the weight of the firebox, which was located behind the rear drivers. This 2-8-2 arrangement proved to be very satisfactory and similar engines were produced soon after for use on railroads in the United States; the type was designated as the Mikado, honoring the ruler of the Japanese, but American railroaders quickly dubbed them "Mikes," and a series of them used on the Southern Pacific that were equipped with Precision reverse gear were known to Espee enginemen as the "screw Mikes."

Following the bombing of Pearl Harbor in 1941, a wave of patriotism swept the nation and some roads changed the designation of the "Mikado" to the "McArthur" type, but the change was never widely accepted. The 2-8-2 shown here bore Baldwin's Shop No. 15203 and was erected in February of 1897 for the initial Japanese order. Steam railroading had been introduced to Japan in 1854 by Commodore Perry's expedition; a miniature 4-4-0 locomotive built by Norris was assembled by engineers from the U.S. Navy squadron and pulled delighted Nipponese around a circular track laid in a field. The model coach was too small to enter, but the Orientals perched on the roof and their robes billowed in the breeze as the train ran at speeds up to 20 miles per hour. (Courtesy H. L. Broadbelt collection)

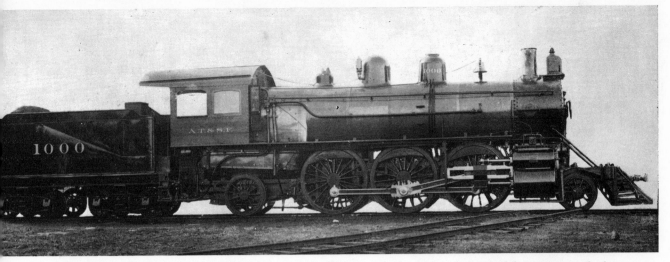

THE PRAIRIE TYPE. The 2-6-2 or Prairie type was a refinement of the old 2-6-0 or Mogul locomotive, with the trailer truck added to carry the additional weight required as the engines grew longer and heavier. The use of the trailer permitted a wide firebox carried above the frames and to the rear of the back pair of drivers; the earlier Prairie types had their trailing axles fitted with inside bearings, as illustrated here, but later locomotives equipped with trailers frequently used the "outboard" style of truck, with bearings on the axles outside the wheels.

In 1901 the Baldwin Works built 45 engines of the Prairie wheel arrangement for the Atchison, Topeka & Santa Fe, and 50 of the same type for the Chicago, Burlington & Quincy. The 2-6-2 illustrated here is a compound built by Baldwin as the Santa Fe's road number 1000. Other roads also ordered Prairie types in limited numbers, but the use of the 2-6-2 in main line road service was never very popular and the type was supplanted by other designs. (Courtesy of H. L. Broadbelt collection)

PIONEER PACIFIC. In 1901 the New Zealand Government Railways ordered thirteen locomotives from Baldwin designed to burn lignite and these engines were built with a 4-6-2 wheel arrangement. The engines were basically a 4-6-0 with the addition of a two-wheeled trailing truck, the latter helping support some of the weight of the lignite-burning firebox, which was both wide and deep; the firebox was carried above the frames and the trailing truck was integrated into the locomotive's spring suspension system by means of long equalizing bars and spring hangers. Although the Strong "Duplex" built for use on the Lehigh Valley R.R. in 1885-86 had a 4-6-2 wheel arrangement, the group of engines shipped to New Zealand by Baldwin were the first large-scale order and their island destination gave rise to the name of "Pacific" as applied to this type.

The Pacific type proved especially suited for passenger service and a great many 4-6-2's were turned out by various builders and were widely used throughout North America.

The locomotive pictured here is New Zealand Government Rys. No. 350, built by Baldwin under construction number 19254; she was fitted with piston valves, Walschaert valve gear, and carried two steam domes. (Courtesy of H. L. Broadbelt collection)

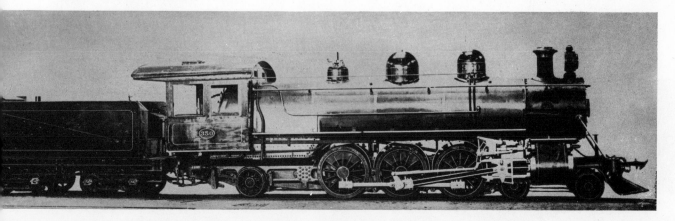

TANDEM COMPOUND. The first tandem compound locomotive built by the Baldwin Loco. Works was constructed in 1902 for the Atchison, Topeka & Santa Fe Railway; in addition to this distinction, it was the heaviest engine Baldwin had built to that time, weighing 267,800 pounds. The engine was a 2-10-0 or Decapod type and was designed to handle heavy freight trains over the Santa Fe's steepest grades.

The tandem compound system embodied two cylinders on each side of the locomotive, placed line-in-line, with the small high pressure cylinder located ahead of the larger low pressure cylinder.

In 1903 the Santa Fe ordered some additional tandem compounds from Baldwin for freight service and these were similar to the Decapod ordered the previous year, but a trailing truck was added, creating the 2-10-2 type which became known as the Santa Fe type. These 2-10-2's had 57 inch drivers and their cylinder dimensions were 19 and 32 × 32 inches; they had a total weight of 287,240 pounds. An engine of this type built for the Santa Fe was among the Baldwin exhibits at the Louisiana Purchase Exposition held in St. Louis in 1904. (Courtesy of H. L. Broadbelt collection)

BULL OF THE WOODS. The geared logging locomotive patented by Michigan logger Ephraim Shay was still in swaddling clothes when this photo was taken at the Cummer Lumber Company's saw mill at Cadillac, Michigan, in 1882. The Shay engine was born in the woods and it was there that the type rose to its height of development, the rapid chant of its unique exhaust ranging from the pines of Michigan to the rain forests of the Pacific.

The Shay engine design incorporated vertical cylinders powering a crankshaft that transmitted its effort to each set of wheels under engine and tender by means of a lineshaft, universal joints, and bevel gears; the flexibility of the engine permitted it to operate over the poorest quality of track and what it lacked in speed was compensated for by its goat-like ability to climb grades of a degree almost unbelievable to rod-engine railroaders. The Shay was a veritable power-house on wheels in terms of tractive effort and the crude early model illustrated here is credited with having drawn a train of 34 loaded cars of logs of the type shown in this frigid scene. The engine pictured appears to have a vertical boiler, with a water tank on the forward platform and a fuel wood bin located behind her cozy cabin; later models featured a more conventional type of locomotive boiler, which was located off-center to the left side of the engine to balance the weight of the cylinders and driving shafts and gears that were mounted on the right-hand side of the locomotive, an arrangement which gave the timber beast a rather lop-sided appearance when viewed head-on.

Lima Locomotive Works built hundreds of Shays and after the patent rights expired a similar engine was produced by the Willamette Iron & Steel Co. of Portland, Oregon. (Courtesy of Smithsonian Institution)

TIMBER BEAST. The Climax locomotive was near kin to the Shay type, in that both were gear-driven and were commonly found ranging the forested mountains where loggers were engaged in harvesting timber. While the Shay was built with two or three vertical cylinders, the Climax gradually evolved into a two-cylinder machine, the pair of cylinders mounted at an angle and driving a counterbalanced shaft that was geared to a line shaft running under the center line of the engine, with gear connections to each axle; the early "Class A" Climax engines used vertical cylinders mounted in the cab behind the backhead of the boiler, and were provided with a sliding gear mechanism by which the engineer could change the gear ratio as the need arose. A number of Climax engines were built with concave wheels for operation on logging pikes where wooden poles were substituted for rails.

The stem-winder shown here is No. 12 of the Polson Logging Company's timber line in western Washington; she was built in the shops of the Climax Manufacturing Company in Corry, Pennsylvania, and carried shop number 409; note the sections of rail used for brake beams on this woodburning lokey. The hose and strainer slung under her cab and tank enabled her to siphon boiler water from trackside sources.

Kissing cousin to the Climax was the Heisler, whose two cylinders were mounted V-fashion and connected to the crankshaft under the belly of the boiler. The wheels in each set of Heisler trucks were connected with outside connecting rods. (Courtesy of Rayonier, Incorporated)

Upper photo shows a 3-truck Climax posed on a flimsy trestle on the Wood & Iverson logging railroad; her tank bears road number 3.

Two-truck Heisler No. 6 operated on the logging road of the Mud Bay Logging Company in the state of Washington. View shows the inclined left cylinder, located to the right of the air compressor. (Both photos, courtesy of Fred Jukes)

Bottom photo shows the Two-spot of the Mason County Logging Company, a two-truck Heisler. Both Heislers shown on this page are equipped with spark-arresting stacks to reduce fire danger in the woods. Unlike the Shay and the Climax, power was geared to only one set of wheels in each Heisler truck, the second set of wheels being driven by the conecting rods visible here; note counterbalancing applied to each wheel. (Courtesy of Jay Golden)

THE LAST MILE. The last milepost has drifted past our cab window and our train ride into the nostalgic yesterdays of steam railroading draws to a close.

The locomotive engineer who has held the throttle on the journey through the pages of memories contained in this album hopes your trip with him has been a pleasant and rewarding one, with the views as interesting as those which attract the gaze of these veterans decorating the roof of a Milwaukee inspection train cruising along the Mississippi near Hastings, Minnesota, in the golden summer of long ago.

The journey back into history is ended, the fires are banked, and your runner bids you a fond farewell. (Courtesy of Mr. Benj. T. Hart)

THE END OF THE TRAIL

The coming of the Diesel locomotive ended the reign of steam on the railroads of America and the Iron Horse began to fade into oblivion after a brief reprieve brought about by the heavy burden of traffic during World War II.

For many old veterans of the rail the coup de grace was a rather humiliating one, the death stroke being dealt by the torch in the hands of the scrapper. Across the land the noble steeds that had served so long and so faithfully were led forth on their final journey, their worn brasses clanking mournfully and their rusting flanges screeching the funeral dirge.

Dry pistons groaned protestingly as shop engines shunted discarded power to rip tracks where the executioners waited. Showers of sparks rained down as the cutting torches gnawed away, reducing the cold boilers and running gear to piles of scrap metal, for even in death the last ounce of value was to be extracted from the inanimate hulks that had once proudly pounded the burnished rail and blasted their glorious chant of power to the heavens.

A few of the valiant breed survived, enshrined in museums or placed on display where future generations could gaze in curiosity upon one of the most fascinating of man's creations.

Mark well the bones of the old slide-valve steamer being scrapped at the Canadian Pacific's shops in Vancouver, B.C., for this scene, ignominiously repeated across the length and breadth of the land, marked the end of an era wherein steam, steel, skilled hands, and a devotion to duty created the undying saga of steam railroading. (Courtesy of Fred Jukes)